Tacitus, Thule and Caledonia

The achievements of Agricola's navy
in their true perspective

Stan Wolfson

BAR British Series 459
2008

Published in 2016 by
BAR Publishing, Oxford

BAR British Series 459

Tacitus, Thule and Caledonia

ISBN 978 1 4073 0274 4

© S Wolfson and the Publisher 2008

The author's moral rights under the 1988 UK Copyright,
Designs and Patents Act are hereby expressly asserted.

All rights reserved. No part of this work may be copied, reproduced, stored,
sold, distributed, scanned, saved in any form of digital format or transmitted
in any form digitally, without the written permission of the Publisher.

BAR Publishing is the trading name of British Archaeological Reports (Oxford) Ltd.
British Archaeological Reports was first incorporated in 1974 to publish the BAR
Series, International and British. In 1992 Hadrian Books Ltd became part of the BAR
group. This volume was originally published by Archaeopress in conjunction with
British Archaeological Reports (Oxford) Ltd / Hadrian Books Ltd, the Series principal
publisher, in 2008. This present volume is published by BAR Publishing, 2016.

Printed in England

BAR titles are available from:

        BAR Publishing
        122 Banbury Rd, Oxford, OX2 7BP, UK
EMAIL   info@barpublishing.com
PHONE +44 (0)1865 310431
FAX   +44 (0)1865 316916
        www.barpublishing.com

In memory of Sally and Adrian

CONTENTS

Lists of maps and photographs 4

Preface 7

Abbreviations of Journals 9

Introduction 10

Chapter 1. Shetland: The Classical Geographical Context 14

Chapter 2. The Manuscripts of Tacitus' *Agricola* 25

Chapter 3. Reassessment of Vocabulary and Sense 29

Chapter 4. The Search for a Harbour 34

Chapter 5. Thule in Contemporary Latin Poetry 47

Conclusion 62

Appendix 1. The *Boresti*: The Creation of a Myth 65

Appendix 2. A Problem of Identification or *Pie in the Skye* 74

Appendix 3. The Coinage of Titus and Agricola's Caledonian Campaign of AD 79 78

Appendix 4. Vettius Bolanus in the North: Fact or Fiction? 88

Appendix 5. *Caledonius*: Allusion and Illusion 98

Bibliography 107

List of Maps

Map of Scotland, showing locations referred to in Classical sources and the suggested route of Agricola's expedition in AD83

The Ancient British Isles: Map reproduced from Mallet's *Description de l'Univers* of 1688 and published at Frankfurt in 1719. It betrays contemporary ignorance of the ancient geography of north-west Europe. *Thule* is depicted as Iceland, the non-existent *Pomona* is resurrected among the Orkneys, the *Aemodae* are presumably the Faeroes, and the Shetland Isles are unlisted. *Ocetis* and *Dumna* are approximately correct. Illustration courtesy of Reinhold Berg, www.bergbook.com

Fines Borei: the area north of the Dornoch Firth, map courtesy of Harvey Maps, www.harveymaps.co.uk

Map of north-east Scotland, showing possible and probable sites, from *The Romans in Moray*, courtesy of Ian Keillar

List of Photographs

The arms of Lerwick

Mosaic of Oceanus and Tethys (2nd- 3rd cent. AD) from Zeugma, now in the Archaeology Museum, Gaziantep, Turkey. Photo from www.theoi.com

Codex Aesinas Latinus 8, folio 63 (description in text)

Guarnieri's transcription (description in text)

Aerial photograph of Lerwick, looking east towards the Isle of Bressay, photo courtesy of Alan Moar, www.alanmoar.flyer.co.uk

The plateau of Scaraben looking east towards the North Sea, photo courtesy of Peter Standing, www.geograph.org.uk

Crop-mark at Balnageith, photo by E.D.B. Jones, courtesy of Ian Keillar

Crop-mark at Boyndie, photo by E.D.B. Jones, courtesy of Ian Keillar

West ditch of installation at Easter Galcantray, photo courtesy of Ian Keillar

Denarius of Titus Augustus with captive reverse, earliest issue (described in text)

German prisoners-of-war beneath a trophy from a scene on the lower section of the *Gemma Augustea*. Note the brimmed Celtic helmet which was adopted by the Roman legionaries.

Roman Military Diploma from Egypt (*CIL*.16.24) from AD79. References in line 3 to the 14th acclamation of Titus, and in line 17 to *the 6th day before the Ides of September*. ie 8th Sept, provide supporting evidence for the earliest possible date for the next acclamation attested in Dio (*RH* 66.20.3).

Denarius of Julius Caesar with captive reverse (described in text)

Denarius of Titus Caesar with captive reverse (described in text). This is on the same file attachment as the denarius of Julius Caesar. The obverses of both coins also appear.

Denarius of Julius Caesar with double-captive reverse (described in text)

Aureus of Titus Augustus with double-captive reverse (described in text)

Denarius of L.Aemilius Paullus with trophy (referred to in text)

PREFACE

The ideas presented in this book originated in suggestions I made to my tutor, J.H. Mozley, during a seminar on Tacitus at Queen Mary College, University of London, in 1957. He approved of these, but noted their incompleteness: I had seen the part, but not the whole. It has taken me nearly half a century before I plucked up the courage to resume where I left off and find a conclusion that satisfied me, and might appeal to others. In 1957 there was no adequate edition of the *Agricola*. The annotated orange-covered text of Church and Brodribb had been chosen in preference to Anderson's edition with its commentary because it was cheaper rather than better. The text, notes and introduction had undergone little change since the middle of the nineteenth century, and long dead German philologists were being cited as if the Franco-Prussian War was still in progress. The publishers probably thought it was; they had no awareness of new developments in Latin scholarship. Sadly the translation of the dynamic duo, more solidly bound and more aesthetically pleasing than Mattingly's paperback, retained the myth of a *snow-covered Thule* being *descried in the distance*—and although the rediscovery of the Jesi codex in 1902 had laid this to rest, it is still accepted by the unenlightened as gospel. Even the enlightened will have been amused to notice its resurrection (with all faults) in 1997 by Ronald Mellor for his *Anthology*. Victorian values have their place in a changing modern world, but Victorian scholarship comes with a *caveat* for readers of the modern era. A good translation should reflect the times as well as the text.

In terms of palaeography the works of Robinson, Perret and Till were indispensable. Robinson was really the first to provide a substantial account of the manuscript tradition, though some of his readings, especially where proper names were involved, were patently incorrect. Perret's ideas ranged from the ingenious to the illogical and his edition was printed on such poor quality paper that some of the pages simply crumbled away as rapidly as his conclusions. Rudolf Till was able to work on the codex in Rome in 1943 and, more importantly, he photographed it with the backing of the local German authorities, the patronage of Heinrich Himmler (who believed that the *Germania* section of the manuscript supported his racist theories about the ancient Germans) and the suspicious eye of Mussolini (whose allegiance was split between backing his German masters and protecting a national treasure from their envious clutches). Till's plates, last located in the Weidener Library at Harvard, provided the facsimiles to be found at the back of his book. I have drawn attention to two sections. A cursory glance at the first of these will demonstrate the hazards to be negotiated by anyone trying to disentangle the mess of *scriptura continua*. The second section is a fifteenth century transcription and is easier to follow. Whether or not the text and corrections are acceptable is one of the issues I hope to raise.

Since the history of Roman Britain during the first century must involve a knowledge of Tacitus' *Agricola*, the student has to decide whether to be content with a translation, which in itself is an act of faith, or to assimilate the Latin as far as is possible, and choose an edition where the commentary not only explains the text, but provides some archaeological background. Sadly archaeology will always outstrip the text, and what was acceptable to, shall we say, Anderson in 1922, is no longer valid in 2008—and our current information will be obsolete a decade from now. Fortunately, whatever scholars do to the text will not alter the general direction of Agricola's career. He still remains the Roman governor of Britain about whom we know the most. We may adopt different viewpoints about him in search of new ideas and minimise or maximise his achievements, but at the end of the day it all comes down to the Latin.

Which editions provide the most reliable text and the most illuminating commentary? The answer, very few. Errors and misconceptions marred the 'revised' edition of Ogilvie and Richmond, although the latter may be exonerated. Ogilvie frequently repeated the errors of Furneaux without bothering to check his sources or their accuracy, while some of Anderson's better ideas were ignored. Forni's invaluable introduction and bibliography compensated for his inadequate text and commentary. Delz and Lund were like a breath of fresh air, though not entirely faultless, while Soverini's recent edition promised much, but produced little that was new. I still await a text and commentary which combine accuracy, clarity and originality. Perhaps repetition is less arduous and less time-consuming than innovation. But there comes a time when the rope has to be replaced before the climber breaks his neck. Haverfield, Collingwood and Richmond did their best to complement the text, but could never stem the tide of progress. Their archaeological contributions were commendable in their day and some of their ideas still hold good. Unfortunately for them, new discoveries, elucidated by new scientific techniques, have frequently necessitated a radical change of direction.

For whom is this book intended, the specialist or the non-specialist? The answer is, for anyone who is interested in the history of Roman Britain in the latter half of the first century. As Courtney puts it: *I hope that all classes of users will be able to pick out severally what corresponds to their individual needs*. This may sound like shopping for laxatives, but the sentiment is sincere. The specialist will forgive me if I don't conform to strict standards by occasional light-heartedness. It is not my intention to match the *gravitas* of those whose status is testimony enough. Readers may ignore the notes altogether if they appear presumptuous, hypercritical or too close for comfort. Likewise, non-specialists may pass over the copiousness of notes and grammatical terms if they find them overwhelming or incomprehensible. I hope that the English translations of words, phrases and sentences will be useful. A *critical* reinterpretation implies judgement. But I prefer to act within my own parameters, not those laid down by others. My approach is based on a blend of common sense and reason. If this combination tells me that something is not quite right, then it isn't right, no matter what scholarly excuses are conjured up or how much ink is spilled over it. This approach may appear arbitrary, unscientific and unorthodox in philological terms. But a subjective approach which produces reasonable results is better than an objective approach which still leaves people in the dark. My intention is to let in a little light. I see textual criticism as a means to an end

My original paper contained an appendix, subsequently expanded to produce the material which appeared on my website (for which see the Bibliography, Wolfson 2002). The website gave me direct control over my material and made it accessible worldwide, with the result that people could contact me and exchange views. The University of the Internet is an establishment I would heartily recommend, provided that the student isn't seduced by the fantasy war-games or virtual reality, entertaining, but pure fiction. The website in its turn has now gone through numerous changes, revisions, corrections and improvements to accommodate recent scholarship and is now presented in a permanent printed form, rather than in a transient electronic form. Quotations, whether in English or in Latin, are printed in italics.

I owe much to those who facilitated my task. To the library staff at the Institute of Classical Studies in London many thanks for their kind and cheerful assistance. To Christine Crick, Justin Blake and my son Adrian for their computer skills, thanks again. I am most grateful to my brother-in-law and sister, Steve and Nite Butler, for the hours they spent in Texas, converting my typescript into a website and then back again onto a disk. Ian Keillar's knowledge of the Moray littoral was much appreciated. My correspondence with Ronald Martin in 2001 was an education in itself and proved vital to me. His incisive, authoritative and sympathetic comments on the text of Tacitus gave me cause to think twice, while pointing me in the right direction. I am deeply in his debt. Mark Hassall's comments on my original paper, and his belief in my ideas, I shall always cherish. Above all my gratitude to Tony Birley whose constant support, advice, encouragement and friendship have been inestimable. Without him none of this would have got off the ground.

I accept total responsibility for whatever changes I have made to the text, for better or for worse, and for any errors which may have crept in. I make no apologies for anything else.

ABBREVIATIONS OF JOURNALS

Acta Arch.	*Acta Archaeologica* (Copenhagen)
AJPh	*American Journal of Philology*
ANRW	*Aufstieg und Niedergang der Römischen Welt*
BMCR	*Bryn Mawr Classical Review*
CFCES	*Cuadernos de Filología Clásica. Estudios Latinos*
Class et Med	*Classica et Mediaevalia*
CJ	*Classical Journal*
CPh	*Classical Philology*
CQ	*Classical Quarterly*
CR	*Classical Review*
CSCA	*California Studies in Classical Antiquity*
EC	*Études classiques*
Euphr	*Euphrosyne*
G&R	*Greece and Rome*
Gymn	*Gymnasium*
HSCP	*Harvard Studies in Classical Philology*
JCPh	*Jahrbuch für classische philologie*
JHS	*Journal of Hellenic Studies*
JRS	*Journal of Roman Studies*
MAAR	*Memoirs of the American Academy in Rome*
MH	*Museum Helveticum*
Mnem	*Mnemosyne*
OJA	*Oxford Journal of Archaeology*
Phil Woch	*Philologische Wochenschrift*
Philolog	*Philologus*
Pop Arch	*Popular Archaeology*
PCA	*Proceedings of the Classical Association*
PSAS	*Proceedings of the Society of Antiquaries of Scotland*
QS	*Quaderni di Storia*
RCCM	*Rivista di Cultura Classica e Medioevale*
REL	*Revue des études latines*
RFIC	*Rivista di filologia e di istruzione classica*
RhM	*Rheinisches Museum für Philologie*
RPh	*Revue de Philologie*
SAF	*Scottish Archaeological Forum*
SAR	*Scottish Archaeological Review*
TAPA	*Transactions and Proceedings of the American Philological Association*
TCWAAS	*Transactions of the Cumberland and Westmoreland Antiquarian and Archaeological Society*
TRSL	*Transactions of the Royal Society of Literature*
WJA	*Würzburger Jahrbücher für die Altertumswissenschaft*

INTRODUCTION

The purpose of this book is to put the achievements of Agricola's navy, apparently understated by Tacitus, in their true perspective, with the proposition that the Roman fleet reached the furthest limit of the known world, Thule, or Mainland, Shetland, where it located a convenient anchorage, possibly in Lerwick harbour. To support this theory, firstly the identification of Thule as Shetland during the classical period from the time of Pytheas onwards is investigated through collation of geographical sources, secondly the earliest manuscript of Tacitus' *Agricola* comes under closer scrutiny at the relevant points than ever before, and finally contemporary literature is reassessed to determine the significance of Caledonia and Thule in the Flavian propaganda machine and to suggest the first Roman presence in the Shetland Islands. The procedures I have followed are based mainly on textual analysis and common sense. The star performers in this scenario have long since gone, Tacitus, Agricola, the unnamed scribe identified as *E*, the humanist transcriber, Stefano Guarnieri, the countless commentators who over the last five centuries, with varying success, tried to shed light on all four.

It is encouraging now to see the role of the archaeologist making its presence felt more and more and linking up with the philologist. The decline of Latin in schools has left a cultural void and a slender rope for the archaeologist to climb at the risk of hanging himself. A little knowledge is worse than none. The importance of interdisciplinary co-operation cannot be understated because the search for the truth requires the blending of all skills. I have cited archaeological sources where they were relevant and I appreciate the effort that goes into providing a practical framework around which the classicist can operate. The same degree of care is required for both disciplines, the only difference being that archaeology involves teamwork, while the textual critic ploughs a lonely furrow. But at least he doesn't have to worry about the season or the weather.

Agricola's British Fleet (*Classis Britannica*) is unlikely to have left any traces of its presence in the north or anywhere else and I doubt very much that we shall ever find the remains of a Roman warship or transport ship in the waters around Scotland or the northern isles. Since the movements of the fleet would generally be co-ordinated with the movements of the army, the location of military installations, whether temporary or semi-permanent, are crucial for determining the northern limits of Roman penetration. I am convinced, even if others are sceptical, that Agricola *did,* as Tacitus tells us, complete the conquest of Britain and that his army and navy reached areas never before considered possible. Military sites along the north-eastern seaboard must reflect the movement of the fleet, and if the fleet sailed well north of the Scottish mainland, then military sites should extend at least as far as Wick in Caithness. The fact that nothing concrete has yet been found beyond the Dornoch Firth should not lead to the assumption that nothing exists. One only has to look at what archaeology has revealed in Moray over the last two decades to realise that the Roman presence is being extended ever further north. The possibility of Agricolan marching camps in Sutherland and Caithness should be considered a probability, and when Tacitus tells us that Agricola reached the end of the island in his final season, why should I disbelieve him, when earlier campaigns have been vindicated by the spade? Archaeology requires money, time and expertise, and without adequate funding the time will not be found for the expert to probe areas which sceptics have considered to be hardly worth the trouble.

Ultima Thule has always had a fascination for both scholar and layman and much ink has been spilled over its whereabouts or even its existence. Strabo had his doubts over two thousand years ago. In modern times Iceland is a prime suspect and still has its supporters, despite the fact that all the evidence points in a different direction. Parochial interests have transferred it to Scandinavia where chemists have named an element after it, *Thulium.* But the literary arguments do not support Norway or Sweden. At the time when Tacitus was writing, Thule was the subject of a romantic novel by Antonius Diogenes, *The Incredible Things beyond Thule.* If we change *beyond* to *about*, we would have an adequate description of modern fiction masquerading as fact. In later years Thule took on a more sinister significance when it was associated with Nietzsche, the Hyperboreans, the Thule Society and the Nazi inner circle. In recent years the name of Thule has been highjacked to advertise bars,

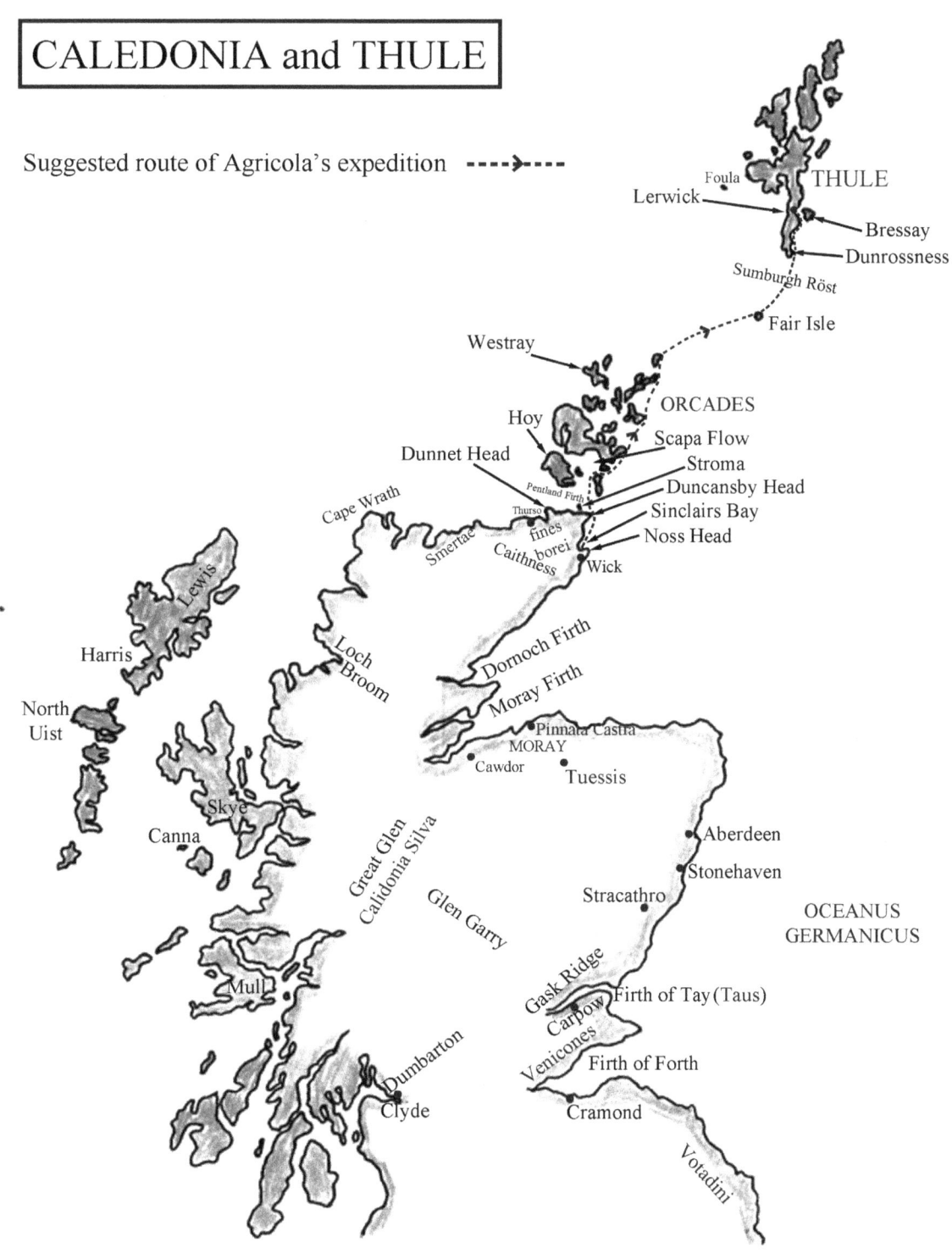

Map of Scotland, showing locations referred to in Classical sources and the suggested route of Agricola's expedition in AD83

hotels and roof-racks. Where actually is Thule? Kavenna's entertaining book, *The Ice Museum*, provides a wonderfully whimsical travelogue on the different locations which may, or do, bear its name. But it is designed to entertain rather than to educate, somewhat like a many-branched tree still looking for its roots. Cassidy's article, *The Voyage of an Island* transferred exploration from the explorer to the island itself which mysteriously turned up in the unlikeliest places according to the whim of any ancient fantasist. My book will explain where I stand. But a study of the motto on the Lerwick coat of arms provides the clue which links Thule, Shetland and Rome.

LERWICK coat of arms

Whether it was good fortune or local pride that extracted this vital information from Tacitus' *Agricola* we may never know. But it was an apt choice, even if those who recommended it did not grasp the full significance of the Latin (to be subsequently explained). It is in fact much closer to home and possibly more relevant to Lerwick than people could ever imagine. The Latin has always been misconstrued, no more so than in 1936 when the great film director Michael Powell produced his documentary, *The Edge of the World*, about life on Foula. The film's introduction is a stark revelation of the island's history. There on the screen title we read, *when the fleet of Agricola, the Emperor, sailed round Britain, they saw from the Orkneys a distant island. They called it the Ultima Thule, the last landfall, the Edge of the World.* Very dramatic! No doubt Agricola would have been thrilled at such a promotion, and I'm sure that the people of Foula were excited that his marines should name their island after a quotation from Virgil. I am sure that Powell himself was too astute actually to believe this; the average cinemagoer will believe anything. *The Edge of the World* is an apt description, since the ancients believed that no one could live beyond it. The fact that *Foula* is a Norse word (Fowl Island) and has nothing to do with *Thule* is immaterial. As was once famously said, *When the legend becomes fact, print the legend*. There's nothing better than a mistranslated Latin quotation to give it some authority.

The Lerwick coat of arms illustrates a Viking ship to show the close connexion between Shetland and Scandinavia in the ninth century. Shetland was only ever accessible from two directions, east and south. The emphasis on an eastern approach from Scandinavia was due to the mass of available evidence, and quite rightly so, but it never occurred to historians that the Romans might have got there eight centuries earlier from the south. There was no archaeological evidence and apparently no written record. There is a certain irony in that the Vikings are given the centre stage, the very people who plundered and destroyed monasteries, the very places where manuscripts were kept from one generation to the next, manuscripts which preserved the Classical tradition, but were burned to illuminate the dark evenings instead of being saved to illuminate the Dark Ages. Yet if just one surviving manuscript can be reinterpreted to show that the Romans had priority in reaching Shetland, then a new chapter may be added to its history.

At this stage I have to confess again that the contents of this book are primarily of a philological nature. Consequently there will be obstacles for the general reader. But you don't have to know how a car engine works in order to drive a car. If readers can negotiate or avoid the minefield and follow my line of thought, they will see what my objectives are. Whether they agree with them is another matter.

Chapter 1

SHETLAND: THE CLASSICAL GEOGRAPHICAL CONTEXT

venient annis saecula seris
quibus Oceanus vincula rerum
laxet et ingens pateat tellus
Tethysque novos detegat orbes
nec sit terris ultima Thule

The centuries will come in the distant years when Ocean is to loosen the chains of the world and a vast land lie open, when Tethys is to uncover new hemispheres and Thule shall not be the last place on earth.

Seneca, *Medea* 375-379

Seneca's reference to *ultima Thule* and *Tethys* is a borrowing from Virgil (*Georg.* 1. 30-31) who, in a dedication to the young Caesar (the future emperor Augustus), prays that the ruler may be protected by the goddess of the sea in his plans for trans-Oceanic conquests and that *farthest Thule* may be subject to him.[1] The hope was that Augustus would achieve what Julius Caesar had failed to achieve—the mastery of the Ocean in the west. Ironically, Augustus' plans were only partially realised, and lay in a different direction. He did not get to Thule, but his desire to explore unknown lands in emulation of Alexander the Great is clear from his own account of his achievements (*RG* 26): *my fleet sailed through Ocean from the mouth of the Rhine to the region of the east to the borders of the Cimbri* (Jutland), *to a place where neither by land nor sea any Roman before that time had gone.*[2] No Roman perhaps, but Pytheas, the Massiliot explorer, had been there three centuries earlier in search of the amber route and, what is more, he had passed through Thule on the way. Seneca's *Medea* is not simply a tragedy unfolding. It is the final episode in the tradition of the *Argonautica*, the saga of Jason and his crew searching for the unobtainable by way of the inaccessible. The search for a new world was always on the agenda, whether for commercial purposes or in the interests of science or purely *to boldly go where no man has gone before*.

Seneca's prophecies have been interpreted by all and sundry as referring to Atlantis, America,[3]

---

[1] It is worth noting that Virgil begins a tradition with this phrase. Not only is Thule the *last* place on earth, but wherever it occurs subsequently in Latin poetry (14 times) it is found only as the *last* word in a hexameter line, despite the fact that there are four other places where it could fit in. The reason for this is probably the author's intention to build up to a climax, where all the epithets referring to darkness, cold, distance or dread provide a foreboding of what is to come.

[2] The account of Tiberius' commission from Augustus is also recorded by the Elder Pliny (*HN* 2.167). Evidence of diplomatic contacts between Rome and the Baltic at this time may be suggested by the discovery of high quality Roman silverware (Jorgensen 2003, 111) in the grave of a local prince at Hoby in West Lolland, a large island to the east of the Danish peninsula. Johansen 1960, 190 links the 'Priam' and 'Philoctetes' cups with contemporary Arretine pottery and dates them right at the beginning of the first century AD. For a similar context one may compare the silver medallion of Augustus from the Lexden tumulus at Colchester (Laver 1927, 25 and pl.62). The juxtaposition of Oikoumene (*the inhabited world*) and Oceanus on the *Gemma Augustea* (Hannestad 1988, 78-82 and pl.51) may well reflect Augustus' ambitions of breaching the barriers of civilisation. D.P. Dobson 1936, 88 suggests that the presentation of *the most sacred kettle* in their country (Str. *Geog.* 7.2.1) by the Cimbri to Augustus, with a plea for his friendship, was in consequence of the impression produced by this expedition.

[3] For Americans, prone to seeing apocalyptic messages in virtually anything, Thule was a godsend. Washington Irving cited Seneca's lines as his motto in *Life of Columbus*. Almost all the biographers of Columbus have cited these lines in their introductions. Columbus himself had translated them into Castilian in his *Book of Prophecies*. Perhaps he was taken in, or merely profited, by an inferior reading in his text of Seneca, where *Tiphys*, the Argonautic pilot, appeared instead of *Tethys*. But he provided himself with a convenient pathfinder, thereby equating himself with Jason. The exploitation of a dubious MS reading to accommodate a dogma or a prophecy is just as bad as the toleration of Dark-Age scribal errors in the name of conservation. The unwavering reliance on vague statements by Virgil and Seneca rather than on the parameters set by the

Mosaic of Oceanus and Tethys

Greenland, in fact anywhere you like, as long as it is somewhere in the remote west or north, as yet undiscovered in the middle of the first century AD. Seneca's long-term view is as astonishing as it is true. What led Seneca to conjure up this forecast may be found in the references to *Oceanus* and *Tethys*. It was this husband and wife team of marine deities which Alexander the Great honoured when he reached the *eastern* limit of the known world. Four hundred years later the same two deities would be invoked by a Greek schoolteacher who sailed with Agricola's fleet in the opposite direction. But Ocean, however much invoked, cannot be appeased. He has to be challenged, as Augustus challenged him, and beaten, as Agricola beat him en route for a harbour in Thule. The only question which Seneca doesn't answer is: *Where is Thule?*

It is generally accepted that Tacitus' *Thule* (*Agr.* 10.4) is Shetland, and that the latter is the *Thule* of Ptolemy (*Geog.* 2.3.14), derived through Marinus of Tyre from Agricola's naval reconnaissance in AD 83, although the Ptolemaic scale of latitude on 63^0N is still one or two degrees off the modern equivalent. It will be argued here that *Thule* is Shetland in *all* the classical geographical sources from the time of Pytheas (c.330 BC), who was the first to record the name, right through to the time of Tacitus. The comment by Bianchetti that the *Thule* of Agricola had supplanted the *Thule* of Pytheas needs to be substantiated, while Aujac's assertion that *Shetland was certainly not Thule* is arbitrary and fails to examine the implications of the time-distance factor laid down by Pytheas.[4] The

---

Greek and Latin geographers allowed Thule to be manipulated by both the famous and the infamous. The poetic myth was more attractive than its prosaic reality.

[4] Bianchetti 1998, 154; Aujac 1988, 329. This is reiterated even more uncompromisingly by Ballin-Smith/Banks 2002, 13: *Shetland was **most certainly** not Thule, in spite of the statement by Tacitus that Agricola's fleet sighted Thule from Orkney.* But, apart from the misinterpretation of the Latin, where does Tacitus claim that Thule was visible from Orkney? To adduce the evidence of a sea captain in support of a non-existent claim adds insult to injury. Then we read, *Tacitus may have been more interested in the use of a near-mythical name as a way of adding glory to the memory of his father-in-law.* Thule was no myth at the end of the first century AD.

observation of Rivet and Smith that the application of the name *Thule* to Shetland by Tacitus and Ptolemy *is not evidence that Shetland really bore the name* implies that Shetland had some alternative name, a notion which I propose to reject.[5] Roger Dion was surely correct in his assumption that when Pytheas reached Shetland *he found the name of Thule attached*.[6] A century earlier Müller, in his notes on Ptolemy, had also preferred Pytheas' Thule as Shetland.[7] Agricola, as will be suggested later, surely knew all about Pytheas and what and where *Thule* was, before he commissioned his naval expedition. There is no good reason to see Thule as *part of a fictional and schematic mapping out of the* world.[8] Hawkes' assertion that Agricola's sailors *would have been told not to expect any Shetlands there* is bizarre.[9] Thule was a reality, not a myth, and the reality was attainable.

Both Strabo (*Geog.* 1.4.2) and Pliny (*HN* 2.187) cited Pytheas' comment that Thule was six days' voyaging northwards from Britain.[10] This would be the time it would take to reach Shetland for a native craft,[11] *not sail-powered, but paddled or rowed*, as Roseman plausibly suggested.[12] It could have involved travelling perhaps from Gills Bay in Caithness to Lerwick, negotiating the *the sluggish and heavy sea* (*mare pigrum et grave*, *Agr.* 10.4), stopping off at Stroma, Orkney and Fair Isle and tackling the formidable Sumburgh Röst. It is in the framework of Pytheas' *six* days, as Jones and Keillar stressed, that Thule must be located.[13] Ogilvie suggested that Thule was Iceland on the basis that six days' sail would cover some six hundred miles.[14] The same view is supported by Cunliffe, who thinks it quite reasonable for boats to achieve some four knots, sustained over a period of twenty-four hours, in Atlantic conditions.[15] This is totally unrealistic.[16] Casson refers to *only two possibilities: Iceland and Norway*, preferring the latter because *Iceland is too far north for oats*,[17] while Thomson ruled out Iceland because it *had no bees for the honey drink* mentioned by Pytheas.[18] But Iceland is out of the question.[19] Norway, as will be shown later, is marginal to the equation.

Any evaluation of voyaging in what the Romans called *Oceanus* needs to be made on the basis of contemporary record of the experience. A crossing from the European mainland to the promontory of Belerium in Cornwall, according to Diodorus' sources (5.22.2), took four days, not one day, as

---

[5] Rivet/Smith 1979, 42.
[6] Dion 1977, 201: *il a trouvé attaché le nom de Thulé*; not to be taken literally, of course.
[7] Müller 1883, 104.
[8] Thus Clarke 2001, 98.
[9] Hawkes 1975, 37. About which one must ask: what would Agricola have called 'the Shetlands' when addressing his sailors?
[10] This point is crucial, since it fixes the limit of Pytheas' voyage. Consequently any references to ice flows, Arctic Circles or nights lasting for six months are no more than hearsay. One must discount the statement of Solinus (*Coll.* ed. Mommsen 1895, 219 l.25) often cited by the unwary, that *Thule was five days and nights sailing from the Orkneys*. Although this would suit my interpretation, the MS tradition of this section is insecure and is accordingly referred to as pseudo-Solinus.
[11] Native boats of plaited osiers were used by the Britons in the North Sea, cf. Luc. *BC* 4.134-5. Pliny (*HN* 6.86) tells us that a voyage in native reed boats from *Taprobane* (Ceylon or Sri Lanka) to the nearest cape in India took four days. The distance is about 80 miles.
[12] Roseman 1994, 155; she notes that *ocean tide and wind conditions would cause a vessel under oar or paddle to travel very slowly*. She has taken this idea from Bentham 1948, 428, who points out that *if it took Pytheas four days to sail from Brittany or Normandy to Cornwall, it seems not altogether impossible that it should take someone (natives) five or six days in among the islands and tides from Wick to Mainland in the Shetlands*. The limit of six days was stressed a century and a half ago by Fotheringham 1859, 502: *six days would not be too many for navigation among the islands forming the two clusters of Orkney and Shetland with their strong tides and other difficulties attending a navigation through northern islands*. Fotheringham was a native of Kirkwall in Orkney and an eyewitness.
[13] Jones/Keillar 1996, 47 n.17. But I reject their view that the Arctic should be part of the equation.
[14] Ogilvie 1967, 172.
[15] Cunliffe 2001b, 126. Selkirk 1995, 183 had earlier conjured up the same figures to produce less than one day's sail from Caithness to Shetland, without evaluating what type of boat might have been used or what conditions were like in the Pentland Firth or Sumburgh Röst.
[16] Braun 1980, 126 is very sceptical about Hawkes' claim for Iceland as Thule: *can we believe in a voyage to Iceland and back...in twice six days with wind and current apparently favourable in both directions*? He himself supports Nansen's *enthusiasm for Norway*.
[17] Casson 1991, 125; likewise Burn 1969, 39. Strabo (*Geog.* 4.5.5) refers to the inhabitants of Thule as living on corn. But cf. Roseman 1994, 136-137.
[18] Thomson 1948, 149. The honey beverage is likewise referred to by Strabo (*Geog.* 4.5.5).
[19] Hyde 1947, 130. We could eliminate Iceland completely if we follow Hogg 1859, 329: *as the chief portion...of Iceland is volcanic, it may not have been in existence at that period*.

Cunliffe imagines.[20] The distance from Land's End to the nearest point of Brittany is some 100 miles, not 400 miles! Caesar's crossing from the vicinity of Boulogne to Dover in 54 BC (*BG* 5.8.2) took some eighteen hours to cover less than thirty miles, and he was not using native boats, while Pytheas (Str. *Geog.* 1.4.3) said that it was several days' sail from Kent to Gaul. Even in Mediterranean conditions, as Casson pointed out, the speed of a fleet could vary from one to three knots according to wind direction.[21] Allowing for twelve hours of continuous rowing or paddling (in Atlantic conditions) at 2.5 knots,[22] it would take nearly three weeks to reach Iceland, which no more fits the description of Thule as *the most northerly of the British isles* (Str. *Geog.* 2.5.8),[23] or *the furthest of the islands around Britain* (Solinus, *Coll.* 22) than it does today. The statement by Rivet and Smith, *all that can be said with certainty is that Thule…was not one of the British isles*, is one 'certainty' which may be discounted.[24] The most northerly of the British isles is Shetland, and this is as far north as any commissioned navigator was likely to travel. Dion tried to resolve the problem of time and distance by suggesting that Thule was Shetland and that Pytheas covered a distance of 550 miles, starting from Galloway,[25] while Bianchetti, following the same starting point, offers a Norwegian fjord as her Thule.[26] But any crossing to Shetland must surely be calculated by the direct route from the vicinity of *Orcas promuntorium* (*Tarve(du)num,* Dunnet Head). It is simply impossible for native boats to cover Dion's estimated 130-150 kms. per day. But at least they both, quite rightly, eliminate Iceland from the equation. Whitaker was too quick to dismiss Shetland on the grounds that *it is not six days' sail from Britain*, without giving any reasons,[27] while André and Baslez state authoritatively that Thule is *undoubtedly one of the Faeroes or Iceland*.[28] Where does such conviction come from? D'Hollander devotes six pages to comparing the merits of the Faeroes, Iceland and Norway, but with no mention of Shetland or Agricola his case collapses.[29] Pytheas was correct in his time allocation, which accords well with a Shetland destination. Hawkes' suggestion that Pytheas made a five day voyage to Iceland from Westray (?) in the Orkney group is pure speculation. His insistence that Thule is Iceland (based on the migration of whooper swans), that Pytheas *heard of it first in North Uist* and that he sailed in a pentecontor, is equally speculative and not supported by the requirements of Atlantic tidal conditions.[30] It is curious that he cites Servius (on Virg. *Georg.* 1.30) as evidence for Thule being Iceland: that author clearly locates it *iuxta Orcades* (*close by the Orkneys*). Cunliffe recognised

---

[20] Cunliffe 2001b, 73, following Hawkes 1975, 29 n. 67.

[21] Casson 1977, 296.

[22] Cotterill 1993, 227 f. produces sensible figures for North Sea navigation in the late third century AD, suggesting that at 2.5 knots and in favourable weather a crossing between Bruges and Kent would take at least fifty-two hours, with at least sixteen hours for a return crossing at the Straits of Dover.

[23] There is no inconsistency, *pace* Roseman 1994, 132, in Strabo's separate statements that Thule was six days' voyage from Britain (*Geog.* 1.4.2) and that it was the most northerly of the British Isles. Taken together, they corroborate the identification of Thule as Shetland.

[24] Rivet/Smith 43. If I have to chose between Strabo and Rivet/Smith I would prefer Strabo, firstly because he had access to material denied to the latter, secondly because they tend to defer to the likes of Hawkes, whose fanciful theories they evidently regard as sacrosanct.

[25] Dion 1965, 445-6; 1977, 201-4. He bases his calculations on Ptolemy's map, which was composed in the Hadrianic period, four and a half centuries after Pytheas. So how could Pytheas have assumed a turning of Scotland? This was caused by Ptolemy's distortion of Marinus' co-ordinates, cf. Jones/Keillar 1996, 48. As Rivet 1977, 48 pointed out, *no competent sea captain ever reported that the general trend of Scotland was from west to east instead of from south to north*. Agricola's *praefectus classis* knew the position of the sun. Ptolemy correctly removed Ireland (*Ierne*) from the Strabo/Eratosthenes location in the remote north to its proper position in the west, while Scotland wrongly takes off in the opposite direction. Whether this was due to the traditional concept that life could not be sustained beyond 63°, or simply to the fact that the area had not been explored (Norway falls into the same category), is open to question. The earliest maps of Britain produce a triangular shape, as may be seen in Diodorus' account (5.21), derived from Eratosthenes. Pytheas' measurements would have provided the data for Eratosthenes' map (Ogilvie 1967, 165; cf. Jones/Mattingly 1990, 18, map 2:3). There is nothing in Tacitus' account (*Agr.* 10.3) or in any other previous one to suggest that Britain took a ninety degree turn along the Wear-Eden axis, cf. Strang's readjustments, 1997, 12 f. Mann 1996, 163 says that *it is quite improbable that he* (Marinus) *had any such observations for Thule*. So where did Ptolemy's co-ordinates come from? Jones/Keillar 1996, 45 suggest that Demetrius' circumnavigation may have provided some information. There is a logic in that, but Thule requires a voyage further north to establish its position.

[26] Bianchetti 1998, 152.

[27] Whitaker 1981, 160.

[28] André/Baslez 1993, 45.

[29] D'Hollander 2002, 95-101.

[30] Hawkes 1975, 37; 34; 44; on the latter point Roseman 1994, 149 observes that a pentecontor *is unlikely to have been chosen by a sensible Greek, planning to venture into completely unknown waters for an extended voyage of exploration.*

Pytheas' achievement as outstanding, *even if only to the Elbe and Shetland, using local ships*.[31] Dilke's comment that later writers were misled into assuming Thule to be Shetland, *whereas it may have referred to the Faeroes*, is fanciful, since a voyage from 'Cape Wrath' would require more than six days to cover 300-350 miles. He acknowledges that Tacitus' *Thule* is Shetland, but is wrong in stating that Agricola's fleet was cruising *near* the *Orcades* and is unaware of the connexion between Agricola and Pytheas.[32] Strobel's suggestion of Fair Isle may also be discounted, for reasons which will later become apparent.[33] Burn was incorrect in assuming that Foula was not six days' sail north of Britain; after all, he himself had earlier stressed the virtual immobility of boats in the Pentland Firth.[34] In asserting the claim for Iceland or Norway he overestimated the capabilities of seafarers in tidal oceans. Are we to assume that Timaeus' island of *Ictis* (Plin. *HN* 4.104, *insulam Mictim*, where the M is a MS dittographical corruption), *six days' voyage inwards* (?) *from Britain*, was some six hundred miles away? Geographically impossible. It is curious that Hawkes claims it would take only one day to cross from Ushant to Belerium (Lands End), yet is happy to allow a six days' voyage from Belerium to the Isle of Wight (on the assumption that this is Diodorus' *Ictis*).[35] The simplest solution to all the divergent problems would be to cut the Gordian Knot and go along with Zehnacker's *voyage imaginaire*.[36] I prefer to unravel it.

According to Roseman, the passage in Strabo (*Geog.* 4.5.5) where Pytheas is criticised is *key in most attempts to identify Thule*. She refers to the Broch at Clickhimin (near Lerwick) and to Hamilton's excavations there, suggesting that Pytheas *did report details that were certainly present in areas he could have observed*. In effect she backs up the view that Pytheas' Thule is Mainland, Shetland when writing of *the reasonable certainty* that Pytheas got as far as $62°$ N (Lerwick is $60°$) and that *his observations could very well have been made in the Shetlands*.[37] Dicks had already found it improbable that Pytheas went much beyond latitudes where nineteen hours would be the longest day (about $61°N$).[38] Carpenter has *as far north as the Shetland Islands, and no farther*;[39] Nesselrath

---

[31] Cunliffe 2001a, 92. He is clearly following Roseman here. But curiously, in his later book, he follows Hawkes, a serious misjudgement. At least he acknowledges, 2001b, 131, the possibility of Pytheas being in Shetland because of the explorer's recording of a place where the shadow of the sun was less than three cubits high, giving a 19 hour day.

[32] Dilke 1985, 136.

[33] Strobel 1987, 202.

[34] Burn 1969, 39; 1949, 94. The 17th century Scottish cartographer, Robert Gordon, made a substantial contribution to Blaeu's celebrated atlas. In his dissertation on Thule in the fifth volume he is very sceptical about the chances of navigating the hazards of the Pentland Firth, 1654, 7: *the strait which lies between Scotland and the Orkney islands is not easily crossed by the inexperienced or without a skilled pilot. What hope then of a Roman voyage to Shetland so that Thule could be found there?... that the Romans saw the Shetland Islands or reached as far as that in ships is a vain opinion*.

[35] Hawkes 1975, 29. Cunliffe 2001b, 77 assumes that *Mictis* and *Ictis* are different, locating the former between the Loire and the Gironde, and applying the latter name to Mount Batten, neither of which is six days' sail *inward* (*introrsus?*) from Belerium. Rivet/Smith 1979, 487-9 produce a sound etymological case for the equation *Ictis* = *Vectis*. The geological possibility of a Solent causeway was proposed by Reid 1905, 284. But this has been scientifically disproved. It is quite impossible to reconcile Diodorus' offshore island with the Pliny/Timaeus location, where there is no reference to Belerium. Rackham's translation of *introrsus* as a description of the island, *lying inward*, is certainly incorrect. Besides, how can *a Britannia introrsus sex dierum navigatione* be translated as *six days sailing up-Channel from the west* (thus Rivet/Smith 1979, 41)? Cunliffe and Rivet/Smith cannot both be right: they are going in different directions, Cunliffe south and Rivet/Smith east. I prefer the latter, but with reservations. The translation *from the west* does not render *a Britannia*, and *introrsus* (*up-channel?*) as a navigational bearing is meaningless. Ancient writers can be very vague in geographical directions. The west is *left*, the east is *right*. So where does *inward* take us? The possibility of confusion between the Pytheas/Strabo six days' sail from Britain to Thule and the Timaeus/Strabo six days' sail from Britain to Ictis (cf. Elton 1882, 40 n.1;Magnani 2002, 148; Roller 2006, 73. n.139) does not negate the validity of the travelling time. Pliny, who has a tendency 'to make a sow's ear out of a silk purse', merely erred in not substituting *Belerio* for *Britannia* when giving *Ictis* as the destination.

[36] Zehnacker 2004, 186. He proposes (174) that Pytheas got only as far north as the Thames Estuary before crossing over to Germany and making for the Elbe.

[37] Roseman 1994, 152, citing Hamilton 1968, 79. Cary/Warmington 1929, 37 reject the idea that Pytheas' Thule is Mainland, Shetland; yet Cary, in his revised version of Tozer's *History of Ancient Geography*, 1964, 288, retains Tozer's *Thule = Mainland* theory, which he and Warmington had ruled out.

[38] Dicks 1960, 184-191.

[39] Carpenter 1966, 183. He argues (180) against Iceland on three counts: a) there is no reason to suppose that Iceland was inhabited before the Christian era, b) there were no natives in Iceland with whom Pytheas could have communicated, c) there is no likelihood that Pytheas would have abandoned his investigation of the Atlantic trade route to steer a course in the opposite direction. The obvious argument was missed, the reference to the *northernmost of the British Isles*, which as

follows suit,[40] as does Angus, who believes that Pytheas got at least as far as Unst (N. Shetland).[41] Dion observes that *in the thought of the ancient geographers Pytheas' voyages did not go beyond the latitude of 61-62⁰*. He provides a route from the Outer Hebrides (?) to Shetland and then on towards Norway.[42] This is much more logical, since a circumnavigation of the British Isles with a continental destination in the Baltic is hardly likely to include Iceland, for which, *pace* Cunliffe, no sound case can be made. References to Arctic conditions need not imply that Pytheas travelled that far north and Aujac notes that *it is probable that Pytheas did not get as far as the frozen sea*.[43] One should distinguish between what Pytheas *gleaned from British sailors*,[44] about conditions in the far north, what he conjured up out of his own imagination—giving later Greek writers good cause for calling him a liar—and what he experienced personally. If Pytheas saw native dwellings on Shetland, perhaps the precursors of the brochs, then the more imposing structures, such as the broch at Clickhimin, would not have escaped the notice of Agricola's fleet commander who would have encountered them already in Caithness and Orkney.

To identify Thule as Mainland, Shetland, requires the elimination of all other possible candidates for the honour. Roseman, following Müllenhoff, proposed that Pliny's *Berrice* could be another name for Shetland, while Zehnacker has no doubts about it and believes Shetland to be the embarkation point for the *real* Thule which he locates in Norway.[45] These arguments are distorted and fail to take account of Pliny's geographical grouping. There is no evidence to suggest that *Berrice* is Shetland and no reference to it in Tacitus, who knew the correct name for Shetland. Hence any voyage to Thule, as stated by Pliny's unspecified sources (*HN* 4.104[46]), must originate either from the south (the Scottish

---

Bunbury 1959, 594 n.4 pointed out *would exclude the possibility of his* (Strabo's) *referring to Iceland.*

[40] Nesselrath 2005, 163: *it seems reasonably certain that Pytheas got at least as far as the Shetlands.* Unfortunately he accepts Cunliffe's Icelandic Thule.

[41] Angus 1934, 170. This falls roughly into Dion's latitude. As evidence that Pytheas reached the Shetlands he cites Pliny (*HN* 2.217), *Pytheas informs us that the tide rises 80 cubits* (120 feet) *north of Britain* and compares it with a 120 foot tide rise recorded in the Pentland Firth. Unfortunately he says that Shetland *must not be identified with Thule*. Roseman 1994, 81 believes that *a true tide of 80 cubits is impossible*. But Pytheas is noting *exceptional* conditions. Roller 2006, 76 likewise dismisses Pytheas' claim: *the maximum range in the Orkneys is 10.4 feet*. In fact in 1862 a tidal surge, over 200ft high, swept across the cliffs at Stroma (Cunliffe 2001b, 103). Roller is also quite confident that *the very nature of Iceland is the strongest proof that Thule can be nowhere else*. In fact it is the weakest link in the chain—Cunliffe and Hawkes have much to answer for. Roller's article is full of vague statements and misconceptions. Of Thule he states that *Vespasian was said to have conquered it* (79, based on Silius, but completely misconstrued), and that *later Gaius* [sic] *Julius Agricola went there*. He then asserts that *obviously these 'discovered' Thules* (ie. Shetland, etc.) *were merely places in the remote north that had little relationship with Pytheas' travels.*

[42] Dion 1977, 196.

[43] Aujac 1988, 329.

[44] Cunliffe 2001a, 93. Pytheas certainly obtained information from others about areas he had not visited, as is clear from his reference to *hearsay* (Str. *Geog.* 2.4.1) and to Geminus of Rhodes, who quotes Pytheas' observation that *the barbarians have shown* us where the sun goes to sleep, cf. Dion 1977, 204-207. Phillips 1969, 194 suggested that Pytheas may have obtained his information on the Arctic Ocean from Celtic or Germanic sources, while Angus 1934, 172 believed that *somewhere north even of Shetland...they told him* (Pytheas) *of a place still further north.*

[45] Roseman 1994, 94; Müllenhoff 1890, 387; Zehnacker 2006, 174, following Dilke 1964, 347. In Zehnacker's view, Agricola thought he sighted Thule in the distance but was forbidden by the emperor to go there. Quite the opposite, as will be shown.

[46] *Some authorities mention other islands also, the Scandiae, Dumna, Bergi and Berrice, the largest of all, from which one sails to Thule* (*sunt qui et alias prodant, Scandias, Dumnam, Bergos, maximamque omnium Berricen, ex qua in Tylen navigetur*). It is curious that Pliny should give a *British* context to a group of islands which are essentially Scandinavian. Thomson's assumption, 1948, 246, that Pliny thought that these were British islands was questioned by Roseman 1994, 94. She writes about Pliny's disjointed account without explaining how a group of Scandinavian islands suddenly appears in a British context. Rivet/Smith 1979, 42 likewise offer no explanation. It was the British context which led Hawkes to assume a reference to the Outer Hebrides, where the *Scandiae* could not possibly be located. In this case *Dumna* is the odd one out and reflects Pliny's misinterpretation of different sources. It was this sort of confusion which led Pliny to assume that *Scandinavia* and *Scandiae* were not the same (cf. Schutte 1917, 136), since he was following Mela for the former, and a separate source for the latter. If a reference to Norway (*Berrice*, as I maintain) is assumed among this group, then the group was misplaced during textual transmission and belongs at the end of sections 96-97, where Pliny describes the area from the Vistula to the Ems. Once Pliny had mentioned Sweden, he should have referred to Norway, misplaced after his account of Britain through confused collation of different sources. Pliny's geographical description of *the outer parts of Europe* (*extera Europae*) goes anti-clockwise: the Polish coast, Denmark, Sweden, Norway, Germany, Gaul, Spain. The direction for mariners is explicitly stated: *you must coast along the shore of the northern Ocean towards the west until you reach Cadiz* (*litus Oceani septentrionalis in laeva, donec perveniatur Gadis, legendum*). The account of Britain and its adjacent islands

mainland and Orkney) or from the east (Norway). I therefore propose that *Berrice* is Norway on the basis that an unattested name of an island, which was conspicuous for its size and grouped with the *Scandiae*, requires a Scandinavian, not British, context.[47] Consequently this would be the first *recorded* contact between Norway and Shetland. Rivet and Smith do not rule out the possibility that Pliny's *Bergi* and *Berrice* are Scandinavian, while Stichtenoth believes that *Berrice* is *the original Scandinavia*, against Hawkes, who makes no valid case for identifying *Berrice* with North Uist in the Outer Hebrides.[48]

Pliny's *Acmodae* (*HN* 4.103) and Mela's *Haemodae* (3.30) are clearly identical and have been erroneously suggested as the Shetland Islands by a range of scholars over the centuries.[49] Such views are based on a reluctance to accept Tacitus' interpretation of *Thule* as part of an ongoing tradition. Mela locates his *Haemodae* (*Acmodae*) in the Baltic facing Germany, and this should have given pause for thought. Mela, who was Pliny's source, lists his island group in the sequence: *Orcades* (Orkney Islands), then *Haemodae*, but makes no mention of the *Hebudes* (Hebrides).[50] Pliny's sequence is *Orcades, Acmodae, Hebudes*. Pliny clearly used a different source for the Hebrides and the other islands off the west coast of Britain which are not mentioned by Mela, and through loss of concentration he confused his sources,[51] and consequently his direction. But Mela, as the earlier source, must be right. It is noticeable that whereas Pliny starts off with the Orkney Islands, moving *south-west* through the Irish Sea into the English Channel, thereby eliminating, by reason of direction, the *Acmodae* as the Shetland Islands, Mela moves *south-east* across the North Sea towards Denmark, Sweden and the Baltic where his seven *Haemodae* are now to be located.[52] Hawkes' assertion that the *Haemodae* were *north* of the Orkney Islands is rather odd, considering that Pliny's direction puts them to the *south*.[53]

(102-104) is a digression from the description of continental Europe, where we find ourselves at the start of 105. The section *sunt qui alias...Cronium appellatur* would fit very comfortably at the end of 97.

[47] *Which might point in the direction of Scandinavia* (Rivet/Smith 1979, 42). This would negate Dion's theory, 1966, 211, of the *probability of an extension of the ancient name for Norway to the Shetland archipelago*. There is no reason to assume that Shetland and Norway ever had the same name, and no basis for claiming that Norway was called *Thule*, especially if it was called *Berrice*. One thing is certain: *Thule* and *Berrice* are both Greek names—and they may both derive from Pytheas' account, especially if, as Dion suggests, Pytheas landed in Norway. *Berrice* is not recorded by any other source. If it is Norway the vagueness of its location is understandable, since Norway was unexplored territory and consequently absent from Ptolemy's listings. Svennung 1974, 9 claims that Agricola would have been familiar with Pliny's reference to Thule and asks whether *Berrice* might be one of the Orkneys. But the Orkneys are distinct from the *Scandiae*.

[48] Stichtenoth 1959, 78, 84 (*das eigentliche Skandinavien*); Hawkes 1975, 34, cf. Rivet/Smith 1979, 41.

[49] Hardouin 1723, tom.1.223 n.3; Thomas 1875, 225; Hergt 1893, 48; Burton 1932, 79; Thomson 1948, 235; Svennung 1963, 12; Hawkes 1975, 37; Rackham 1989, 199; Cunliffe 2001b, 93; D.J. Breeze 1999, 36; Freeman 2001, 54; Rivet/Smith 1979, 241. The failure of Rivet/Smith to translate (76) the whole sentence in Mela is misleading. Roseman 1994, 90 likewise does not cite beyond *contra Germaniam vectae*. Burn 1969, 37 also fails to examine the entire sentence, assuming, like Anderson 1922, xl, a confusion with Ptolemy's *Aebudae*. Since when were the Hebrides located in the Baltic?

[50] The appearance of the Hebrides in Pliny (the first time they appear in literature), but not in Mela, would have been the result of reconnaissance of the Western Isles during the northern campaigns of Cerialis, who may deserve more credit than he is usually given. Before Pliny's time Roman knowledge of the smaller islands to the west of Britain did not extend further north than Anglesey (*Mona*, Rivet/Smith 1979, 419). Pliny's earlier Greek sources, clearly responsible for naming the Western Isles (e.g. *Andros*), may have required confirmation through Roman naval involvement.

[51] This would easily occur if Pliny was faced with two words of similar spelling, *Haemodae* and *Haebudae* (or *Aemodae* and Ptolemy's *Aebudae*). There was clearly scribal error at some stage. Rivet/Smith 1979, 241 did not rule out the possibility that the two groups were the same. Their unquestioning acceptance of Ranstrand's reading in Mela was never a sound basis for this theory. Tillisch 2005 is incorrect in using the spelling *Haemodes*. So is Pedech 1976, 72, who assumes they are the Hebrides, reached, as he claims, by Pytheas. Berry 1977, 125 translates *Hemodes* from a pointless edition of 1493 with a facsimile text on facing pages! *Haemodes* is a mountain range located by Mela to the east of the Black Sea. This error goes back to Blaeu and Camden.

[52] Dilke 1990, 286, reviewing Silberman's edition of Mela, says of the *Haemodae*: *mention of Germany takes on more sense if applied to the islands of what is now Denmark, and to Norway-Sweden, regarded as an island*. I concur with this, except that Sweden and Norway should be taken as *two* separate 'islands'.

[53] Hawkes 1975, 37.

20

The Ancient British Isles: Map reproduced from Mallet's *Description de l'Univers* of 1688 and published at Frankfurt in 1719. It betrays contemporary ignorance of the ancient geography of north-west Europe. *Thule* is depicted as Iceland, the non-existent *Pomona* is resurrected among the Orkneys, the *Aemodae* are presumably the Faeroes, and the Shetland Isles are unlisted. *Ocetis* and *Dumna* are approximately correct. Illustration courtesy of Reinhold Berg, www.bergbook.com

Any interpretation of the work of Pomponius Mela depends ultimately on a ninth century Vatican MS of dubious quality, generating even more dubious texts, and there is no firm guarantee that one interpretation is better than another.[54] But the most recent editions, commentaries and translations, follow Müller in punctuating the text.[55] They all put the *Haemodae* in the western end of the Baltic Sea, *contra Germaniam vectae in illo sinu quem Codanum diximus. ex iis (S)codanovia...ut magnitudine alias, ita fecunditate antestat* (Mela 3.6 [54], *bearing opposite Germany in that gulf we have called Codan. Of those Scodanovia stands out above the rest, not only in size, but also in fertility*).[56] But they do not explain Pliny's anomalous sequence of islands. None of the options on offer is satisfactory and I have serious reservations about all of them.[57] Mela calls his *Codanovia* (Sweden) the largest of the *Haemodae*, while Pliny (*HN* 4.96) described it as the *most famous of the islands in the Codan Gulf, of undiscovered size*, without realising that *Scadinavia, Scandiae* and *Acmodae* are part and parcel of the same group.[58] This is the consequence of inadequate source collation. Ptolemy fails to mention the *Haemodae* and *(S)codanovia* (Pliny's *Scadinavia)*, using the term *Scandiae* (*Geog.* 2.11.16) instead, and listing only four islands (including south Sweden) in a bay which Pliny describes as *refertus insulis* (*HN* 4.96 *crammed with islands*).[59] The location and number of the islands between the Bay of Kiel and Halsingborg suggests that seven is more apt than the four, which include Sweden, and that Mela and Pliny were closer to the correct number. The name *Haemodae* had become obsolete by Ptolemy's time, just as the Scythians, Pliny's *prisca appellatio* (*the old term*), are replaced by the Sarmatians. There is nothing to connect the *Haemodae* with Shetland, Ptolemy's *Thule*.

Any account of what is now called Scandinavia should contain some reference to Norway. Ptolemy's failure to produce any names or co-ordinates for Norwegian locations simply reflects the uncertainties about the area in earlier writers, due possibly to the belief that people could not live in such latitudes, inadequate or incomplete exploration (as in the case of Sweden), the reluctance of merchants to reveal their lucrative trade routes, and the absence of Roman military and naval involvement that far north.

The same codex, which reads that *Thule is adjacent (apposita)* to *the coast of the Belgae*, is seriously at fault here, since an isolated Thule cannot be *adjacent* to any coastline, especially one situated west of the Rhine.[60] Vossius correctly emended it to *opposita (facing)*, which gave Thule its requisite isolation and correct bearing.[61] But no adequate explanation was given for *Belgarum* (retained by

---

[54] *Vaticanus latinus* 4929, cf. Barlow 1938, 87: *the sole remaining authority*.

[55] Silberman 1988; Brodersen 1994; Romer 1988; Berry 1977; following Müller 1883, 104, note on Ptol. *Geog.* 2.3.14.

[56] Alonso-Núñez 1988, 52 believes this to be the Kattegat and the western Baltic. He suggests that Scatinavia/Scodonavia is the southernmost part of Sweden and equates it with Scandia. This may be accepted, but not his location of Thule halfway up the west coast of Norway. His rendering *Thule seen at a distance* cannot possibly imply that the Romans got a glimpse of Norway. For the use of *vectae* in this passage cf. Mela 2.3 (37).

[57] The reading here is controversial. Salmasius and Vossius read *Vecta* as a name, but this is a later usage (cf. Rivet/Smith, 1979, 488). In any case the Isle of Wight does not face Germany, and this reading is ruled out by *ex iis* which can only refer to a *plural* antecedent, i.e. *Haemodae*. Gronovius' *ex insulis* (*of the islands*), 1782, 281, cannot be an expansion of *iis*. Grienberger's *exit* (*emerges*), 1921, 1199, is totally unnecessary, while Frick's suggestion of *eximia* (*outstanding*), which Parroni supports, 1984b, 355, merely duplicates *antestat*. Parthey began his next sentence with *in illo sinu*, but *ex iis* is not likely to appear in the *middle* of the clause. Ranstrand was not prepared to commit himself and obelised *ex iis*. The MS reading *Vecti* claimed in *RE* VII 2182 does not exist. The word order *septem Haemodae...ex iis Codanovia...antestat* is reminiscent of Mela 2.7: *sex sunt...ex his Peuce notissima et maxima* (*there are six...of these Peuce is the biggest and most famous*).

[58] He uses the form *Scadinavia*. But the ending in *-ovia* is more likely.

[59] Pekkanen 1987, 552 claims that the *sinus Codanus* comprises the *whole* Baltic. But the whole Baltic is not crammed with islands. Silberman 1989, 579 points out that the '*sinus Codanus*' can only represent the *south of Sweden and the area between the Skagerak and the bay of Kiel*. I suggest that Lolland was one of these islands and should be listed among the *Haemodae*. Mela's knowledge of the *Haemodae* probably derives from Roman contact with the Baltic, which had been ongoing since the time of Augustus. This would come via Germany, either through trade, military reconnaissance or treaties with chiefs, cf. the Hoby grave (n. 2 above). Pliny had served in Germany during his earlier military career and may have had access to information on the Baltic coast. His reading *Acmodae* must be a scribal error for *Aemodae*. Apart from Lolland and S. Sweden the *Haemodae* should also include the two other large islands, Funen and Zealand, and perhaps Mon, Falster and Aero. Blaeu in his atlas of 1654 correctly located the *Haemodae* in the Baltic and named six of those I have listed. He omitted Sweden.

[60] It is surprising that Parthey retains this reading in his edition.

[61] Vossius 1658, 57. It is strange that modern editors have not adopted the Vossian emendation, while translators (e.g.

Vossius) which bears no geographical relationship to Thule. Abraham Gronovius conjectured *Belcarum* (*of the Belcae*), since Mela had already referred to Scythians called *Belcae* (3.5 [36]).[62] But the Scythians, according to Mela, lived on the borders of Asia, which hardly comes under the heading of north-west Europe.[63] Silberman's map is distorted in order to accommodate this conjecture, with the result that Thule and the *Orcades* appear in the same latitude. The MS error involves only one letter and, although *Belgae* and *Belcae* are attested forms, they are geographically flawed. *Bergarum* (*of the Bergae*), which appears in Camden, would fit neatly, and Hawkes, Rivet and Smith and Silberman noted it as a possibility.[64] It might refer to the natives of *Bergi* or *Berrice*, located in Norway. Shetland would be *Bergarum litori opposita* (*opposite the shore of the Bergae*) because it lay on exactly the same line of latitude as Bergen (60°N) at a distance of 220 miles. Dion was sure about this and talks of the *Bergae* as *partie du littoral norvégien où se trouve aujourd'hui Bergen* (*indication précieuse en ceci qu'elle confirme l'identification de Thulé avec les Shetland*).[65] Silberman also was right to explore the possibility of a link here, commenting that *si l'on rapproche Bergae de Bergen, on est tenté d'identifier Thulé avec les Shetland, en face de Bergen*.[66] But his translation *opposite* in this commentary note contradicts the *next to* in his translation of *apposita*, and there is no point in his reference to Jordanes (*Get*. 3.22), whose *Bergio* is used in connexion with the Goths and should relate to Sweden (*Scadinavia*). I do not subscribe to the view of Whatmore and Dion that *Berrice* is a corruption of *Nerigos* (*not* a MS reading, but a conjecture of earlier editors), to be linked with *Norge*, although the end-product is the same.[67] Equally speculative are Hawkes' attempts to link the inferior MS variants, *Vergon* and *Verigon* with *Rerigonius sinus* (Loch Ryan).[68] Roseman's suggestion that *Berrice* might be one of the *Bergi* is reasonable, insofar as there could be a link between the two, but her proposal that *Bergi* could be an earlier name for the Shetlands does not tie in with her *Baltic* location for the *Scandiae* which appear in the same sentence.[69] Ninck fancifully claimed that *Berrice* was *Pomona* (Mainland, Orkney).[70] But the name is a fantasy, conjured up by the errors of misguided Elizabethan scholars. How can a non-existent *Pomona* be the largest island of all? In any case *Dumna* (allegedly Lewis[71]), listed in the same group, is larger than any in the Orcadian archipelago.

Rivet/Smith 1979, 42) persist in rendering the participle as *opposite*. *Apposita* means *adjacent, adjoining, next to*. Clearly editors have been misled by the incorrect definition in *OLD*, as meaning *opposite*, which has no more justification than the assumption that the English words *opposite* and *apposite* are synonymous. *TLL* is correct in equating *apposita* with *vicina*. How can Thule, *the furthest of islands,* and six days' sail away from Britain, be *adjacent* to any coast?

[62] Gronovius 1782, 1029.

[63] *East of the Vistula*, Parroni, 1984b, 356. Strabo, *Geog*. 1.2.27, notes that the ancient geographers, such as Ephorus, used the term *Scythians* to embrace all the northern peoples and that subsequent discoveries allowed further refinements such as *Celtiberians* and *Celtiscythians*. Mela located them by the river Don and the Caspian Sea. By Ptolemy's time Scythia was firmly located in Asia. Its northern limit was never established.

[64] Camden, *Britannia* 1588; Hawkes 1975, 34; Rivet/Smith 1979, 42, 76; Silberman 1988, 288.

[65] Dion 1977, 279: *part of the Norwegian coast where Bergen is today* (*a precious clue in confirming the identification of Thule with Shetland*). A connection between *Belcae*, *Bergae* and *Bergen* is discussed in full by Magnani 2002, 182 f., who agrees with Dion and stresses a Norwegian rather than Scythian location. Journes/Georgelin 2000, 104 f., apart from regarding the *Haemodae* as Shetland, resurrecting the impossible *Nerigon* and putting Pytheas in Iceland, assume that the *Bergae* - *Bergen* link is a fact rather than a probability. The connection between *Bergae* and *Bergen* was made by both Camden (cf. previous note) and the cartographer Ortelius (*TOT* 192, 57), who used the historian's data for his atlas. Camden noted the textual anomaly and refers to Thule as *opposite Bergen* (*Bergae, not Belgae, as has been wrongly and corruptly written*).

[66] Silberman 1988, 288: *if Bergae is linked with Bergen, one is tempted to identify Thule with Shetland, opposite Bergen*. This observation is inconsistent with his translation, *près du littoral des Belcae*.

[67] Whatmore 1913, 319; Dion 1977, 279 n.20. Cassidy 1963, 596 reads *Nerigos* and assumes it to be the Isle of Lewis.

[68] Hawkes 1975, 34. It will have been noted by now that Hawkes faces considerable criticism. His work is almost entirely speculative and comes with a *caveat*.

[69] Roseman 1994, 94.

[70] Ninck 1945, 220. Ninck fell into the same trap which deludes present-day Orcadians who persist in applying the name *Pomona* not only to Mainland, Orkney, but to taverns and restaurants. The error stems from a 16th century misinterpretation of a passage in pseudo-Solinus (ed. Mommsen 1895, 219, 1.25): *ab Orcadibus Thylen usque quinque dierum ac noctium navigatio est; sed Thyle larga ac diutina pomona copiosa est* (*from the Orkneys to Thule the voyage takes five days and nights; but Thule is extensive and abundant in the prolonged yield of its crops*). Buchanan (1506-1582), following the *Scotichronicon* of John of Fordun (1871, 1.2.11), had assumed that 'Pomona' was a second island, Orkney, distinct from Thule (presumably because both islands appeared in the previous sentence) and writes in his *Rerum Scoticarum Historia*: *Orcadum maxima multis veterum Pomona vocatur* (*The largest of the Orkneys is called Pomona by many of the ancients*). The creation of myths in the context of Romano-British history will be examined later.

[71] It is generally assumed that Dumna is Lewis and Harris in the Outer Hebrides. But Ptolemy's co-ordinates place it on the

A link with Bergen (Norse *Bjørgvin*, hill pasture, cf. *OE Beorg* and modern *borough* and *broch*) should not be ruled out. Bergen, like Lerwick with which it now has close maritime links, has a conspicuous harbour, geared to the needs of the fishing industry which would have been a distinctive feature of Norwegian and Shetlandic lifestyles in the Iron Age. The Greek version, *Berrice* (perhaps a duplication of *Bergi*[72]) may well reflect the mountainous Norwegian landscape, as described by bilingual traders operating via the Skagerrak between the Graeco-Roman and Celtic worlds. Yeames refers to an archaic Greek statuette, allegedly excavated at Bergen, and suggests that it reached Bergen as a result of the trade in amber.[73] He goes on to say that *from Jutland to the south of Norway is not an incredible voyage for a sailor in the sixth century*. Roman imports into Hordaland may well have come in through Bergen.[74] Dion proposed that Pytheas on the final stage of his journey proceeded from Shetland to Norway, where he landed not far from Bergen.[75] This might explain the origin of the claim put out by Pliny's unnamed sources who would have assumed that if one (Pytheas?) could travel from Shetland to Norway, then the reverse was also possible. But Dion's theory of *two* Thules, a smaller one, Shetland, and a larger one, Norway, can hardly pass muster.[76] Are we to assume that when Pytheas reached Norway, *he found the name of Thule attached* there as well?

If Sweden can be treated as an island, why can't Norway (*Berrice*) be regarded by Pliny as the *largest of all* (*maximam omnium*)?[77] The points to emphasise are that *Thule* and *Berrice* cannot both refer to Shetland, that neither the *Haemodae* nor the *Bergi* should be identified with the Shetland group, and that Iceland cannot be listed among the British Isles any more than Cyprus can be called the furthest of the islands around Greece

---

same longitude (30°) as Orkney and Shetland. Why do Pliny's sources place it in a *Scandinavian* context ? The *Ravenna Cosmography* provides a list of the western isles, a list which includes Skye (?), Canna and Bute, but ominously makes no mention of *Dumna, Bergi* or *Berrice*. Strang 1997, 13, referring to the turning of Scotland, says that Ptolemy *dropped off the larger islands at convenient places; Thule at 35° and the Orcades at 55°, trying to maintain some sort of visual integrity in their relative positions above Scotland*. But Lewis is *larger* than Shetland and surely merits the same consideration. Why does Shetland receive five sets of co-ordinates from Ptolemy, while Dumna gets only one? Why should Dumna be moved, when Thule and the Orkneys are not? Why cannot Dumna maintain some sort of *visual integrity* and be identified with Hoy (Anthon 1850, 213) ? Or why can it not be moved further to the east in Scandinavia where Pliny apparently locates it? Ptolemy makes no mention of *Berrice* or *Bergi* because exploration had not embraced Norway (cf. *Geogr.* 1.5), and such places were hearsay (*sunt qui prodant...*).

[72] Whether *Bergos* is preferable to *Vergos*, the reading of the superior MS (*A*), is open to question. B and V are frequently interchanged in proper names during transmission of texts, cf. *Batavorum/Vatavorum* (*Agr.* 36.1), *Boudicca/Voadicca* (*Agr.*16.1). Stichtenoth 1959, 84 suggested a possible derivation for Berrice from the German *Bär* (*bear*), assuming a connection with the Greek *arktos* (*north*) and the constellation of *Ursa Major*.

[73] Yeames 1906, 284 f.

[74] Hansen 1987, 439 gives a list of Roman imports found in Hordaland and now in the Bergen Museum.

[75] Dion 1977, 202-204.

[76] Bianchetti 1998, 152 pointed out, quite rightly, that Pytheas would not have given the same name to two different places.

[77] Selkirk's argument, 1995, 183, that Norway *is not an island*, is pointless. Sweden is not an island either, but Pliny believed it was. It is the ancient conception which matters, not the modern reality.

Chapter 2

THE MANUSCRIPTS OF TACITUS' *AGRICOLA*

longa est iniuria, longae
ambages. sed summa sequar fastigia rerum

The damage is protracted, as are the complexities. But I will trace
out the main points

Virgil *Aeneid* 1.341-2

In the absence of archaeological evidence, unlikely to be conclusive in support of Agricola's naval movements, literary evidence must be scrupulously examined at source and philological arguments proffered for a radical reinterpretation of Tacitus' statements on the role of Agricola's fleet in the north. In order to understand the points which will be subsequently clarified a very brief explanation of the manuscript format and tradition is necessary.[78] My own opinions are integrated with this.

The standard texts of Tacitus' *Agricola* are based on a ninth-century MS from the Benedictine monastery at Fulda in Germany, the *codex Aesinas latinus 8*, referred to as *E*.[79] This resurfaced in 1902 at Jesi in Italy, after a disappearance of more than four hundred years.[80] The three other MSS, all written in the 15th century, are ultimately derived from *E*.[81] So only rarely can they be introduced as evidence. Unfortunately *E*, which is written in Caroline minuscule, exists only from chs. 13.1 to 40.2 (ff. 56-63), together with a palimpsest (f. 69) with some decipherable readings from 40.2 to 43.4. The rest of the manuscript is a 15th-century transcription of the missing or damaged sections in the hand of S. Guarnieri: these sections are referred to as *e*. *E* contains corrections, both in the text itself, where they are referred to as E^2, and variants written in the margin, E^{2m}. The readings of both E^2 and E^{2m}, being contemporary with *E*, are just as valid as, and, in some cases, superior to, those of *E*, especially in the interpretation of proper names.[82] The last point is important in the light of the argument I shall propose. In tackling minuscule, one is confronted not only with continuous script, often with no spaces between words, but with the similarity of letter forms, so that *c* and *t* are often indistinguishable, while upward strokes sometimes make it hard to determine whether we have *in* or *un* or *m* or even *ut*. At the same time, the scribe or his corrector occasionally produces a blend of inspiration and nonsense, so that we cannot tell whether we are dealing with a sober idiot or a drunken scholar. Yet for all the complaints made by Furneaux, quoted below, the text is quite reasonable when compared with the First Medicean MS of the *Annals*: this, like its junior counterpart, originated from Fulda about the same time and leads one to conclude that it was the creation of a drunken idiot. Who in a sober state would make the title of the work *an integral part of the text which he evidently made no effort to construe*?[83] In all probability the exemplar for the *codex Aesinas* was also written in minuscule, and

---

[78] For the history and interrelation of the manuscripts, cf. Sleeman 1914, xxxviii-xlv; Robinson 1935, 1-78; Lenchantin de Gubernatis 1945, v-xxii; de Saint-Denis 1956, xxiii-xxx; Mendell 1957, 257-293; Koestermann 1964, v-xxvi; Ogilvie 1967, 80-90; Till 1979, 7-10; Delz 1983, i-vii; Turner 1997, 587-589; Pohlmann, 2003, 153-60.

[79] General consensus assigns it a ninth-century date: those who follow Wissowa, e.g. Anderson, Spilman and de Saint-Denis, have no support for the tenth. There was also a MS of the *Agricola* at Monte Cassino in the 12th century. Whether it was the same as the Fulda MS or a descendant is open to question, cf. Ogilvie 1967, 81.

[80] *E* is the Oxford abbreviation for the codex. Further refinements are added by Murgia 1977, 324 n.2. Till 1979, 7-10 and Soverini 2004, 45 use *H* (for Hersfeld) for the Caroline section and *E* for the 15th-century transcriptions. Delz 1983 assumed that the Hersfeld and the Aesinas were the same. That they were different was proposed by Mendell 1949, 134 f.; 1957, 257-293 and Schaps 1979, 28-42, and supported by Winterbottom 1983, 411.This was challenged by Murgia and Rodgers 1984, 145-153, cf. Magnaldi 1997, 133). For the history of the codex, past and present, cf. Brugnoli 1961, 68-90, Schama 1995, 75-81 and Niutta 1996, 172-202. The codex currently resides in the Biblioteca Nazionale in Rome, where it is labelled *Cod. Vitt. Em.* 1631.

[81] Codex Toletanus 49,2 (*T*); codex Vaticanus 3429 (*A*); codex Vaticanus lat. 4498 (*B*).

[82] Cf. Perret 1950, 99 f.; Koestermann 1964, xii; Murgia 1977, 339.

[83] Oliver 1951, 235.

any brilliant conjecture by the marginal corrector is probably due less to his intelligence than to the availability of an alternative exemplar.

Richard Dawkins coined the term *memes*, units of information stored in the human memory bank.[84] His theory was that the transmission of information from one individual to another *ad infinitum* went through different stages of distortion until it was so far removed from its source as to be barely recognisable from the original. When the information is verbal, it is impossible to retrace its path. Unlike Virgil's *Rumour*, which *mobilitate viget viresque acquirit eundo* (*flourishes by movement and gathers strength as it goes*), it gets weaker in its progress until the shout becomes a whisper. But with the written word there is basis for hope. Tacitus wrote his *Agricola* in AD 98. It passed from the author to the bookseller/publisher who furnished a team of copyists to transcribe it. Even at this early stage transcription errors would occur. Tacitus could not check everything published under his name. We shall never find a MS with his autograph and it would be interesting to know what he would have made of the work reassembled in a German monastery in his name over seven centuries later. What we possess is a reflection in a distorting mirror and so far we have not succeeded in straightening the image to the point where we can say with complete confidence that all of this is what Tacitus wrote. Furneaux referred to *the corruptions and other difficulties of the text which are proportionately more numerous than in any other work of Tacitus*.[85] This was written four years before the discovery of *E*, which in fact solved very few of the problems that troubled Furneaux.

Where variations occur through contemporary or humanist corrections the judgement of editors has given rein to wild speculation. If two different readings are on offer, one must be wrong—but which one? And why do we prefer one to the other? If Tacitus is referring to a *part* of Agricola's *forces* (*partem virium*) and the scribe writes *vinum* (*Agr.* 25.1, *wine*) in the margin, the likelihood is that he was dreaming about the next glass of Benedictine.[86] In that case the correct version is obvious. Blurred vision, whether induced by wine or candle fumes, may lead to the addition of an extra syllable and produce the opposite meaning. Thus *cognitum* (26.1, *discovered*) becomes *incognitum* (*undiscovered*), perhaps reflecting a subconscious guilt that there might be a spot check. The worst scenario is where the marginal corrector offers a reading, *reducit* (38.2, *led back*), which takes Agricola in the opposite direction (south), when *E* reads *deducit* (*led down*), meaning that Agricola took his army down from the hills into the coastal plain to the north, where the island ended.[87] Sadly this error still has its supporters. Fortunately there is a general consensus on what we can leave untouched; but a hundred different editions reflect the same number of viewpoints. We still end up with a hundred different images of Tacitus, and they cannot all be right. Still, even a distorted image is better than none.

Any experienced teacher knows how easy it is to trace the source of a dubious piece of homework. The detected student copies it piecemeal without a mistake, and, by being faithful to the original, which contains the same peculiar errors, he gives himself away. Had he been intelligent, he would have made a few mistakes on purpose. The Dark Age scribe, whether or not he knows what he is transcribing, is also making his mistakes unconsciously. But he is not trying to cheat or to tell future generations how incompetent he is. The mind-numbing routine takes its toll; the cloistered discipline of the ill-lit *scriptorium* requires that the maxim *humanum est errare* is not to be entertained.[88] But do his superiors actually check his work for errors? Does he want to transcribe it in the first place? Is it some sort of religious penance? Or is there nothing else to do between prayers? It is not simply writing

---

[84] Dawkins 1976, ch.11.
[85] Furneaux 1898, xi. He goes on to say (5): *the difficulties of scholarship are greater in it than in any other part of the works of Tacitus*.
[86] There is no reason why a scribe's attention should not be preoccupied with something else. Ogilvie 1991, 1722 is unhappy with *paenitentiam* (*Agr.*31.4 *repentance*) and would prefer Wellesley's *poenam* (*punishment*). He describes the scribe's action as *an example of a monastic corruption...in which a scribe's mind is influenced by theological thoughts.* So why not *oenological* thoughts?
[87] The marginal correction is probably due to the scribe's quite justifiable assumption that Agricola had reached the end of the island and could go no further; hence a *return*. He did not consider the fact that the battle had been fought in a mountainous area and that a *descent* to the coastal plain was inevitable in order to regain contact with the fleet.
[88] The comments here are aimed at the general reader. For a thorough understanding of the workings of a medieval *scriptorium* see the magisterial study by Newton 1999.

practice. One would like to think that the motive was to save the past for the benefit of the future. But what the student and the scribe have in common, apart from the obligation to complete a thankless assignment, is that they both cause a degree of aggravation for the teacher and the editor. The teacher will laugh it off because of the naivety of the culprit, the editor will be filled with self-doubt because he is treading a path along which his predecessors have already stumbled. He knows, however much he refuses to admit it, that the next generation of editors will consign his work, at best to oblivion, at worst to the scrutiny of others. This is the price you pay for putting your head on the line. You allow the reviewers to justify their existence. Your *memes* may be taking you away from, rather than towards, Tacitus. Editors have milked every possible interpretation from the manuscript, trying to make sense by juggling nuances of different words, by readjusting the order of individual letters, where the scribe's eye has strayed, by bracketing sentences which suggested duplication, in fact by competing with each other in the quest for innovation. There are still dubious words and sentences in the *Agricola*, and even more dubious explanations which are perpetuated in so called 'revisions'.[89] There are passages which contain nonsense, that still need to be corrected, and the worst scenario is when the explanations for these are more nonsensical than the nonsense they are supposed to explain.

The editor's function is to elucidate the text, not to obfuscate it by putting the blame on Tacitus and accusing him of lack of conciseness. Such excuses are unacceptable. The textual critic likes to think he has come up with something new. There is nothing wrong with that, provided it makes sense and is an improvement on previous theories. Learned journals are the playground for new ideas and the graveyard for bad ones. Unfortunately the transformation from new to bad is usually only a matter of time. Library stacks are like mortuaries where the bodies, individually numbered, are taken out to be inspected by the curious before being duly interred, occasionally exhumed and ultimately forgotten until resurrection day. The same applies to the 'authoritative' texts of the *Agricola*, which mark the acme of indigenous scholarship, whether it be in England, Germany, France, Italy or anywhere else. Whereas in the codex the corrections are a by-product, in the printed texts they have become an industry, where rival variant readings jostle with each other to secure recognition, while the editor's suggestion stands proudly in the text, perhaps protected by a dagger with which subsequent editors will stab it to death. The relegation of these discards to the bottom of the page is virtually a death sentence. The graveyard is expanding, when it should be contracting and soon there will be no more room for the corpses. The reader who is confronted with ten different editions is spoilt for choice— Tacitus himself would have insisted that there shouldn't be one. It is quite right that scholarship should be in a state of flux and that problems require new approaches. At the end of the day we should be thankful that Tacitus is still subject to investigation. Otherwise philologists would be working in supermarkets.

Since the *Agricola* is (as already said) absolutely essential to the study of Roman Britain in the first century, writers on the topic who are not Latinists have to resort to translations which are based on the Latin texts, which themselves are based on the MSS. This puts them at a disadvantage because they may be drinking from a contaminated stream without being aware of it. Such writers feel they have to give a brief explanation to the general public about the manuscript tradition in the hope that the reader will not look too closely into it. In some respects they are right: references to manuscripts at the beginning of a chapter may not be an inspiring start to gain the attention of the reader. But it is all a matter of degree. A Latinist reading an academic journal is likely to fall asleep when faced with a hundred pages of palaeobotanical references, when all he needs is the brief concluding paragraph which tells him what a Roman has had for breakfast. It was not my intention to write for an ever decreasing circle, nor at the same time to deceive the public by professing to know what I didn't. The bottom line is that the manuscript is the ultimate source and its interpretation will always be subject to controversy. The problem lies in determining which interpretation is acceptable, and why.

---

[89] The optimism exuded by Furneaux in 1898 is repeated by Ogilvie 1991, 1721: *Of the clear corruptions, I am confident that a number have been so far remedied that any new dramatic cure is unlikely.* Why should any cure be *dramatic* or *unlikely*?

Tacitus *Agricola* 38.3-4, Codex Aesinas Latinus 8, folio 63, verso (from Till 1943)

Note how a scholar has inserted 'space-bars' in lines 7-8 to facilitate reading where continuous script might create problems:

quo/novarum
gentium animi/ ipsa transitus

There was no good reason for the scribe to compress the words here, since there is adequate space on the lines. It raises the question of whether he knew the meaning of what he was actually transcribing. Ethnic and place names were written down as they were pronounced, irrespective of spelling. The spelling of the word *Brittanniam* in line 4 is quite common, but we find elsewhere in the MS *Britanniam* and *Brittaniam*. The scribe was not too concerned, since in his mind they all sounded the same. There was no standardisation in the spelling of proper names. The marginal variants are indicated in the main text by a small dash over the relevant word.

Chapter 3

REASSESSMENT OF VOCABULARY AND SENSE

semper ego auditor tantum numquamne reponam

*Am I always to be merely a listener and shall I never have something
to say in return ?*
                                                                Juvenal, *Satires* 1.1

We may begin with an analysis of what Tacitus tells us about *Thule* (Mainland, Shetland) in *Agricola* 10.4:

hanc oram novissimi maris tunc primum Romana classis circumvecta insulam esse Britanniam affirmavit, ac simul incognitas ad id tempus insulas, quas Orcadas vocant, invenit domuitque. dispecta est et Thule, quia hactenus iussum et hiems appetebat. sed mare...perhibent
   (ed. A.A.Lund)

It was then that a Roman fleet for the first time[90] circumnavigated[91] this coast of the remotest sea and established that Britain is in fact an island. Then too it discovered the islands, hitherto unknown, which are called the Orcades (Orkneys), and subjugated them.
   (tr. A.R. Birley)

The fleet is involved in three activities: an east-west voyage around northern Scotland for the first time;[92] then the reduction of the Orkney Islands; but what is its role in the last section, as translated below, by Mattingly and by Aujac?[93]

*Thule, too, was sighted by our men, but no more; their orders took them
no farther, and winter was close at hand...*

On entrevit aussi Thulé; interdiction d'aller plus loin, et l'hiver approchait...

---

[90] For initiatives attributed to Agricola, cf. Lund 1980, 275-282.
[91] Not a *complete* circumnavigation of the island, as suggested by Forni 1962, 125. It simply means *sailed round*. The Usipian mutineers had done the same in the reverse direction (*circumvecti Britanniam*, *Agr.* 28.3), cf. Liv. 10.2.4; Plin. *HN* 2.167. Augoustakis in his abstract for the 2008 conference misquotes Tacitus, *Romana classis tunc primum circumvecta insulam* (*the Roman fleet then for the first time sailed round the island*). Tacitus does not say this. One cannot make assumptions from half a quotation. The suggestions of Ogilvie 1967, 282 and Durant 1969, 43 of a voyage round the west coast via the Irish Sea and the Channel to a southern base for the winter defies both logic and strategy. Nor is there any reason for the fleet to <u>complete</u> a circumnavigation which would merely take it back to its starting-point in north-east Scotland. For an evaluation of the problems here, cf. Burn 1969, 59; Strobel 1987, 202 n.19; Hanson 1991a, 140-142. I find it inconceivable that after its intense campaigning along the east coast of Scotland and its voyage to the Orkneys and Shetland the fleet should be commissioned to sail *all the way round* Britain, a voyage which would not be completed before the end of the year, by which time the fleet would be at the bottom of the Ocean. Hoffmann's suggestion (2001), based on Cassius Dio, and perhaps influenced by Urban 1971, 21-28, that the circumnavigation took place in AD 79, cannot be entertained. Dio should never be used in evidence against Tacitus
[92] This is not strictly true, unless the previous exploratory mission of Demetrius involved only a few ships, rather than a fleet. In any case assumptions that Demetrius' voyage involved the Western Isles (thus Ogilvie, 1968, 33) are unfounded. Plutarch (*De defect. orac.* 18, 419e) merely refers to *deserted islands scattered around Britain* and that Demetrius visited the nearest of the inhabited ones. The islands referred to may have been the Orkneys, not the Hebrides. Tacitus makes no mention of the Hebrides. They were irrelevant since they did not figure in Agricola's plans for conquest. But an exploratory voyage to the Orkney Islands may have been the prelude to their conquest (cf. Wainwright 1962, 65). Demetrius' voyage should be linked to naval intelligence. He was only part of a team. One can hardly suppose that Domitian commissioned him as a prototype of Columbus or Darwin. There is too much self-advertisement and fiction in Demetrius' story-telling to make it totally convincing, let alone put him in the Western Isles. The comment by Clay 1992, 618 that the islands were the *Scillies* may be dismissed.
[93] Mattingly 1948, 60; Aujac 1988, 340.

The French translation is equivalent to its English counterpart. But I maintain that both of them, and most other translations hitherto produced, do not reflect the Latin. The interpretation of *dispecta est* is crucial. It does not mean *sighted*,[94] nor *seen from far off*,[95] nor *glimpsed*.[96] The verb *dispicere* is an exact synonym for *perspicere*, paralleled in all its nuances: *to pick out with the eyes, to distinguish* (Suet. *Nero* 19.1; Curt. *HA* 4.12.20), *to examine closely, to inspect thoroughly* (Tac. *Ann.* 13.27.3).[97] All compounds of *spic/spec-* must initially embrace the *physical* concept of looking. The prefix *dis-*, as in the English *dis-sect*, reflects an *analytical* observation, which one would expect from naval surveyors, marking *different* points along the coast. *Dis-spic-spec-* has its exact parallel in Greek, *ana-scop-scept* which means *examine well* (Polyaen. *Strat.* 2.31.1; Paus. *GD* 10.25.4, cf. the English parallels, *dis-solve* and *ana-lyse*). Nowhere in any lexicon is it translated as *sighted*. The definition of *dispecta est*, which *OLD* and *TLL* offer, is arbitrary. Since it was always assumed that the verb meant *was sighted* or *glimpsed*—an unsubstantiated assumption based on the misconception that Agricola's naval officers could not have reached Shetland—few bothered to question the possibility of a different meaning. *OLD* should have cited this example right at the beginning of its second group of definitions (554.2), where the *physical* examination should precede the *mental* one. Volusenus returned, *perspectis regionibus omnibus* (*BG* 4.21). This was a *close examination of all the coastal areas* (of Kent) in a reconnaissance mission to locate suitable harbours for Caesar's invasion force in 55 BC. Thule *was closely examined* for similar reasons. Whence else, but from a close inspection, was Marinus able to confirm five sets of co-ordinates for Ptolemy's Thule?[98] This verb puts the Roman fleet in the coastal waters of Mainland, Shetland. The translations of Borzsák (in Hungarian), *was thoroughly* (or *well*) *examined* and A.R. Birley, *was thoroughly viewed* can be the only correct

---

[94] Stephenson 1894; Strut 1912 (*seen*); Acheson 1938; Mattingly 1948; Burn 1969 (*clearly sighted*); Dion 1977 (*en vue*); Rivet/Smith 1979; Till 1979; Handford 1986; Spaltenstein 1990); Hanson 1991a; Coleman 1988; Clarke 2001; Cunliffe 2001b; Freeman 2001 (*saw*); Magnani 2002; Salles 2002; Mason 2003; Rivet 1977, 62 through misinterpretation produces a false conclusion, *the fleet sighted it, but did not land, so that the old conception of it* [as an island rather than an archipelago] *remained unshaken*. Bosworth 2004, 557 is incorrect in saying that Thule *had come under observation*. This leads him to the conclusion that by keeping away from Thule Agricola showed *a prudence which Alexander* [being reckless] *would never have entertained*. Agricola made no personal visit to Thule—but his fleet did.

[95] *Seen/sighted/descried from far off/ at a distance/in the distance*: Orelli 1848; Church/Brodribb 1869; Andresen 1880; Davis 1892; Furneaux 1898; Pearce 1899; Anderson 1922: Gudeman 1928; Thomson 1948; Smith, 1987; Aujac 1988; Benario 1991; Romm 1992, 148 (*glances into the murky distance*); Wijsman 1998. Michelet 2006, 123-126 devotes an entire chapter entitled, *Britain in the Distance*, where Agricola is accorded less than his due. To support his interpretation of *distance* (*il verbo indica qui il 'distinguere' da lontana qualcosa*) Soverini 2004, 157 cites Caesar's description of Gergovia (*BG* 7.36.2), *qua dispici poterat* (*where it could be seen at a distance*). MS corruption from *de-* to *di-* is a commonplace, and editors such as Greenough, Kennedy and Edwards who read *qua despici poterat* (*from where a bird's eye view was possible*) are surely right. When an elevated position is referred to, the sense requires a bird's eye view from that position, not a *distant view* from the plain. Caesar had already examined the location closely, *perspecto urbis situ* (*BG* 7.36.1). So what need of distance? In fact, after his long-winded digression on the Aedui, he refers back to Gergovia with *ut erat a Gergovia despectus in castra* (*BG* 7.45.4, *as there was from Gergovia a view down into the camp*). For the impersonal use of *despicere* cf. Livy 44.6.8, *ut despici vix sine vertigine...possit* (*so that one cannot look down without feeling giddy*, cf. Amm. Marc. 19.5.4). In Caesar, *to be seen from a distance* is *procul videri* (*BC* 1.41.4). Cravioto 2003, 78 informs us that *Thule was sighted. It is worth noting that they didn't dare sail in the direction of this island.* No reference to instructions.

[96] *Barely sighted/glimpsed*: de Saint-Denis 1956; Forni 1962; Gorrichon 1974; Romm 1992. This would imply *vix conspecta est*. Pedech 1976, 73 asserts that *not even Agricola's fleet got as far as Pytheas. It merely glimpsed at best the Shetland Islands*. There can be nothing more amusing than a criticism levelled by someone who knows nothing against someone who knows still less. Ghael 1838, 482 criticises a certain Mr Logan, who entertained his own views about Ireland and Thule. Apart from citing the Latin as *despecta est* the indignant Ghael is at pains to point out that Agricola's *navigators had occasional glimpses of it* (Thule) *wrapt in snow and storms*. Church and Brodribb would have been proud of this.

[97] *dispiceret quisque sua merita* (*each should closely examine his services*), cf. Quint. *IO* 2.8.6; Amm. Marc. 14.9.1.

[98] There is no evidence to suggest that Marinus (and Ptolemy) obtained any co-ordinates on Thule directly from Pytheas, although, as will be suggested later, such data could have been available to Agricola. The necessary bearings for Thule would in fact be confirmed by Agricola's navigators, and subsequently made available to Marinus. Rivet/Smith 1979, 146 suggest that the bearings *are presumably based on an estimate made by the fleet*. This could be partly the case: the fleet need not have gone further north than Lerwick and may have estimated the rest of the coastline. The island follows the 90° distortion of northern Scotland. Ptolemy's co-ordinates make it roughly twice as long as its width. The correct measurements would make it about 13 miles shorter in length and about half of Ptolemy's width at the widest point. Carpenter 1966, 183 makes a sweeping assertion that *it is an <u>unchallengeable</u> inference that Ptolemy's data for the location of Thule <u>must</u> go back to Pytheas, since no one else in antiquity ever claimed to have visited that island*. Romm 1992, 157 likewise denies any visit. Rivet/Smith 1979, 42 suggest that the Greek form of *Thule* was never Latinised due to the fact that *no one from the ancient world ever found it again*. This contradicts what they earlier stated about the bearings taken by the fleet. At all events, I hope that these assertions will soon be laid to rest.

interpretations.[99] Ogilvie was right to reject translations reflecting a sighting—although he contradicts himself elsewhere.[100] Such versions are illogical and imply that the fleet commander was given instructions to reach a point where Thule could be seen in the distance. This was not a sight-seeing excursion or a 'Spot the Thule' competition. The emphatic position of the verb shows that it was more than a glimpse or sighting. If Thule was visible, it was accessible to Agricola's fleet. Ogilvie was also correct in his view that *the fleet must have sailed on to the Shetlands*, but his comment that *their orders only went as far as viewing* introduces a restriction which simply does not exist in the Latin. Why does every translator have to introduce words such as *only* or *no more*? Mattingly and Aujac produce a series of co-ordinate sentences and fail to translate *quia* (*because*), as do Rivet and Smith.[101] A causal clause is crucial here because it explains *why* Thule was closely examined. Andresen's observation that *quia* tells us that the island *was not approached, but only sighted from a distance* contradicts both Latin and logic, and stems from the failure to understand *dispecta est*.[102] Where did the *distance* come from? If we strip away the gratuitous restrictive terms we have a simple translation:

A close examination of Thule also was made because they had been instructed to go this far.

Agricola's instructions were clear enough: *Sail on to Thule and examine it closely.* But were they instructions *to* or instructions *from*? The impersonal form of the verb, *iussum est* (lit. *it was ordered*), is a device by Tacitus to disguise the fact that Domitian had authorised the expedition, even if he did not initiate it.[103] Tacitus' point of Agricola's fleet reaching the *ultima Thule* of Virgil and Seneca is a triumph of the reality of exploration over poetic myth. The *Thule* which is to serve Augustus, does not. It will serve Domitian if he chooses to extend the exploration to conquest. As will be argued in the next paragraph, Agricola could make a good case for what at first sight might appear to be a gamble with the fleet. I suggest that the strategic objective, like that of Volusenus, was to make a survey of the Shetland coast and confirm the location of the same harbour which Pytheas had used four hundred years earlier. Agricola had plans for possible future involvement. Cunliffe's observation, *it seems they sailed as far as Orkney*, is superficial and dismissive and does not respect the Latin and its implications.[104]

It is tempting to reflect on the possibility that Agricola's expedition to Shetland may have taken its origin from his earlier years, when c. AD 56, as a young student at university in Massilia (*Agr.* 4.2),[105] the home town of Pytheas, he would have imbibed not only traditional philosophy, but also the seafaring aura of the town,[106] the four hundred years of Pytheas' legacy and the works of Pytheas, the *Massaliot philosopher*.[107] Even today, as Cunliffe noted, the city of Marseille has a statue of Pytheas in its stock exchange, staring out across the harbour.[108] There is no reason why a similar statue could not have occupied an equally important niche in Massilia during the principate of Nero. More detailed documentation of Pytheas' travels in the Ocean, not originally designed for general consumption, in order to protect Massilian commercial interests in the fourth century BC,[109] may have been accessible

---

[99] Borzsák 1992; A.R. Birley 1999, 9, following Ogilvie's translation, 1967, 172.
[100] Ogilvie 1967, 172; contradicted at 35 and 283.
[101] Rivet/Smith 1979, 93. Columba 1935, 256 was one of the few people to see the illogicality of the sentence. *It seems to me*, he writes, *that some phrase must have dropped out after 'Thule' such as 'and no further, however*. He saw a problem which did not exist.
[102] Andresen 1880, 168.
[103] This would be counter to D.J. Breeze's observation, 1988, 16, *although there is no positive evidence that Agricola acted on instructions from his emperors* a point which he later (2007, 30) contradicts, *it would be wrong to assume that he acted on his own initiative*. See Appendix 4.
[104] Cunliffe 2001a, 415.
[105] Cf. Richmond 1944, 42 and Aujac 1993, 18. Strabo (*Geog.* 4.1.5) says that *at the present time Massilia has attracted also the most notable of the Romans, if eager for knowledge, to go to school there.*
[106] It is possible that the original role of Forum Iulii as a *naval* base may also have impacted on the young Agricola (A.R. Birley, *pers.comm.*).
[107] Cleom. *Cael.* I.4.208-210. Magnani 2002, 137 suggests that Tacitus' reference to Thule seems to reveal some recollection of Pytheas' account. He did not realise how close he was to the truth.
[108] Cunliffe 2001b, 1.
[109] Pytheas was probably funded by a Massilian merchant consortium, which would certainly have been cautious in screening

in Massilian records once the 'the statute of limitations' had lapsed and Oceanic charts were general knowledge.[110] Agricola's subsequent transfer from a studentship in Massilia to a senatorial tribunate in Britain would have sharpened his curiosity to find out for himself, as well as from books and maps, what lay in the far north of the island and beyond, hence *noscere provinciam* (*Agr.* 5.1, *he got to know his province*). On this basis Agricola would know exactly where Thule was and where to find a suitable harbour, since he would be following a tradition of which he had first-hand knowledge and he would have had over twenty years to put his plans into operation. Consequently the expedition to Shetland would be based on sound planning and sound bearings, not on chance. Pytheas, the pathfinder, had made it easy for Agricola. One is almost tempted to accuse Tacitus of suppressing the true facts (he may have exaggerated about the Orkney Islands being *undiscovered* and overstated the *circumnavigation* of Britain) in order to exaggerate the voyage into the *unknown* (successful propaganda, to judge by Silius Italicus' *ignotam Thylen, Pun.* 3.597, *unknown Thule*) and to credit Agricola with a daring enterprise under false pretences. Dion noticed the tendency in Polybius and Strabo to devalue the role of Pytheas in the interests of Roman patriotism.[111] But whatever motives we ascribe to Tacitus, the fleet deserved fuller treatment. Perhaps Lund's attribution of initiatives to Agricola needs re-examination. One thing is certain; Agricola would never have commissioned his fleet commander to risk his ships in uncharted waters out of sight of the coast. Tacitus, Marinus, Ptolemy, Strabo and Pliny were correct in locating Thule within secure sailing range of the Scottish mainland and Orkney. What a singular honour for his *alma mater* that Agricola could be as closely associated with Thule as Pytheas!

The comment made by Tacitus, *et hiems appetebat...sed mare pigrum...perhibent*, is distinctly odd. The approach of winter cannot be a reason for the reconnaissance of Shetland. Yet this is the implication of the texts currently on offer. De Saint-Denis, following Furneaux, with some logic placed a colon directly after *iussum*, and both Wex and Urlichs saw that *sed* was misplaced.[112] No one has provided a reasonable explanation for why *sed* should begin the next sentence. It *is,* as Heubner (*contra* Forni) noted, adversative.[113] Guarnieri's transcription (referred as *e*) repeats *et hiems* in successive lines, *& hiems appetebat & hiems sed mare* (a curiosity which Till and subsequent commentators have ignored), reflecting, perhaps, variant doublets in the archetype rather than his own carelessness. There appears to be a problem here; the sense requires a reversal of *et* and *sed*,[114] i.e. *sed hiems appetebat, et mare... perhibent* (*but winter was approaching, and they say that the sea...*). This part of the codex is only Guarnieri's transcription of the missing section and it is quite possible that the reversal of the conjunctions is correct. It is ironic that *Vaticanus* 4498 (*B*, generally ignored through its glaring inaccuracies) reads *sed hiems appetebat et mare*, a reading perceptively adopted by Schulz.[115] In any event, it should have appeared among Ogilvie's variants, since a contrast in sentences and sense is quite apparent.[116] De Saint-Denis was correct to acknowledge *B*'s reading. The conjunction may have arisen from a misinterpretation of (*hiem*)*set*(*mare*) by Guarnieri in his transcription.[117] It is more

---

any information which Pytheas brought back. Any suggestion that Pytheas was sponsored by Alexander the Great does not consider the immediate needs of Massilia (cf. Roseman 1994, 154), but merits some consideration in so far as it might explain why the Carthaginians, in fear of Alexander, would allow Pytheas a passage through the Pillars of Hercules (if his travels were entirely by sea) into the Atlantic whose routes they monopolised. I would see Pytheas' mission as primarily commercial, then scientific. Pytheas would only have published what was in the parameters of his remit. Massilia and Alexander did not share the same objectives.

[110] The protection of Massilian interests may be seen in Scipio Aemilianus' failure to obtain information about Britain from those he interviewed at Massilia (Str.*Geog.* 4.2.1, cf. Chevallier 1984, 91.

[111] Dion 1977, 273.

[112] De St. Denis 1956; Furneaux 1898; Wex 1852; Urlichs 1875.

[113] Heubner 1984; Forni 1962.

[114] We find an unnecessary *sed* in 16.3, where *E* reads *lascivi sed Trebellius* which E^2 then replaces with the equally meaningless *lascivir' sed Trebellius...*. In this case the contraction for *et* should replace *sed* which has no business being there.

[115] Schulz 1865.

[116] Murgia 1977, 324 lists three emendations in *B* which are relevant to Guarnieri's transcription. I believe we can now add a fourth.

[117] *set* = *sed*. This interchange of consonants is quite common, cf. *Agr.* 18.1, 24.2, *aut* for *haud*; 18.2, 21.2, 22.4, 29.4, *aput* for *apud*; 23, 27.1, 28.3, 29.4, 30,3, 33.2, 34.1, 37.2, *adque* corrected to *atque*. A similar case involving *sed* is found at *Agr.* 10.3, where *e* reads *unde & in universum fama est transgressis unde & universis fama sed*. The awkward *est* before *transgressis* is clearly, as pointed out by Wölfflin 1867, 144, a metathesis of *set* (= *sed*). We have two conjunctions, when

apt to link the approach of winter with sailing conditions in the next sentence where there is an attempt to define the North Atlantic Drift Current (Gulf Stream). Roman ships, approaching the main island, would have to negotiate the formidable Sumburgh Röst.[118]

> neum tenuatur hancoram no
> uissim maris tunc primum
> romana classis circumuecta
> insulam esse brittaniam affir
> mauit: ac simul incognitas ad
> id tempus insulas: quas orcha
> das uocant inuenit domuitq;
> Dispecta est & thyle quia
> hactenus nissum & hiems ap
> petebat & hiems: sed mare pi
> grum & graue remigantibus
> perhibent ne uentis quidem: pro

**Tacitus *Agricola* 10.4-5, Guarnieri's transcription (*e*)
of the missing section of the codex, folio 55, recto (from Till 1943).**

Guarnieri has clearly distinguished between the words to make his transcription 'reader-friendly'. But the second half of the first line does not follow this pattern:

hancoram no.....

The compression of the two words *hanc oram* (*this coast*) in a maritime context may have been due to the ninth century scribe (*E*) losing temporary concentration so as to produce a metonymous version of *anchoram* (*anchor*), a possibility rendered more likely by the alternative spelling (for *ancoram*) found in all the instances where the word occurs in the Medicean MSS of Tacitus, *anchorarum, anchoris*. Sailing around an *anchor* is, of course, nonsense, such as was noticed earlier in the confusion between *virium* and *vinum*. But the scribe, consciously or otherwise, is merely replacing one object with another. At all events Guarnieri should have recognised the problem and separated the two words. Nowhere else in his transcription of the *Agricola* does such compression occur. There is enough evidence elsewhere in the MS to suggest that Guarnieri, as well as *E*, was not always aware of what he was transcribing. The spelling *Brittaniam* in line 4 is routine for Guarnieri. In the seventeen instances where he refers to Britain or Britons only once do we find the single *t*. Carelessness produces the repetition of *& hiems* in line 10. If this duplication appeared in his exemplar, Guarnieri is guilty of failing to correct it. If it did not, Guarnieri has no excuses. The sad fact is that he appears to have destroyed or discarded the damaged exemplar which could have shown where the responsibility lay.

---

only one is required. For the replacement of a MS *et* with a correction *sed* cf. Stat. *Silv.*5.2.3.
[118] Nicolson 1984, 11.

The scenario, as I see it, is that the Roman fleet was instructed to return to winter anchorage at the end of the military campaigning season,[119] sailing, I suggest, from a bay in Caithness to a base somewhere on the Clyde (Dumbarton?). It would be no problem to overrun the Orkneys.[120] The opportunity to follow in the wake of Pytheas and to reconnoitre Shetland was too good to be missed and might never occur again. It would require no great time to cover the distance from Scapa Flow to Mainland, Shetland, to make a detailed report of the coastline, to instil fear in the natives by its very presence in a major harbour and then sail back to its winter base on the Clyde with the claim that it had been the first time that any Romans had reached, let alone 'sighted', Thule.

---

[119] It has been suggested that campaigning summers are defined by the spring and autumnal equinoxes, Raepsaet-Charlier 1991, 1843 n.165. But there is no need for such rigidity, which implies a two-season campaigning year of winter and summer. This contradicts Tacitus' statement that summer was already over and winter was approaching. There must be a period between the end of summer and the approach of winter. The interpretation of *winter quarters* is a point in question, since troops could be sent to *hibernacula* at the height of summer (*Ann.* 2.23.1). Strobel 1987, 203 set the battle of Mons Graupius in AD 84, at the end of July or early August and the voyage of the fleet anywhere between mid-August and the end of September. If the battle occurred in the far north well beyond Moray, there is no reason why the fleet should not have started out in early September. This would leave ample time for operations in the Orkneys and Shetland before returning to a winter base. I would incline to the view that a campaigning summer would end whenever it suited the governor.

[120] The Roman fleet would never have had the time to overrun more than a handful of some seventy islands. The conquest of offshore islands is given an *aura* of achievement scarcely merited. The conquest of the Isle of Wight is overplayed (Suet. *Vesp.*4.2), as is the reduction of Anglesey (Tac. *Ann.* 14.29). But those two islands did not constitute the type of obstacle which the Orkney brochs (over a hundred) would present to Agricola's marines.

Chapter 4

THE SEARCH FOR A HARBOUR

puppesque tuae pubesque tuorum
aut portum tenet aut pleno subit ostia velo

Your ships and the young men of your company are holding the harbour
or approaching its entrance under full sail

Virgil *Aeneid* 1.399-400

The triple commission of the fleet, outlined at *Agr.* 10.4, i.e. the circumnavigation of northern Britain, the conquest of the Orkneys and the voyage to Shetland, should be paralleled at 38.3-4. The circumnavigation is again referred to: *He instructed his fleet commander to sail around (northern) Britain, praefecto classis circumvehi Britanniam praecipit*. The landing on the Orkneys is implied, as Furneaux, Heubner, Saddington and Soverini noted, by *forces were allocated for that purpose, datae ad id vires*.[121] But there appears to be no mention of Shetland where there ought to be. The answer lies in the enigmatic and contentious sentence presented thus in the standard editions:

et simul classis secunda tempestate ac fama Trucculensem portum tenuit, unde proximo Britanniae latere praelecto omnis redierat

This is translated by Handford as follows:

At about the same time the fleet, which, aided by favourable weather, had completed a remarkable voyage, reached Trucculensis Portus. It had started the voyage from that harbour, and after coasting along the adjacent shore of Britain had returned intact.[122]

Now any translation is only as good as the text on which it is based. But if the manuscript is corrupt and goes unchecked, then so is the text, and consequently the translation is valueless.[123] The above is a well-intentioned, yet seriously flawed, attempt to do justice to Latin which, even translated less freely, would still be virtually meaningless. But introducing into the translation words which are not there in the Latin (*had completed a remarkable voyage, it had started the voyage*) is at least better than introducing into the original text, as some editors have done, extra Latin words (*profecta, starting out*) which cannot possibly be there. Tacitus would never sacrifice logic to alleged conciseness. Editors have looked in vain for excuses to justify this sort of nonsense.

It has often been assumed that the mysterious *Trucculensis portus* was the winter station of the fleet.[124] But there is no basis for this assumption, apart from the fact that no sensible Roman governor would allow his fleet to spend the winter in some remote spot in the far north of Scotland.[125] Why would

---

[121] Furneaux 1898, 149. *Vires* implies more than just naval strength. Manpower would be required for armed landings both on the Orkneys and on the north coast of Scotland. The fleet was only part of Agricola's resources (*partem virium, Agr.*25.1). Church /Brodribb 1869, 82 correctly translate as *military force*, while Sleeman 1914, 119 refers to '*troops*' to make landings. See also Heubner 1984, 111 (*Diese Streitkräfte waren bei dem Landeunternehmen auf den Orkneys eingesetzt*); Saddington 1990, 228 (*marines (vires) were provided*); Soverini 2004, 270 (*si trattava evidentemente delle truppe che sbarcarono sulle isole Orkneys*).
[122] Handford 1986.
[123] Burn 1969, 59 states that *the translation on the face of it is not difficult* and goes on to produce a version based not only on rejected readings (*omni*), but on a misinterpretation of the uninterpretable.
[124] Ogilvie 1967, 282 f.; Reed 1971, 147 f. This assumption was quite rightly rejected by Burn 1969, 59, Strobel 1987, 202 n.19 and Hanson 1991a, 141.
[125] Strobel 1987, 202 n.19.

Tacitus bother to mention it, when he does not tell us where the *army* was quartered for the winter? Rivet and Smith were correct in referring to Tacitus' reticence on place names.[126] But to state that Tacitus names it because *it was the furthest known place on the mainland* will convince no one. The *furthest known place* was Ptolemy's *Tarved(un)um* (Dunnet Head) which ultimately derives from Agricola's reconnaissance reports. Besides, how do we know it was on the *mainland*? Nowhere in the monograph does Tacitus name any military base or even civilian settlement in Britain. Consequently any obscure geographical reference in the *Agricola*, whether to a harbour or to a tribe, should be regarded with the highest suspicion. Tacitus was not interested in presenting geographical *trivia* in his biography and we should not be fooled by Dark Age dyslexia.

After the battle of Mons Graupius the combative role of the army was finished. Its installation in winter quarters was not due to the imminent approach of winter,[127] but to the fact that its campaign was virtually over. The battle was won, the enemy was demoralised and hostages were taken from tribes in the extreme north. But the role of the fleet was not over; its triple commission had yet to be implemented. More to the point, the naval arm of Agricola's forces merits the same consideration as his land forces. The fleet cannot compete on the same terms as those in the field; its function is to transport and terrorise. It cannot win a victory over the natives because they have no combat vessels. Its victory has to be over the elements, *tempestatum ac fluctuum adversa* (*Agr.* 25.1, *the dangers of storms and tides*) or over *Oceanus*. It was the *threat*, posed by the fleet to a people unfamiliar with large-scale seaborne operations, which enhanced its prestige, enabling it to compete on equal terms with the land forces. But the fleet needed an achievement to match Mons Graupius. That achievement would be the conquest of the Ocean barrier—to reach Thule.[128] So during the *lentum iter* (*slow march*) of the army,[129] the fleet, far from returning immediately to a winter base, was assigned the commission of circumnavigating north-west Scotland from east to west, receiving the submission of the Orkney Islands and reconnoitring Shetland (for the reasons mentioned earlier).

Into this equation comes *Trucculensis portus*. How do we interpret this curious and contentious location which has spawned a plethora of translations.[130] These vary from the "leave it as it is school" of Handford to the buccaneering *Port Trucculum* of Starr; from the Norwood and Watt absurdity *Trucculene Harbour* to the equally impossible *harbour of Trutulium* offered by Church and Brodribb, and further back to Roach Smith's *Trucculensian harbour*?[131] *Trucculensis* would suggest a noun *Trucculum*. But no such place is recorded in any geographical source. We might try to relate it to a known archaeological site. But unless it occurs in Ptolemy or is attested elsewhere, this would be pure conjecture. We may follow Hanson's optimistic, but mistaken, suggestion that *there is no indication in the manuscript that the place-name* portus Trucculensis *is seriously corrupt*.[132] Could we account for it as a transcription error such as *Truxelensis*, *Truxulensis* or *Traxulensis portus*? Or as a circumlocution for a less familiar location recorded elsewhere, such as *Tunocelensis portus* or *Ugrulentum portus*, or the distortion of a more familiar one, *Rutupiensis portus*? Since I do not consider any of these to be the winter base of the fleet nor believe that Tacitus would have bothered to mention it, the validity of all six suggestions requires examination..

Truxelensis was offered by Smith.[133] Without acknowledging the existence of an alternative MS

---

[126] Rivet/Smith 1979, 49.
[127] The end of summer does not necessarily imply an end to campaigning, cf. *Agr.* 18.2, *quamquam transvecta aestas...ire obviam discrimini statuit* (*although the summer was passed...he decided to confront the danger*). Likewise Ostorius Scapula began his campaign in Britain *coepta hieme* (*when winter had begun, Ann.* 12. 31.1).
[128] The interpretation of Agricola's aims by Romm 1992, 149 can only be described as curious: *a boundary imposed by nature...must forever be closed and divine anger would destroy any further expeditions sent out to explore it.* If *Oceanus* was angry with Agricola, he never showed it by destroying the fleet.
[129] This may have been due to the need to allow his troops a breathing space as well as to impose their terrifying presence on the natives.
[130] A brief summary of the possibilities may be found in Soverini 2004, 270 f., who offers nothing new.
[131] Handford 1986; Starr 1960, 154-155; Norwood/Watt (undated); Church/Brodribb 1899; Roach Smith 1850, 3.
[132] Hanson 1991b, 1743. This is where the archaeologist and philologist part company. There is *every* indication that the phrase is seriously corrupt. The claim that *some sentences have required careful emendation, but do not seriously affect any historical interpretation* ought to be reconsidered.
[133] Smith 1987, 42.

reading, he proposes that some such adjective is formed from a noun *Truxulum*, itself a cursive(?) script corruption of *Fl.* [i.e. *flumen, river*] *Uxelum* and says that this river is associated with *Uxelum*, which *can be identified with reasonable confidence, through Ptolemy, as the fort at Ward Law in Dumfriesshire and hence the river name Uxelum must refer to the Nith* (he identifies *Novius* in Ptolemy with *the inlet of the Urr Water*).[134] He then suggests that the forts at Ward Law and Lantonside *functioned as the naval base of portus Trucculensis*. Stretching a MS reading to produce a hypothetical noun corruption in order to create a hypothetical adjectival corruption is a rather circuitous route towards establishing a hypothetical naval base—which would have been of no interest at all to Tacitus. Smith does not explain why Tacitus did not simply write *Uxelum*. But why would Tacitus bother to mention such an obscure place?

Andrew Breeze's philological arguments reflect the Celtic rather than the Classical approach and are worth quoting, if only to see how narrowly he missed the target: *Tacitus' Truccu- should thus perhaps be emended to Truxu-...An original truxu- may also explain the variant Trutulensis. Emendation here of -cc- to -x- has, among other advantages, that of being milder than others proposed for Trucculensis...If then the reasoning above is sound, we might take Tacitus' Trucculensis Portus as Truxulensis Portus, located at Loch Harport, Skye...Such an interpretation seems to make archaeological and linguistic sense.*[135] But does it? His explanation for *Trutulensis* was heading in the right direction, but he needed to evaluate the codex at source. The marginal variant *trutulensem* is preferable in any case, as will be shown later, and any argument involving *E*'s reading falls short, unless confusion between minuscule consonants is properly accounted for. There is no archaeological evidence from Skye, despite Mackie's suggestion, to link it with Agricola, and any Roman naval base would surely be on the mainland so as to be close to the army.[136] Surely such a large island would have been mentioned by Tacitus? Furthermore, in this monograph Tacitus goes out of his way to avoid mentioning major British locations, let alone minor ones. Breeze, like Smith, has created a hypothetical toponym. It is interesting that both create a root *trux-* without appreciating its Latin application. In this instance Classical and Celtic philology cannot be reconciled. It is much easier, albeit negative, to assume that such a place did not exist.

Most recently Alison Grant[137] introduced the unlocated *Traxula* (*Rav. Cos.*108₂₄) into the equation. She does not claim personally that this is the River Test, but relies on Richmond and Crawford, while the Rivet and Smith[138] objection is relegated to a footnote. This leads to a connexion with a location around Southampton (*arguably Portus Trucculensis*) which she proposes as the starting-point from where the fleet *originally* set sail for campaigning in the north. But the fleet is surely Agricola's fleet, not a projection of Vespasian's from the Claudian era. Vespasian initiated the *Flavian* conquest. *Originally* is irrelevant to the events of Agricola's governorship. Her *adjacent shore* (rather *the nearest side*) is interpreted as the south coast, whereas *proximo* can, in fact, refer to any *side* of Britain relative to the fleet's destination. The reliance on Andrew Breeze's *Truxulensis portus*, which he located in the *north*, to support an argument in favour of a vague Southampton area, is really a case of reaching for a lifebelt which does not exist. One shaky hypothesis is no sound basis for another. Neither one is valid for the reasons cited earlier. Furthermore it should be borne in mind that Tacitus'

---

[134] A possibility according to Rivet/Smith 1979, 484. But cf. Strang 1997, 21.
[135] A. Breeze 2002, 310.
[136] Mackie 2001, 432. See Appendix 2. Southern 1996, 375 is quite specific that *in this area* (north of the Clyde) *there is no archaeological evidence whatsoever to support combined naval and land operations at any point in Agricola's campaigns.* This may be the case, but it does not rule out the possibility that military and naval operations had taken place in the area.
[137] Grant 2007, 111-112 and n.153
[138] Richmond/Crawford 1949, 47; Rivet/Smith 1979, 475 are correct in their view that there is no phonetic equation between the words *Test* and *Traxula* (Ekwall 1928, 401 had suggested *Trest* as the true derivation) to confirm any connexion. Their verdict that it is *unknown, but apparently a river in southern Britain* should be upheld. Accordingly the creation of a hypothetical adjective *Traxulensis* from an unidentified river leads nowhere. Why, in any case, would a harbour be named after a river ? The conviction that Ptolemy's *Great Harbour* (*Megas limen*) equates with a non-existent *Traxulensis portus* is hardly helped by the suggestion that *Leuco Magno* (*Rav. Cos.* 10621) is possibly a *misreading of the transliterated Greek 'mega limani'*. This is surely the *Leucomagus* of Rivet/Smith 1979, 389, cf. *Noviomagno* in the MSS for *Noviomago*. Even without what I assume to be a typographical error for *Megas limen*, this is really stretching the bounds of credibility. Hind 2007, 100-101 offers a range of possibilities for the *Great Harbour* and favours *portus Adurni* (Portchester) of the *Notitia Dignitatum*. This identification, although dubious in itself, has better credentials than a fictional *Traxulensis portus*.

objectives are to boost Agricola's credentials and to impress his readers. Would contemporary Roman society be more impressed by a round-trip to an unheard of Southampton than by a newsworthy (cf. my comment on p.49) voyage to the fabulous *Thule* (as will be suggested later) ? Grant's hypothesis finds no support in any Silver Age sources. Her list of alternative theories treads a well worn path; these deserved a much more thorough study. The failure – not for the only time- to examine and evaluate the Latin at *source* has led to misrepresentations at crucial points in *Agr.* 10.4 and 38.4. These lapses undermine, rather than underpin, her arguments. *'Trucculensis' portus* must be interpreted in the context of the *whole* Tacitean sentence, not treated in isolation nor supplemented with superficial comments about *considerable disturbance of the Latin*. These mask an unawareness of the philological issues. Over-reliance on the ubiquitous and outdated Ogilvie and Richmond edition, as if it were gospel, is no substitute for independent thinking. As with the other ill conceived hypotheses, listed earlier, the question has to be asked as to why Tacitus would be concerned with geographical *trivia* in his monograph. The answer is that he would not. Consequently all theories based on hypothetical and obscure toponyms may be discarded. There is nothing in the *Agricola* to imply a *complete* circumnavigation of Britain (cf.28.3 and my note 91) and the general consensus (cf. Hind 1974, 285) is against this. The suggestion that such a voyage was a *conquering of 'Ocean'* and *Vespasian's triumph* carries little conviction. *Ignota Thyle* demands recognition.

Tunocelensem was proposed by Hind, basing his emendation on *Itunocelum* of the *Ravenna Cosmography*.[139] This was aptly disposed of by Rivet and Smith, but survived to be included among the rejected readings in the edition by Winterbottom and Ogilvie.[140] Its omission by subsequent editors is understandable. It is hardly likely that an obscure place-name, whose noun form itself is highly dubious, could have generated an adjective worthy of mention by Tacitus. Hind does not explain why Tacitus did not simply write *Tunocelum* or, better still, *Itunocelum* (sited in the Solway Firth). His comment that *although the best manuscripts (?) read "trucculensem", there is a variant "trutulensem"* is curious. The three 15th century MSS derive from the Caroline codex (*E*), the *only* one which is the best—because it forms the basis of the rest. In fact *trutulensem* (E^{2m}) has greater validity. It is optimistic to claim that *tunocelensem* will lead to the clarification of the context and the elimination of a difficult reading. How could *trucculensem* be a corruption of *tunocelensem*? Hind then begs the question when he writes *Tacitus' name "trucculum"*. I support the observation of Hanson that this location is *highly improbable*.[141] The entire sentence, not just one word, requires explanation.

Ugrulentum was suggested by Reed, who does not provide a precise location, merely the vague *somewhere north of Loch Broom*. Commenting on Richmond and Crawford objection that *trutu- has the best authority*, he says, *this (sc.trutu-) can now be seen from Ogilvie's app. crit. to be untrue; rather, if anything "truccu-" has the best authority*.[142] There is nothing in Ogilvie's *apparatus* to support the superiority of *truccu-*. In fact Ogilvie points out that the corrector *has the same authority as E itself*, although even he seems unaware that *E* is usually inferior to E^{2m} in the spelling of proper names.[143] Murgia suggested that *trucculensem* was influenced by *truculentus (ferocious)*, an idea taken up by Maxwell.[144] This might well occur to a 9th century copyist, but is hardly a welcoming sight to a sea-sick marine. Till believed that *trutulensem* was due to the corrector's disapproval of the double -*c*.[145] Reed's suggestion derives through Furneaux from an idea by Hübner, who tried to establish a similarity with the *Ugrulentum* of the *Ravenna Cosmography* (435.2.1).[146] Unfortunately Reed fails to

---

[139] Hind 1974, 285.
[140] Rivet/Smith 1979, 478-479; Winterbottom/Ogilvie 1975, 27—this edition did, at least, correct some of the misconceptions which had appeared in the Ogilvie/Richmond edition of 1968.
[141] Hanson 1991a, 141.
[142] Reed 1971, 147-8; Richmond/Crawford 1949, 47.
[143] Ogilvie 1967, 87; cf. at n. 42 above on this point.
[144] Murgia 1977, 339; Maxwell 1990, 70 f. This notion has recently been perpetuated by Fitzpatrick-Matthews (2006) who rejects (and rightly) Hind's theory and follows the route *Trucculensem → Ugrulentum → Trucculentum*. There is no reason for the double consonant in an alleged connexion with the Latin adjective. Not only is one non-existent name derived from another, but we have a corruption of the intermediate name which may actually be correct.
[145] Till 1943, 69. But cf. Perret 1950, 99 f.
[146] Hübner 1881, 545; Furneaux 1898, 149 f.

explain how *Ugrulentum* could possibly be corrupted to *Trucculensem*. Dillemann at least attempted to trace a pattern of distortion, even if it was not convincing, and was prepared to admit that any connexion between *Ugrulentum* and the 'Tacitean' reading was *without cogency*.[147] But against *Ugrulentum* is the fact that it does not appear in Ptolemy's list. As with the previous two suggestions: why would Tacitus bother to mention it ?

Rutupiensem (*of Richborough*) was suggested by Murgia.[148] His route is *rutupiensem→rutulensem→trutulensem*. This is more plausible than the previous three suggestions. The idea began with Rhenanus, who suggested *Rutupensem*.[149] But *Rutupiensem*, an alternative offered by Lipsius, should retain the extra vowel from the noun *Rutupiae*. Lipsius' suggestion found support in the commentaries of Ogilvie and Richmond and of Borzsák, while Saddington is non-committal.[150] Hind says that this was *not likely to have suffered corruption to "Trucculensem"* (nor was *Tunocelensem*), but he does not expand on E^{2m}'s reading, as Murgia does. Further, his argument against *Rutupiensis* on the ground that *Rutupinus* is the *normal adjective* is invalid, since his examples are drawn from Latin poetry, where *Rutupiensis* would be metrically impossible. However, the link between such an adjective and a well-known harbour such as Richborough does not explain why Tacitus did not merely write *Rutupias*, the normal literary usage (Amm. Marc. 20.1.3; 27.8.6). Since vocabulary links between Ammianus and the *Agricola* are numerous (as will be shown later) there can be no valid grounds for a circumlocution. Hanson produces a convincing case against this suggestion.[151]

Besides this, the philological argument is undermined by the logic of naval strategy. With the army wintering in the north it is hardly likely that the fleet would be based in the south-east.[152] It is equally implausible that it would begin and end its voyage, as Murgia suggests, at Richborough, which it was unlikely to reach until mid-November—when conditions in the Irish Sea and the Channel would be virtually impossible to cope with. If it was planned for Agricola or his successor to renew the campaign the following year—for the circumnavigation suggests reconnaissance as much as exploration—then surely the fleet would have remained in the north.[153] We cannot rule out the possibility that it was actively involved off northern Scotland until AD 86-87.[154] The taking of hostages in the extreme north, as well as the evidence for permanent military installations as far as the Moray Firth, implied by the names in Ptolemy and further corroborated by archaeology, reflect Rome's commitment in the furthest part of the island. Nor can the conquest of the Shetland Islands by Agricola's successor be ruled out. This could be one of the reasons why the Thule episode is understated by Tacitus. Suffice it to say that Agricola *may give the impression of having revealed it to posteriy* (*potest videri ostendisse posteris, Agr*. 13.1—a judgement referring to Julius Caesar and Britain).

---

[147] Dillemann 1979, 70.

[148] Murgia 1977, 339. The strongest case against his reasoning is the fact that the adjective *Rutupinus* already existed in the middle of the first century (cf. Appendix 5) and whether we follow Ammianus or other sources which provide variant nouns, *Rutupis, Ritupis* or *Ratupis,* there is no reason to create a fictitious adjective as an alternative to a valid one. Murgia's suggestion is supported by Strobel 1987, 202 n.19, whose arguments against Reed and Hind are sound enough. But Strobel has not evaluated the textual problems.

[149] Rhenanus 1533.This suggestion was taken up by Hasted 1790, 686, who describes it as *the best reading*. This is a classic instance of what can happen when a topographer relies on a scholar instead of checking the source for himself. His subsequent extrapolation on Agricola's circumnavigation is built on non-existent foundations.

[150] Lipsius 1574; Ogilvie/Richmond 1967, 282; Borzsák 1992, 101; Saddington 1990, 228: *It is not certain that this* (*Trucculensem portum*) *can be regarded as the fleet's base in Britain and, if so, whether the emendation to Rutup(I)ensem...can be accepted*. He suggests the possibility of a temporary base in the north of Britain.

[151] Hanson 1991a, 141; 1991b, 1743.

[152] Hanson 1991a, 14: *nor does reference to a base on the south coast of England seem entirely relevant to Tacitus' narrative at this point*. Hind 1974, 288 says that *it would not be unlikely that the fleet proceeded at a leisurely fashion southward around the Romanized part* (*proximo?*) *of the province to its place of origin*. He fails to take into consideration the season, the time factor, weather conditions, tides or naval strategy—nor does he suggest the *place of origin*. Was it to the place where they started this circumnavigation, or some base on the south-east coast?

[153] *Evidently in preparation for another year of campaigning Agricola...sent his fleet north to explore and report*, Welch 1965, 150.

[154] Starr 1960, 155 notes that following the recall of Agricola *the British fleet may have held a station on the north-east coast during this period.* A base in the north can certainly be accepted; but whether on the east or the west side is open to question.

Some scholars have elected to retain the reading in *E*, attempting to conjure up ingenious, and sometimes amusing, derivations. Burn offers a Celtic root for *truccu-*, identifying it with the Welsh *Turk* or *Twrch* (boar).[155] Rivet and Smith suggest that the harbour lay at the mouth of a river *Truccula* or *Trucculus*, an unsuccessful attempt to dispose of Ogilvie and Richmond's suggestion of Richborough.[156] They then offer an even more speculative suggestion: that the name is based on a Celto-Latin *tructa* (trout), a river *Tructula* (little trout), *a half-joking name conferred by the Roman fleet*. Are we seriously to contemplate zoological derivations which disregard the superior reading of E^{2m}?

Watson proposed Montrose as a distinct possibility. Forni, following Anderson and MacDonald, suggested that the harbour was Carpow or Cramond, on the assumption that the fleet sailed *all* the way around Britain in the middle of winter—as if it had nothing better to do.[157] But the circumnavigation should imply a winter base on the *west* coast, perhaps at Dumbarton. Hanson saw *portus Trucculensis as a point in the extreme north which the fleet reached before returning along the other side of the island to its unnamed base*.[158] Reference to the *extreme north* is very sound. Unfortunately the rest of his sentence is in direct contradiction to the Latin where *returning* occurred <u>before</u> *reached*. This is the fundamental difference between the perfect and pluperfect tense. The concept of *returning* is the sticking point, if we wish to retain the obvious anti-clockwise direction together with a base on the west coast. Tacitus is not being deliberately obscure and it is highly unlikely that this is what he wrote. And why would he refer to some vague point in the extreme north of Scotland? A location on the Scottish mainland is not confirmed by Tacitus. Why does the harbour merit a mention unless its significance were linked to some momentous navigational feat?

So where does all this leave us? It was surely never likely that Tacitus would have referred to some insignificant harbour when there were more challenging options for the fleet.[159] Would his readers have been any more enlightened by the reference to an obscure location, which no one had ever heard of before and was unlikely to hear of again? Thule is an entirely different matter. The impact of a Roman fleet reaching a harbour there would be considerable, going some way to exploding a myth. Furthermore, as will be shown later, this would be reflected in contemporary literature. It is much easier and more logical to assume that the harbour in question is a reference to Shetland, relating to the third leg—the most prestigious in terms of propaganda—of the fleet's commission and reflecting a navigational achievement worthy of record. For whatever reason, Tacitus may have underplayed it. It may be suggested that the main clause should be corrected to:

> *et simul classis secunda tempestate ac fama trux Tulensem portum tenuit.*

This may be translated as:

> *And at the same time the fleet, its ruthlessness enhanced by rumour and favourable weather, reached Shetland harbour.*

The adjustment is minimal. *Trux*, meaning *ruthless, threatening, fearsome*, in conjunction with the ablative case, is relatively common in Tacitus. If it can be applied to a cohort in the *Annals* and to a battle line in the *Histories*,[160] it is certainly applicable to a fleet whose effect on the natives would be

---

[155] Burn 1969, 59. The idea of a Welsh hydronym which Rivet/Smith 1979, 49 dwell on led them to accept Sandwood Loch (Sutherland) as a possibility. But, as Andrew Breeze points out, 2002, 309, *twrch*, which is applied to Welsh torrents, hardly fits Sandwood Loch, which is tranquil.

[156] Rivet/Smith 1979, 479. A. Breeze 2002, 309 believes that they have misinterpreted this and suggests that *trwch* means *fracture* or *cleft*, thereby suggesting a name *Breach Harbour*. He makes a valid point that *archaeology and philology may advance knowledge by fruitful collaboration*. One may add: perhaps *palaeography* might have a contribution to make.

[157] Watson 1926, 7 f.; Forni 1962, 224; Anderson 1922, 141; Macdonald 1919, 135 f.

[158] Hanson 1991a, 141. Saddington 1990, 228 likewise misinterprets the Latin, *the fleet returned to an otherwise unnamed port*. Tacitus does not say this. The fleet *held* the harbour. The pluperfect tense, the MS 'redierat' is not the main verb.

[159] So Strobel 1987, 202 n.19: *geringfügig*.

[160] *Ann.* 4.7.3: *quam* (sc. *cohortem*) *Romanus...tumultu trucem...instruxerat* (which, menacing in its uproar, the Roman had

impressive and intimidating (*Agr.* 25.1, 25.2). *Fama trux* relates both to the past record of the fleet and to its anticipated impact on those unfamiliar with its terror, a daunting prospect in Shetland harbour.

The two MS readings merit comparison:

truc-culensem E   tru-tulensem E^{2m}

E is in the habit of confusing *c* and *t* (as is common in minuscule).[161] Perret elucidates the problems and makes a strong case for the superiority of E^{2m}'s readings of proper names.[162] Till's comment on *trutulensis* that E^{2m}'s *conjecture has no guarantee* is no longer accepted.[163] The corrector, if anything, is guilty of omitting -*x* rather than of avoiding the double -*c*. The last three syllables should be identical. Latinised Greek names often drop an *h*.[164] To create an adjective from an island is easy enough, e.g. *Cretensis* from *Crete*. Thus, it would be perfectly natural to describe the harbour as *T(h)ulensis portus*. It did not have an individual name such as *Tunocelum* (?) or *Ugrulentum*, which would only be given when a presence was established there.

No other correction comes closer than *tru<x>tulensem* to the reading of E^{2m}, which is now preferred, *trutulensem*. Tacitus' use of *simul* clearly shows the fleet reaching this harbour at the same time as the army reached its *hiberna*. At this point it must be stressed that a voyage to Richborough,[165] a distance of some fifteen hundred miles, could have taken up to three months—if any admiral were rash enough to consider the prospect of such a long voyage in deteriorating weather conditions in the Irish Sea. Are we to assume that the *lentum iter* (*slow march*) and *transitus mora* (*protracted passage*) of the army took this long? If we allow some twenty days for the conquest of a scattered Orcadian archipelago, followed by a breathing space and an expedition to Shetland, the army during that time could have covered the distance from Caithness to the isthmus, via the Great Glen,[166] where it would encounter the *novae gentes* (*Agr.* 38.3, *new tribes*).[167] Agricola by a display of arms along the western flank of Caledonia might well claim that he had encompassed the whole of it.[168]

The specific mention of a harbour suggests that Agricola's naval officers had seen something to impress them. This would rule out Fair Isle. The most obvious location would be Lerwick, of which Nicolson says: *opposite [this] lies the island of Bressay, six miles long and curved parallel to the Mainland shore, to provide the natural barrier which makes Lerwick harbour one of the finest in northern Europe.*[169] Reaching Shetland harbour is even more impressive than simply reaching Shetland. The precise reference to *Thule Harbour* might be an Agricolan translation from the Greek of Pytheas, something like *Thoulaios Limen*. Detailed maritime locations would have been noted by the explorer and 'kept under wrappers' in Massilia. One may recall Cunliffe's suggestion that Pytheas may have reached a safe anchorage in Bressay Sound.[170] The Roman fleet would have located the same station, not really surprising, if it had access to Pytheas' marine charts. The fleet's achievement lies in the triumph over nature and the elements, and matches the victory at Mons Graupius. It is noticeable that *Agr.* 39 begins with *hunc rerum cursum* (*this course of events*) rather than *hanc*

---

drawn up). *Hist*. 4.46.3: *cum...aciem telis et armis trucem...aspicerent* (*when they were looking at a battle-line fearsome with its missiles and weapons*).

[161] Cf. *inicium* 13.3; *spetium amititiae* 24.8. For further examples, cf. Till 1943, 45 and 78 and Anderson 1922, 54.
[162] Perret 1950, 99-100.
[163] Till 1943, 69: *Seine Vermutung hat keinerlei Gewähr*.
[164] Cf. *RIB* 121 and 201: *Tracum*.
[165] Ogilvie 1967, 282 f.
[166] Henderson 1985, 332. Hanson 1991b, 1770 says that *a route back via the Great Glen would imply a more northerly location for the Boresti and Mons Graupius*. Precisely. But we can eliminate the Boresti. See Appendix 1.
[167] *Agr.* 38.3. Ogilvie 1967, 282 locates these *new nations* between Moray and Aberdeen. D.J. Breeze 1990, 59 suggests a return route through Glen Garry and Strathtay. Jones/Mattingly 1990, 76 f. note the mountain route taken by Edward I. Hanson 1991, 140 lists plausible alternatives for a marching route south.
[168] It is quite possible that Tacitus' description of the western sea-lochs (*Agr.* 10.6) was partly derived from Agricola's march south, cf. Ogilvie 1967, 42.
[169] Nicholson 1984, 13.
[170] Cunliffe 2001b, 132-133.

Aerial photograph of Lerwick, looking east towards the Isle of Bressay, photo courtesy of Alan Moar, www.alanmoar.flyer.co.uk

victoriam (*this victory*), a phrase which combines triumphs both on land and on sea.[171]

The introduction of *trux* eliminates the awkward syllepsis involving *secunda*: the ablative cases are causal; it was the fine weather and its previous record (cf. *Agr.* 25.2, 29.2) which allowed the fleet to pose such a threat. This was no random phrase by Tacitus; he was looking for something to balance a similar description of the *army*. The *variatio* is clear:

> *fama ferox exercitus* (*Agr.* 27.1)
> *the army, formidable* (or *emboldened*) *through the report*

The entire clause *unde...redierat* is untranslatable and meaningless as it is presented in all the standard editions, and no one has yet provided a satisfactory explanation for it.[172] If my suggestion of *T(h)ulensem portum* is correct, then *redierat* is impossible, since you cannot return from a place you have never visited. The clause must reflect what *had* happened to the fleet from the time it left the Scottish mainland to the time it anchored in Shetland harbour. Since *unde* with the pluperfect tense

---

[171] So A.R. Birley 1981, 78 and 2005, 91.
[172] Grant 2007, 111 rejects my suggestions, despite the fact that the Silver Age poets point in this direction. Her own proposals founder on a mistranslation of the Latin: *according to Tacitus' text, the fleet was said to have returned to the harbour 'from which it had set out'*. This, of course, is nonsense. As a result her subsequent arguments are invalid. Textual criticism is not something one can fudge. Resurrecting the old chestnuts is perfectly admissible, if only to demolish them. But it will not solve the problems of textual corruption. A thorough study of the palaeographical issues is essential before any pronouncements on Latinity can be made. Grant makes no reference to the marginal variant. Two points must be added. Firstly, the fleet would not return to a southern port while the army was still based in the north, as Hanson correctly noted. Secondly, it is nowhere implied that troops <u>landed</u> on Shetland: the fleet reached Thule Harbour, showed the flag and terrified the natives. That was all it was meant to do.

always *precedes* the main verb in Tacitus (*Hist.* 2.6.61, 4.29.8; *Ann.* 15.10.1, 16.21.7), questions must be raised about the validity of *unde*, to see whether it should be retained. An *independent* clause with the pluperfect tense is normal Tacitean usage and often introduces a reason or an afterthought (*Agr.* 6.4, 9.3, 38.3). The subordinate clause appears in the MS thus:

unde proximo Brittanniae (Britanniae E^2) latere prelecta (lecto E^{2m})
omnis (omni E^2) redierat.

The codex clearly poses problems here, producing a mixture of injudicious guesswork and scribal error, leading ultimately to bemusement rather than elucidation. But attempts to establish a connection between *unde* and *redierat* have created unacceptable linguistic contortions by editors and commentators and must be considered failures.[173] Each part of this clause requires close study.

The interpretation of *proximo* has always produced a dilemma for commentators who could not understand what *nearest* referred to. Tacitus, despite his geographical vagueness, would not have left us to hazard a guess. There is no need to assume, as Burn proposed, a proximity to the *harbour*.[174] How can a *side of Britain* be *nearest* to a harbour? For Ogilvie *it might be the shore adjacent or nearest to Rome*. How can it possibly be *adjacent to Rome*? And where is the word for *shore*?[175] It is remarkable that in his 'revised' version of Hutton's edition he actually inserted *litore* (an old conjecture by Pichena) into his text, without bothering to revise Furneaux, whose faulty commentary he used as his starting-point. Ogilvie was trying to establish a connexion between *proximo* and Richborough, which has already been discounted as the fleet's winter base in AD 83, when the army was based in the north. If the circumnavigation began in the far north-east (Caithness, as will be argued later) *proximo* cannot refer to the *southern* side, nor to the *eastern* side, as Gudeman proposed.[176] Tacitus himself had already stated that Agricola's fleet had sailed around the *coast of the remotest sea* (*Agr.* 10.4, *hanc oram novissimi maris tunc primum Romana classis circumvecta*) to confirm that Britain was an island. This must mean the *furthest side of Britain*, not the *nearest*. Roy translated *proximo* as *furthest*, trying to reconcile the irreconcilable,[177] while Andresen made the absurd claim that *the nearest side of Britain is the coast of the remotest sea*.[178] The furthest side of Britain should be the area from Duncansby Head via Cape Wrath to the Clyde. The possible interpretations of *proximo* are summarised by Hutton, who associates the word with the part of the

---

[173] Scholars have attempted to bridge the gap by linking *unde,* not with *redierat*, but with a participle. Furneaux, following Orelli and Ernesti, links *unde* with the unacceptable marginal reading *lecto*: *the sense being 'quo' litore* (sic) *inde lecto, redierat*. But *quo litore*, apart from being wrong, is ambiguous. He justifies this with the comment that *clearness is sacrificed to conciseness*, 1898, 150. Anderson 1922, 141 similarly proposes that *'unde' is taken only with 'praelecto'*. There is no parallel in Tacitus for such a use of *unde* in a subordinate clause. For Ogilvie, unhappy with the suggestions of his Oxford predecessors, *'profecta' is to be understood with 'unde'*, 1967, 283, a concept taken up by Heubner 1984, 112 and Borzsák 1992, 101, while De Saint-Denis and Zúñiga actually introduce *profecta* into their texts, *unde profecta proximo Britanniae latere lecto omni redierat* (*setting out from there and hugging the nearest side of Britain, it had returned*), thereby producing two participles instead of one and resurrecting the long discarded readings of Furneaux. No one has yet been able to explain *redierat.* Madvig 1873, 569 thought this reading to be *unsustainable* (a view which I endorse) and recreated the text to read *unde proximo anno latere lecto omni reditura erat* (*from where it was to return after hugging all the nearest side the previous year*). This is even more unsustainable. There is no point in introducing *anno* in reference to some *future* event outside the term of Agricola's governorship. The imperfect subjunctive, another of his suggestions, would imply that the fleet commander had been given instructions *to return*. What else was he supposed to do? Both before and after the discovery of *E* the problem has defied solution because scholars have insisted on retaining the concept of *return*. Attempts to relate *redierat* to the maritime events of AD 81 and to suggest that there were two separate half-voyages (Sleeman 1914, 119; Burn 1969, 53; MacKie 2001, 432. Hanson 1991a, 141 calls this *an unnecessary convoluted explanation*) would require the insertion of *biennio ante* (*two years before*), and, as pointed out by Maxwell 1989, 70, *the sense of the passage demands that a complete circumnavigation* (*of Scotland*) *should have been made in the final year of Agricola's governorship*. The fact that no destination is given in this clause should have aroused suspicion. One does not return *from* without returning *to*. *Redierat* lacks a destination, and Andresen's comment, 1880, 209, that *qui portum tenet, rediit* (*whoever holds the harbour has returned*) overlooks the fact that *unde* cannot imply a destination. The lengthy arguments put forward by Soverini 2004, 271 f. merely present the views of previous scholars without adding anything new or perceptive.
[174] Burn 1968, 316.
[175] Ogilvie 1967, 283, in consequence of citing as a parallel *proximumque Galliae litus* (*and the nearest shore of Gaul*). Handford's translation is unfortunately based on Ogilvie's text.
[176] Gudeman 1928, 75.
[177] Roy 1793, 25.
[178] Andresen 1880, 208.

coast nearest to the fleet.[179] This tells us nothing. *Proximo* must surely refer to the side of Britain nearest to the fleet's destination,[180] and if its destination was Orkney and Shetland, then the nearest side is Caithness.

All the modern editions of the *Agricola* read *praelecto*. But this is no more than a 15th century conjecture, a reconciliation of the two variants, because *lecto* was considered un-Tacitean.[181] *Lecto,* if such a form existed, would be all right for Livy, but not for Tacitus, and suggests a conjecture either by E^{2m} or by his exemplar. But *praelecta* is a different problem altogether because although *praelegere* is Tacitean usage and, in my opinion, a Tacitean neologism, there is no evidence that in its *maritime* sense it has a past participle. With the meaning of *to coast along, to skirt, to hug*, it never occurs in the perfect tense in any prose writer, either in its simple or compound form, for obvious reasons: you reach your destination *while coasting,* not *after coasting.* The shoreline does not stop after you reach your destination. It would be implied by the perfect tense that the fleet had completed its coasting and was now out in the open sea.[182] *Latus praelegens* (*hugging the side*) would be acceptable and the present participle of the simple verb is paralleled in Livy (21.51.7, *oram Italiae legens Ariminum pervenit, he reached Ariminum while skirting the Italian coast*). Friis-Jensen, who produced the two past participle parallels from Livy[183] and Propertius[184] for *TLL*, had doubts himself as to whether such forms existed.[185] But how can you support one conjecture with two others, particularly when a valid case can be made against all three? Till regarded *E*'s *praelecta* as the fault of the copyist who had made the participle agree with *classis,* and he described it as a *grammatical impossibility*.[186] I suggest that Till was only half correct: the agreement is right, the verb is wrong. Corruption occurs in two stages, *praevecta→praeiecta→praelecta*.[187] *Praevecta* (*sailing on*) is an attested form and is more valid than *praelecto*, a conjecture paralleled only by other conjectures, whose usage is highly dubious and whose introduction creates an ablative absolute where there is no need for one.[188] The fact that Tacitus uses the verb *praelegere* twice elsewhere has prejudiced editors against the possibility that it could not be used here. They have ignored the fact that the verb *praevehi* (*to sail on*) had already been used to describe the voyage of the Usipi in the reverse direction (*ut miraculum praevehebantur, they were sailing on like a mirage, Agr.* 28.1). The humanist corrector (*A*) merely compounded the error by assuming it lay in the ending rather than in the stem. There were only ever two options: either radical correction or rejection of the whole clause as a gloss. The fleet had been given instructions *to go ahead. Praevecta* is here almost equivalent to *praemissa,* which Tacitus had already used to describe the advance activity of the fleet, *praemissa classe quae…terrorem faceret* (*Agr.* 29.1, *the fleet was sent ahead to cause terror*).[189]

---

[179] Hutton 1914, 344.

[180] Soverini 2004, 272 is mistaken in his suggestion that the use of *proximo* in relation to the fleet's departure point is less convincing. If I am sailing from England to Boulogne, do I start off from Liverpool or Folkestone?

[181] Ogilvie 1967, 283.

[182] The middle verb equivalent *praevehi* (*to sail past, on*) produces a past participle *praevectus,* cf. *oram Achaeae et Asiae…praevectus, Rhodum…petebat* (Tac. *Hist.* 2.2.3, *having sailed on past the coast of Achaea and Asia…he was making for Rhodes*). In this instance we may, as in English, *sailing on past,* infer a completion of a coastal voyage. A present participle *praevehens* would be impossible, being transitive.

[183] Livy 21.51.7: *praelecta est ora* (*the coast was skirted*). This was originally suggested by Madvig for the meaningless *periectas oras* of the earliest MS (*codex Puteanus*). He failed to note that Livy always uses *legere*. Weissenborn's later conjecture, *praevecta est oram* (*sailed on past the coast*), perhaps based on continuous script *pvectaestorâsed*, is more convincing, since a *middle* verb, followed by an *impersonal* verb, *in Ebusam insulam transmissum* (*a crossing was made to the isle of Ibiza*) is followed shortly afterwards (22.20.10) by a similar pairing, *inde flexa retro classis reditumque in citeriora provinciae* (*then the fleet turned back and returned to the nearer parts of the province*).

[184] Propertius 1.8.19: *praelecta Ceraunia* (*Ceraunia skirted*). But the earliest MS (*codex Neapolitanus*) reads *praevecta,* a reading which most editors have retained. *Post victa* (*after conquering*), suggested by N. Heinsius (cf. Sil. *Pun.* 15.509-510), is preferable to *post lecta* (*after skirting* Mueller), unparalleled with this meaning. The host of suggestions, originally proposed for the true Propertian reading, should have alerted scholars to a reconsideration of *E*. One thing is certain: there is no evidence in the MSS for the maritime use of *praelegere* before the second century AD. Tacitus' innovative use of such *transitive* verbs appears in his later works, cf. *praefestinans* (*Ann.* 5.9.3. *hurrying past*).

[185] Friis-Jensen 1985, 175.

[186] Till 1943, 69: *grammatisch Unmögliches*.

[187] The second stage of corruption is a commonplace in the First Medicean of the *Annals*, where the *lect-* root is found, cf. *prolectae servientium patientiae* (3.65.3), also *circumlectam* (2.11.2), etc.

[188] It is worth noting that *oram… circumvecta* had already been used for the same voyage.

[189] Onesicritus, the helmsman of Alexander the Great, is referred to by Seneca (*Ben*.7.2.5) as *praemissus explorator*,

Ogilvie says that *omnis* emphasises that *the whole fleet returned intact*.[190] But this very statement undermines his theory. The Tacitean sentence has only *one* adjective, not both. The suggestion that *omnis* means *intact* cannot be supported. Its literal meaning is *all* and in this sense it must be accompanied by a qualifying adjective such as *integer* (*intact*) or *incolumis* (*unharmed*). Unfortunately the examples which he cites from Caesar (*BG* 4.36.3, 5.23.6), where both adjectives are used, further subvert his argument; in Caesar it is *incolumes*, not *omnes*, which is used predicatively.[191] The predicative use of *omnis* in the singular is not found in Tacitus or in any other historian. *Incolumis redierat* (*had returned safely*) would be perfectly acceptable in normal circumstances, even if it didn't make sense in this context, but not *omnis*, which here is decidedly odd and uncomfortable.[192] Benario's translation, *without loss*, would imply that Tacitus actually did write *incolumis*.[193] The Rivet and Smith version, *it had all returned*, shows how awkward a direct English translation can be.[194] Was the corrector (*E²*) apparently unimpressed with *omnis*? Did he remove the terminal consonant to make *omni* agree with *latere* (*all the nearest side*), thus creating, as Ogilvie says, *a weaker sense and an unparalleled word order*?[195] I think it more likely that he misread it as '*omni-sre-dierat*, i.e. a metathetical distortion from *res* to *sre*. We find a similar confusion between *est* and *set*.[196]

It is also possible that *E*'s exemplar contained doublets which included *omnia*. In that case the *-a* belongs to *-dierat* and was lost through haplography. The only certainty is the last three syllables, *-dierat*. Yet *omni* was good enough to deceive Andresen, Furneaux, Koestermann and Burn. Persson claims that *omni* is emphatic and that *the fleet had sailed round the northern side of Britain, and in fact the whole of it*.[197] Apart from failing to offer an explanation for *proximo*, Persson seems to forget than any completed circumnavigation (which a past participle implies) is hardly likely to involve less than the whole side. Büchner is convinced that *the Hersfeld corrector has rightly emended 'omnis' to 'omni'*, without explaining why he regards *omnis* as an unsuitable word.[198] But no good case can be made for creating an isolated *omnis* and then claiming that it means *intact* or *without loss*. *Omnis* must stand directly next to *classis* to make any grammatical sense. Till argues that its position is emphatic, but produces no true parallels for a predicative use.[199] If it is retained in its position, it must agree with something else. It might be in the *accusative* case (=*omnes*). Its very position in the clause suggests that it might be the object of a verb such as *adierat* with the missing noun being *res*: *resadierat→redierat*, the error caused in *scriptura continua*.[200]

The *unde* may be partially dispensed with. As may be seen from Till's photocopy of the codex the *un-* of *unde* bears a resemblance to *-uit* of *tenuit* and would be a case of dittography. We now have an independent clause and the text will read:

---

commissioned to *look* for wars in the unknown sea, while exploring the route between the Persian Gulf and India.

[190] Ogilvie 1967, 283. Lund 1981, 124 equates *omnis* with *integra* or *incolumis*. This would imply from the examples in the following note that Caesar was repeating himself. *Omnis* means *all*, not *intact*, as Hind 1974, 285 translates. If Tacitus had intended to say *all the fleet* he would have written *omnis classis*. Forni 1962, 224 cites Horace, *Carm*. 3.30.6: *non omnis moriar*? Does Horace really mean that he will not die *intact*? For the same reason Heubner's example from Quintilian is no parallel.

[191] In both instances *omnes incolumes* is plural and directly adjacent to its noun or pronoun. In Tacitus *omnis* appears to be singular, totally isolated from *classis* and used predicatively; quite un-Tacitean.

[192] For the predicative use of *incolumis* in the singular, cf. *Ann*. 1.18.3, 6.14.2, 6.30.4, *Hist*. 2.29.3.

[193] Benario 1991, 51

[194] Rivet/Smith 1979, 97.

[195] Ogilvie 1967, 283 (cf. Heubner 1984, 101). *Omni* should precede *proximo* (cf. *omnis propior sinus*, *Agr*. 23, cited by Soverini 2004, 272 in a different context, without realising that it demolishes his own theory of *omni* following the participle). Burn 1969, 59 preferred *omni* in his translation, *after the exploration of all the adjacent side of Britain*. Exploration may well have been on the agenda of the fleet, but *praelegere* does not mean *to explore*, as Acheson 1938, 83 also translates, nor, as Benario 1991, 51 suggests, *to reconnoitre*. An explanation of *adjacent* is also required.

[196] Cf. note 114 above.

[197] Persson 1927, 83-84: *die Flotte hatte die nördliche Seite Britanniens umsegelt, und zwar die ganze*. His citation of the earlier reference to the voyage, *hanc oram...circumvecta* (*Agr*. 10.4) shows that *omni* would in fact be superfluous.

[198] Büchner 1955, 292: *Der Korrector des Hersfeldensis hat 'omnis' mit Recht zu 'omni' verbessert*; he calls '*omnis*' *ein nicht passendes Wort*. But *E²*'s conjectured *omni* is hard to justify.

[199] Till 1979, 72.

[200] Schoene 1889, 37 is the only editor, as far as I am aware, to assume that *omnis* required a noun next to it, but his proposal, *omnis reditus erat*, involving a shorthand version *redit'erat*, stretches credibility to the limit.

Thulensem portum tenuit; de proximo Britanniae latere praevecta omnis res adierat.

...reached Shetland harbour; having sailed on from the nearest side of Britain, it had encountered every scenario.

The nearest side of Britain for a voyage to Orkney and Shetland would, as already suggested, be Caithness.[201] What Tacitus is saying is that Agricola's fleet had faced both *prosperas res* and *adversas res* (*ups and downs*) from the time it left the coast of mainland Scotland.[202] The *prosperas res* would be the "discovery" and conquest of the Orkney Islands, the *adversas res* would be the hazardous sea currents on its voyage to Shetland. But the fleet had faced and triumphed over all the challenges. *Omnis res* (*all eventualities, situations, fortunes*) is virtually equivalent to *omnem fortunam*. The verb *adire* is normal usage for *facing* or *handling* situations, as Livy illustrates with *ad omnem adeundam simul fortunam* (25.2.1, *to face every eventuality together*).[203] *Res* (plural) and *fortuna* should be interchangeable, both words meaning *fortune, circumstances* in terms of both fate and finance, or, with the appropriate form of *omnis*, simply *everything*. The language of the entire sentence is couched in terms as if Tacitus were describing a routine maritime operation. Furneaux may well be right in suggesting that the expedition was understated because Agricola had not been personally involved in it.[204] But, equally, Tacitus may have been aware that Agricola had merely followed the course plotted by Pytheas, and he could not attribute too many initiatives to Agricola in a monograph in which his father-in-law had already been overindulged. There is even the possibility that Domitian had authorised the expedition on the proviso that Agricola should not risk his life—not that Tacitus would ever admit to such. But in terms of achievement the conquest of the Ocean to reach Thule is equivalent to scaling Everest to reach the summit. The objective is in triumphing over the challenge and laying claim to be the first Roman to do so.

---

[201] This solves Ogilvie's dilemma on the relevance of *proximo*. It is in the Sutherland-Caithness area that the battle of Mons Graupius should be located. Keppie 1980, 84 favours *a fairly* northerly site because it only made sense to send the fleet north, if the starting point was well up the NE coast, thus minimising its voyage. I would support this, although I prefer his reference, Keppie1986, 11, to Tacitus' implication that the battle site *lay close to, and perhaps even in* sight of, the sea, and far away in the very north of Britain.

[202] Although the neuter plural *omnia* is regular usage in Tacitus for the subject and object form, *omnis res* (pl.) cannot be ruled out for the object form (the nominative *omnes res* is understandably avoided on grounds of euphony), cf. Sall. *BJ* 69.2, *omnis res exsequi* (*to carry out everything*). Surely this phrase combines both *res prosperas/secundas* and *res adversas*. Statistically the neuter plural subject and object forms *prospera/secunda* and *adversa* are five times more common in Tacitus than their synonymous phrases.

[203] For the use of *omnia adire* to mean *to tackle everything*, cf. Livy 26.20.4, 34.18.3.

[204] Furneaux 1898, 150.

Chapter 5

THULE IN CONTEMPORARY LATIN POETRY

est locus Hesperiam quam mortales perhibebant

There is a place which men used to call the western land

Ennius, *Annales* 1.24

The achievement of Agricola's fleet in reaching the furthest limit of the western world ought to find some echo in literature contemporary with Tacitus. Modern scholarship has failed to note the voyage to Shetland and consequently has either missed its impact on late Silver Age literature or completely misinterpreted what the Flavian poets have written.

Juvenal launches a bitter tirade against contemporary morality:

> *arma quidem ultra*
> *litora Iuvernae promovimus et modo captas*
> *Orcadas ac minima contentos nocte Britannos;*
> *sed quae nunc populi fiunt victoris in urbe,*
> *non faciunt illi quos vicimus…*
> Sat. 2.159-163

Our arms indeed we have pushed beyond the shores of Ireland and the recently captured Orkneys and the Britons satisfied with the shortest night.[205] *But the things which occur in the city of our victorious people are not done by those we have vanquished…*

The poet's comment that the Roman army had advanced beyond the shores of Ireland may be, as Courtney says, an exaggeration, an echo of Agricola's dealings with an Irish prince and the governor's own assessment of the requirements for conquest (*Agr.* 24.1-3).[206] The *recently captured Orkneys* can be dated to AD 83.[207] The word *recent* cannot be taken back too far, and if Juvenal drafted a version of this c. AD 92, when we know that he was in Rome (Mart. *Ep.* 7.24 & 91), he certainly did not revise it when he finally published it some fifteen years later.[208] But to whom is the poet referring with his

---

[205] Courtney 1996, 148 notes that this passage is *very Tacitean in content* and cites *nox clara et extrema Britanniae parte brevis* (*the night is bright and short in the most northerly part of Britain, Agr.* 12). If the night is short in the most northerly part of Scotland, then Juvenal's superlative form *minima* must refer to the area even beyond that. There is no need to replace *minima* with *nimia* as Martyn 1996, 80 proposes on the grounds of pointlessness of Britons being '*minima contentos nocte*'. I see nothing in the *Agricola* which in fact supports '*nimia*' (Martyn 1974, 345). There is no reason to suppose that Juvenal was being ironic. People living in the Shetland Islands are more than happy with the shortest nights and Juvenal was aware of it. The difference between *brevis* and *minima* is a matter of latitude; the further north, the shorter the nights (five hours in Shetland).

[206] Courtney, *ibid*. The evidence for a Roman presence at Drumanagh in the Irish Republic at the end of the first century has yet to be evaluated, as the site is currently *sub iudice*. From such a site and its links with the interior and with merchants crossing the Irish Sea would come the sources for Ptolemy's map. Gudeman 1898, 302 f. was convinced that Tacitus was referring to an invasion of Ireland at *Agr.* 24 on the basis that *transgressus* referred to the Irish Sea. This theory was ably dealt with by Haverfield 1899, 302 f. A link between Juvenal and Ireland in AD 81 was suggested by McElderry 1922, 154, who proposed that the satirist may have served in northern Britain at the time. Higgins 1998, 407 f. offers some valid reasons why Domitian would not have sanctioned an invasion of Ireland, while di Martino 2003, 16 interprets the *unknown tribes* as Irish and spends thirty four pages on Agricola's *first invasion of Ireland in AD 82*. For a compact evaluation of the Classical sources on Ireland, cf. Raftery 2005, 176-181.

[207] For the dating of Agricola's governorship to AD 77-84, see Büchner 1960, 172 ff. (actually favouring '77-83'); Gallivan 1981, 189; A.R.Birley 1981, 73-81; Eck 1982, 299 f.; Campbell 1986, 197-200; Maxwell 1990, 114 f.; Hanson 1991a, 40-45; Raepsaet-Charlier 1991, 1842; A.R. Birley 2005, 77 f. See Appendix 3 for further evidence.

[208] There is no specific time span for *modo*. Quintilian uses *nuper* (*recently*) in the same loose way. Writing c. 94 about Caesius Bassus (*I.O.* 10.1.96) who died in 79, he says, *quem nuper vidimus* (*whom we saw recently*). Courtney suggests that

Britons satisfied with the shortest night? Britain and its people were already well-known and no longer topical at the time Juvenal was writing. Reference to Ireland and the Orkney Islands should reflect Flavian military intentions, and this geographical group should also include Shetland[209]. I believe that Juvenal's *Britannos* is a poetical circumlocution for the natives of Shetland.[210] In Shetland on 21 June the sun is above the horizon for 18 hrs. 52 mins.[211] The *shortest night* can only be experienced by those Britons who lived furthest away to the north, i.e. the Shetlanders. Furthermore Juvenal is employing the rhetorical *tricolon auctum* (*three-stage build-up*), with the last group being singled out for special attention. Shetland was the climax, the furthest limit of the fleet's activities. Rome's brilliant achievements at the ends of the earth, where the natives are uncontaminated by Roman vices, are sharply contrasted with the moral decline of Rome itself.[212] The present inhabitants of Shetland will be pleased to know that their Iron-Age counterparts did not share the degenerate activities of the more sophisticated Romans. The irony here, of course, is that their fellow Britons in the south had already become addicted to the very vices which Juvenal criticises.[213] The conquest of Shetland may have been on Agricola's agenda, but it never materialised.[214] It did not stop Juvenal (*Sat.* 15.112) from remarking sarcastically that even Thule, let alone Britain, *was now talking about hiring a teacher of rhetoric*.[215] Such was the invasive nature of imported Greek culture. But the point to note here is that Juvenal is referring to events which were in the recent past and were still topical, even if they no longer made headline reading.

Agricola's military strategy for AD 81-83 was undoubtedly outlined in Rome by Domitian, and just as the credit for the fleet commander's achievement would be given to Agricola, so the governor's success would ultimately be attributed to the policy of the emperor, despite the subjective anti-Domitian comments made by Tacitus in *Agr.* 39. Domitian employed a network of freedmen to act as advisers and intermediaries and also to do his 'dirty' work for him. It would be ironic if the *libertum ex secretioribus ministeriis* (*Agr.* 40.2, *a freedman from one of the more senior palace departments*) who, as Tacitus suggests, had been commissioned by the emperor to bring a special dispatch to Agricola, were on the staff of Abascantus, Domitian's *ab epistulis* (Secretary of State), the man who was probably involved in updating the emperor on the progress of the Caledonian campaigns. Statius refers to Abascantus' responsibilities in relaying the emperor's instructions to the different war-zones of the empire and in finding out

---

modo covers about 20 years. It is somewhat surprising that Courtney, noticing the *Tacitean* nature of the lines with the reference to the Orkneys, then claims that Thule (*Sat.* 15.12) is merely a reference to somewhere at the end of the world. Having noted that Tacitus' Thule is Shetland he could have linked it with the Orkneys.

[209] The bracketing of Ireland, the Orkneys and Shetland is repeated by Claudian, describing in the fourth century the activities of Count Theodosius in the far north, *maduerunt Saxone fuso/ Orcades; incaluit Pictorum sanguine Thyle;/ Scottorum cumulos flevit glacialis Hiverne.* (*the Orkneys were drenched with Saxon slaughter, Shetland grew warm with the blood of the Picts, ice-bound Ireland wept for the heaps of the Scots*). *De IV Cons. Hon.* 31-33, cf. Dion 1966, 210. In this parallel *Thyle* cannot be a general reference (*pace* Wijsman) to Britain which Claudian had already referred to in line 28. But it does illustrate how Roman military involvement in the far north becomes virtually a *topos*.

[210] *Britanni* can be anyone living in the British Isles. It is regularly used by Tacitus to describe the Caledonians, while Diodorus (5.32.3) employs it to describe the Irish (cf. Freeman 2001, 35-36) It is therefore equally applicable to the people of Shetland. Shetland is a British island. Its inhabitants are Britons.

[211] Ogilvie 1967, 182; Nicolson 1984, 17. Strabo points out (*Geog.* 2.1.18) that *the longest day has nineteen equinoctial hours*.

[212] It is interesting to note that Pliny (*HN* 6.89), in describing Taprobane (Ceylon or Sri Lanka) as *extra orbem a natura relegata* (*banished by nature beyond the confines of the world*) points out that it was *not* free from Roman vices. But the eastern limits of the world had a far more advanced culture than Shetland.

[213] Cf. *Agr.* 16.3, *seductive vices*; 21.2, *the refinements of evil ways*.

[214] This point needs to be qualified. Agricola was recalled to Rome in spring of AD 84. But the Romans maintained a presence in Caledonia until AD 87, and there is no reason why Agricola's successor should not finish off what Agricola began and complete the conquest of Shetland. In which case references in the Silver Age poets to the conquest of Thule under Domitian may well be true. Tacitus would obviously not mention the achievements of Agricola's successor.

[215] Although Thule had lost its mystery by the end of the first century, it did not stop writers from indulging their fantasies. It is quite possible that Antonius Diogenes, a contemporary of Juvenal and Martial, used Agricola's expedition to Shetland as the inspiration for the title of his novel, *The Incredible Things beyond Thule*. Martial's patron, Faustinus, may be the same man to whom Antonius wrote a letter, describing his work: Bowersock 1994, 37. A connection between the author's family and the Flavian era is suggested by the third-century sarcophagus from Aphrodisias bearing the name *Flavius Antonius Diogenes*, Jones/Smith 1994, 468. Nauta 2002, 68 n.96 is not convinced of any connection between Antonius and Faustinus. But he makes no link with Agricola's expedition to Thule.

> *Quid Rheni vexilla ferant, quantum ultimus orbis*
> *cesserit et refugo circumsona gurgite Thule*
> Silvae 5.1.88-89

...what the standards of the Rhine are bringing, how far the furthest limit of the world has surrendered, and Thule, around which the ebbing floodtide roars

News of foreign victories was always brought in laurelled dispatches and the emperor accorded the usual imperatorial acclamation. Doubtless Domitian's success in Germany would receive official recognition at the expense of Agricola's success in Caledonia, although both occurred in the same year.[216] The implication in Statius suggests that Domitian would bathe in the reflected glory of victories, in whatever part of the world they occurred. The language of Statius regarding Thule should be treated with utmost caution. References to darkness, noise and inaccessibility are a delusion and take their origins from Pytheas.[217] When Polybius and Strabo call Pytheas a liar, they are not far short of the mark. The facts are much simpler. Shetland is and was a habitable island, probably trading with Norway as early as the Iron Age. Obviously tidal conditions are different from the Mediterranean and would be noticeable to those sailing north from mainland Scotland for the first time. Later Latin writers, such as Claudian, perpetuated the myth because it made for a 'good read'. Exotic locations like Thule stir the imagination. Where does it occur in poetry? At the *end* of the line. All the rest builds up to it.[218]

Statius was more concerned with flattering Domitian than with promoting the glory of Agricola, who meant nothing to him.[219] But these lines would relate to Agricola's campaigns, since *ultimus orbis* must refer to Britain as opposed to the eastern *orbis*,[220] while Thule, as in Juvenal, is recognised as being separate from it. The only part of Britain which could have *surrendered* to Domitian is Caledonia (AD 81-83).[221] Thule represents a triumph in hitherto inaccessible areas, but the triumph lies in the conquest of the Ocean to reach *Thulensis portus*. Statius' vocabulary, *refugo circumsona gurgite*, is a good description of Dunrossness, a long peninsula projecting into Sumburgh Röst, *which can be heard breaking even on a calm day*.[222] It would be from naval reconnaissance reports and eye-witness accounts that such a description of the wave-lashed coastline originated.[223] It did not require the type of fantastic embellishment which Germanicus' sailors brought back from their unfortunate experiences in the North Sea (Tac. *Ann.* 2.24.) in AD 16.

Silius Italicus in a remarkable tribute to Domitian presents Jupiter reassuring Venus that Rome will prosper as much under the Flavian dynasty as it did under the Julio-Claudians:

> *exin se Curibus virtus caelestis ad astra*
> *efferet et sacris augebit nomen Iulis*
> *bellatrix gens bacifero nutrita Sabino;*
> *hinc pater ignotam donabit vincere Thylen*
> *inque Caledonios primus trahet agmina lucos*
> Pun. 3.594-598[224]

---

[216] For a detailed analysis of Domitian's receipt of the title *Germanicus*, see the appendix in Buttrey 1980, 52-56.
[217] Cf. Stat, *Silv.* 3.5.20, 4.4.62;
[218] See note 1.
[219] See Appendix 4.
[220] Cf. *in ultimos orbis Britannos* (*into the Britons, furthest in the world*), Hor. *Carm.*1.35.29 f.; *divisos orbe Britannos* (*the Britons separated by the world*), Virg. *Ecl.* 1.67; *cum cetero orbe Vespasianus et Britanniam recuperavit* (*Vespasian recovered Britain also together with the rest of the world*); Tac. *Agr.* 17.11, *dierum spatium ultra nostri orbis mensuram* (*a length of days beyond the measure of our world*), Tac. *Agr* 12.3. Statius clearly differentiates between Britain and Shetland.
[221] Gibson 2006, 111 was quite right in linking *cesserit* to the victory at Mons Graupius, but his reference to Thule evoking *Agricola's circumnavigation in AD 84* misses both the point and the date.
[222] Nicolson 1984, 12 f.
[223] This is not inconsistent with Tacitus' reference to *mare pigrum* (*sluggish sea*). A sea may be sluggish in open tracts, but it has to break ashore.
[224] Bauer's text here is preferable to that of Delz.

Thereafter shall godlike excellence rise up from Cures to the stars, and the reputation of the deified Iuli shall be enhanced by the warrior family reared on the berry that grows in the Sabine land. Hence (?) the father shall present unknown Thule for conquest and shall be the first to haul his columns into the Caledonian forests

The story of the rise of the Flavian family from its humble origins at Cures in Sabine territory to dominate the world under three successive emperors (AD 69-96) is well-known. But the interpretation of these lines, especially with reference to the deified Julian family, Thule and Caledonia, has been less than convincing.

E. Birley wrote that *a senator* (i.e. Silius), *surveying in Domitian's lifetime the record of the Flavian dynasty, attributes to Vespasian the first penetration into the groves of Caledonia and the discovery and conquest of Thule, and that in the early years of his principate.*[225] The key word here is *principate*. Momigliano rejected this view on the basis that the adjective *Caledonius* was used *loosely or at least irresponsibly* and he referred it to the Claudian invasion of AD 43,[226] without considering that Caledonia was inextricably linked to the Flavian family from AD 69 onwards and that the presence of the Roman army in the area close to the *Caledonian forest* had been mentioned by Pliny c. AD 70-71, when Vettius Bolanus and Petillius Cerialis (Vespasian's kinsman, surely his son-in-law) were governing Britain. Are we to assume that Pliny also was using the term *loosely or irresponsibly*?[227] Smallwood, following Nesselhauf and followed by Fitzpatrick, is quite confident that *Silius refers to events prior to Vespasian's reign, almost certainly to the Claudian campaigns.*[228] This confidence cannot be justified, as will be shown. Wijsman was correct in suggesting the possibility that *Caledonius* was influenced by Agricola's expedition to Scotland,[229] but incorrect in describing it as *a piece of sheer flattery of the emperor and his father*.[230] Such views are misplaced and should be re-assessed in the light of my interpretations in the *Agricola*.

Furthermore, Momigliano made no attempt to explain the significance of *Thylen*. In the late Silver Age poets this invariably, *pace* Wijsman, refers to the *furthest* parts of Britain and the western world, where Pytheas' myth of almost permanent night (and almost permanent day) was elaborated, embellished and propagandised to flatter Flavian patrons, who knew full well the reality of the situation. Once the Romans had reached Thule and reports of the mission were received at court, everyone in Rome would have been aware that the place had lost its mystery,[231] as Juvenal's sarcastic comments illustrate. It would be pointless to use *Thule* to describe Britain. Thule (Shetland) cannot be linked with Vespasian in AD 43, but it can be linked to the Flavian involvement in Caledonia, which may go back as early as AD 70. (Where did the concept that Thule = England (*sic*) ever originate?[232])

---

[225] E. Birley 1946, 79=1953, 14.
[226] Momigliano 1950, 42. See Appendix 5. Momigliano's views were effectively countered by E. Birley 1953, 19, who did not rule out the possibility of Vespasian having been commissioned by Plautius to operate in the north. But Caledonia is a step too far. Vespasian's priorities lay in the south, and with no reference to northern campaigns in Tacitus, Suetonius or Dio the matter is still open to question. McGing 1982, 19 f. draws the wrong conclusions from the verses of Silius and Valerius Flaccus. Nowhere does either of the two poets relate Vespasian's achievements to the Claudian conquest. To state that we have a *grossly exaggerated picture of the part played by Vespasian in Claudius' British campaign* merely reiterates outdated views and totally misses the point, and by supporting Momigliano (24, n.22) against E. Birley, whose introductory sentence he quotes verbatim, he compounds the error. Dihle 1994, 76 notes Silius' reference to *the conquest of Scotland under Domitian*, but does not explain the Silian context.
[227] In view of Pliny's close relationship with Vespasian he is unlikely to have distorted events which occurred during the latter's principate.
[228] Smallwood 1962, 171; Nesselhauf 1952, 233; Fitzpatrick 1989, 28. See Appendix 2.
[229] Wijsman 1998, 319. These misconceptions are an amplified version of his notes on Valerius Flaccus, 1996, 153.
[230] Río Torres-Murciano 2005, 89 regards *Caledonia* as a *synecdoche* for *Britannia*. This completely misses the point. Vespasian's achievement lies in initiating the conquest of Caledonia. This is a contemporary allusion, not a throwback to a previous generation. I disagree with D'Espèrey's comment on Valerius Flaccus, 1986, 3073, that *contemporary allusions are rare and of little significance*. Rare they may be, but far from being *of little significance*.
[231] Cf. Aujac 1988, 340. This may explain why Antonius Diogenes set his novel *beyond* Thule. Whatever impact Agricola's expedition had on contemporary society was lost or forgotten in subsequent centuries when Thule once more resumed its mythological status.
[232] Spaltenstein 1987, tom. I, 249: *'Thyles' peut même désigner toute l'Angleterre*. This misconception (see Appendix 5) is repeated in his edition of Valerius Flaccus, 2002, 29, where *Caledonius* is subjected to the same mistreatment. He was

The parallel dedication which Momigliano and Smallwood cite from Valerius Flaccus (*Arg.* 1.7-9) raises similar questions on dating and will be examined later. These five lines from Silius should be seen as a prelude to Domitian's ultimate conquest of Scotland, not simply dismissed as *hyperbole*.[233] The Flavian connexion with Thule and Caledonia, from conception to conquest, covers the years AD 69-83. The Claudian invasion belongs to the achievements of the *sacri Iuli* (the Julio-Claudians) whom the Flavians will surpass. What Julius Caesar and Claudius began, Vespasian and his family will complete. Jupiter is merely humouring Venus (as he does in the *Aeneid*), from whom the Julian dynasty claimed descent. This is Silius' tribute to Virgil, from whom he borrowed the concept. But Silius knew better and, whatever concessions he makes to epic convention, it is hardly likely that he would subordinate the achievements of the Flavians to those of the Julio-Claudians.[234] There would in that case have been no point to the panegyric.

These lines relate not only to the early years, as Birley suggested, but also to the final years of Vespasian's principate, when Agricola was commissioned to push ever further north. Braund has since attempted to reconcile the suggestions of Birley and Momigliano, noting that *Silius Italicus presents as ongoing Vespasian's conquest which began with Claudius and proceeded into the reign of Vespasian through the agency of others*.[235] This appears to make sense, if an overall view is taken, although I do not see why there should be an allusion to Claudius: the panegyric is directed towards the Flavians, not to the dynasty they replaced. But how far *into the reign of Vespasian*? I believe that the reference to Caledonia has been updated by Silius to cover a period of four years from AD 79-83, from the time when Agricola invaded Caledonia to the time when he reached Thule. In retrospect, he was able to see both the beginning and the end of Roman involvement in Scotland, both the legacy and its fulfilment. By *the agency of others* Braund presumably refers to the expansion following the Civil War, when *Vespasian recovered Britain also as well as the rest of the world* (*Agr.* 17.1). A topical allusion, however, would set the seal on the emperor's plans for Britain right up until his final year and would include the early years of the governorship of Agricola, the emperor's agent (*legatus Augusti pro praetore*). Braund mentions Domitian's involvement in Britain, citing Plutarch's account of Demetrius (*De Def. Orac.* 410a, 434c) and the latter's imperial commission of exploration.[236]

But to claim that Tacitus denies Domitian any credit for the conquest of Britain is an oversimplification of the purpose of the monograph. The conquest of Britain did not feature as highly in the list of Domitian's priorities as it did with Agricola and Tacitus.[237] All the same, it was significant enough to be alluded to by Statius and Silius in their references to Thule, and the fact that Domitian allowed Agricola two more years, to show his paces, suggests more than a passing interest. What Vespasian had begun, Domitian could claim credit for completing. Tacitus makes no mention of Vespasian as the man who commissioned Agricola to invade Scotland, no mention of Titus, who authorised consolidation,[238] no mention of Domitian as the man who promoted the push to the extremity of the island. Failure to mention their role is not a denial of it. Once Agricola became governor of Britain he, not his Flavian superiors, is depicted by Tacitus as the initiator. The reverse process may be seen in the poetic tradition. The problem is in striking an even balance. Breeze is probably right in attributing Tacitus' reticence on Domitian's more positive achievements to the fact that Domitian was dead at the time of publication and *damnatio memoriae* (*condemnation of memory*

---

correct in his observation that '*Thylen' renvoie à Agricola.*

[233] So Gibson 2006, 209, who associates these lines with Vespasian's part in the Claudian invasion.

[234] The 'competitiveness' between the two dynasties may be seen in Vespasian's dream (Suet. *Vesp.* 35) of the balance, where Claudius and Nero appear in one side of the scales, while Vespasian and his two sons stand on the other. Evans 2003, 258 stresses the point of Flavian ambitions, *Silius' Jupiter makes explicit that the Flavian dynasty.....has exceeded the achievements of Augustus' line*. So how does this tie in with her translation that the warrior family *shall increase the fame of the deified Julii*? To *increase* is not the same as to *exceed*.

[235] Braund 1996, 150.

[236] Braund 1996, 150; cf. Ogilvie 1967, 32-35. On the imperial commission cf. Wainwright 1962, 66. Saddington 1990, 228 suggests that Plutarch's reference to Demetrius being sent *by the emperor* might imply a central, rather than Agricolan, initiative. This would confirm my own view that it was Domitian who authorised the extended voyage to Shetland, cf. p.36 and n.103.

[237] Cf. Davies Pryce/Birley 1938, 151.

[238] D.J. Breeze 1988, 16: *presumably on the advice of Agricola*.

ie. *consignment to oblivion*) was in full swing.[239] But this does not explain why Titus, whom Agricola would have known personally, is not mentioned at all in the monograph.

Galimberti makes an interesting, albeit extravagant, proposal that Silius' lines could refer to Vespasian as campaigning in the north of Britain in AD 43. He even suggests Vespasian's presence in the Orkneys that year, using this as a reason for Agricola's expedition to the Orkneys: Agricola had been commissioned by Vespasian in AD 78 (?) to re-establish at some time during his northern campaigns the link with the Orkneys which Vespasian had allegedly forged nearly forty years earlier.[240] But Silius makes no mention of the Orkneys. Galimberti sees in Mela's *ignotarum quoque gentium victor* (3.6. [49], *conqueror of unknown nations also*) a veiled allusion to a Claudian expedition to the Orkneys.[241] Yet Mela's language, Claudius *is now revealing*, can only refer to southern Britain. Vespasian was involved in the submission of the Isle of Wight. What Galimberti should have pursued was the possibility of confusion between Wight and the Orkneys in the account of Eutropius (7.13.3).[242] Galimberti defers too much to Momigliano, failing to realise that any reference to the last decade of Vespasian's life, the principate, the highlight of his career, had apparently disappeared from Silius' account. Or had it? Note the sequence of his campaigns. Why is the emphasis put on events in northern Britain, if not because Vespasian's generals had been enjoying success there? Why does the British campaign precede the German one, when a Claudian allusion should assume the reverse, a point which Smallwood noted, but could not explain?[243] Josephus (*BJ* 3.1.4) knew the correct sequence for the Claudian epoch: Germany first, then Britain. But Germany was of no real importance, and is referred to by Silius (and Statius) only because of Domitian's involvement there. Germany does not even rate a mention in the dedication of Valerius Flaccus, who knew exactly where Vespasian's reputation lay. The answer to the Silian sequence lies in attributing a decade of British campaigns, the culmination of Vespasian's connexion with Britain, to Vespasian's principate, which Silius could simply not ignore. What better way for the emperor to end his career than to commission the conquest of Scotland and bring the entire island under Roman control? Having been so successful in the eastern part of the empire *before* he attained the principate, he needed no incentive to take on the western part *after* he had attained it. Herodian (*Hist.* 3.14.2) noted that Septimius Severus wanted victories in Britain to go with those in the east and the north. Alexander the Great had similar ambitions, as did Julius Caesar (and Adolf Hitler). The common objective was conquest of the known world, and if Vespasian had lived for a further two years the conquest of Caledonia and the western world might have been completed by AD 81.

The rest of Silius' Vespasianic resumé is a survey of the late emperor's career under Claudius and Nero, merely for the record.[244] Their reputations (*nomen*) will be enhanced (*augebit*) by their agents,

---

[239] D.J. Breeze 1996, 35.

[240] Galimberti 1996, 74. This is not an entirely original theory, since Torrentius in 1574, in order to accommodate Pliny's location of *Vectis* in the Irish Sea, suggested that Vespasian had campaigned there *or had stormed some other island further to the north*, although Torrentius made no connexion with the Orkneys in citing Eutropius.

[241] This must surely refer to the conquests under Plautius. I do not see his involvement in the Orkneys. What would be the point ?

[242] See Appendix 2.

[243] Smallwood 1962, 171 n. 2.

[244] In the next two lines, *reget impiger Afros/ palmiferamque senex bello domitabit Idumen*, we have references to the last two important stages of Vespasian's career (the proconsulship of Africa and the Jewish War) before he assumed the principate. Momigliano refers to *senex* as an indication by Silius that Vespasian's career builds up to his old age. But this interpretation of his career completely ignores the principate, the most important part of his life. It does not take much to work out that if Vespasian was *senex* at the time of the Jewish War, then he must have been *senex* during his proconsulship of Africa two years earlier. You do not suddenly become a *senex*. Perhaps the poet is using this word *loosely or at least irresponsibly*. Silius' introduction of *pater* and *bellatrix gens* early on in the panegyric has put the Flavian dynasty in a nutshell. What he does next is to show the achievements of the component parts. First, the achievements of the *senex*, next, those of the *iuvenis*. Domitian is still alive, but Jupiter refers to the achievements of his boyhood (*puer*, 608). These age differences are a Silian perspective of three Flavian emperors at different stages of their lives, almost as if one were looking at an album of family photographs. I believe that the deified Vespasian and Titus are presented by Silius as they were at the time of their death, as *senex* and *iuvenis*, for enrolment among the members of the divine fraternity over which Jupiter presides. Why else would Jupiter describe Titus as *iuvenis* (incorrectly translated by Duff as *son*) and then refer to his achievements of some decade earlier as *primo in aevo* (*in his early years*, 606)?

Vespasian and Titus (*bellatrix gens*), through service in Germany and Judaea.[245] But it is only in Britain that Vespasian will determine his own policy of expansion.

The context provided by Silius should be linked to those who represented the emperor in Britain, from the time of Bolanus to the governorship of Agricola. Titus and Domitian will continue their father's legacy until the conquest is completed. It is possible that the emperor, perhaps as early as AD 69, drew up for the *magni duces* (*Agr*.17.1, *great generals*)—from whom Tacitus' prejudice has excluded Bolanus—the plans leading ultimately to the conquest of Caledonia.[246] But he died in June AD 79, a few months after the start of Agricola's third campaigning season. Yet Silius was correct. Detailed policy decisions were made by Vespasian, probably during the course of the winter, and he lived long enough to see his plans being implemented by the last of his appointees. The *agency of others* tells us that he was controlling events by proxy, and despite his illness *muneribus imperatoriis fungeretur* (Suet. *Vesp*. 24.2, *he was carrying out the functions of the Imperator*).[247] Flavian apologists (Jos. *BJ* 3.1.24, *Agr*.13.3), just as they emphasise the role of Vespasian during the Claudian invasion, credit him, and with justification, for a policy implemented during his principate by a succession of governors. Whether or not the emperor comes to Britain in person is immaterial; he deserves the credit for the successes of his legates, whom he has personally commissioned. This is why the imperatorial acclamations on the coinage are so relevant. No doubt Vespasian was fully aware by the middle of AD 79 that time was running out for him. Hence the need to get Titus fully involved. Hanson states that *Vespasian's death meant that the successful advance to the Tay was credited to Titus*.[248] Dio's comment that Titus *received the title of imperator for the fifteenth time* as a consequence of the events in Britain in AD79 is not inconsistent with the developing situation. If Agricola's fleet was causing havoc on the Caledonian littoral in April/May, Vespasian would have received news of it in June, shortly before he died, and Titus, no doubt involved in his ailing father's policy decisions, felt justified after the death of his father in getting some reward for his contributions.[249] Silius' account may well

---

[245] Wistrand 1956, 5 suggests that *augebit* is equivalent to *addet* and that the Flavian family will add its name to the pantheon which includes the Julio-Claudians. I can see his point in that the new dynasty would be accorded the same prestige as the old one. But, if anything, Vespasian wanted to put the Julio-Claudians in the shade. The expression *nomen augere* simply means *to enhance the* name, a common usage, cf. Cic. *Dom*. 19. Silius faces a dilemma in that he addresses Venus as the patron goddess of both families. But it is quite clear that Vespasian intended his family to outdo the Julio-Claudians. See Appendix 3.

[246] It is impossible to accept the observation of McDermott/Orentzel 1979, 51: *Flavian policy seems to have been against expansion and despite absence of comment it seems unlikely that Vespasian anticipated the campaigns in the north with which Agricola indulged himself*. The literary and archaeological evidence suggests otherwise; and how can Agricola's campaigns be classified as self-indulgence? These authors' suggestion that Vespasian appointed the *iuridicus* Salvius Liberalis to keep a check on Agricola, because the emperor had reservations about the governor, needs to be substantiated. The fact that Tacitus *never mentions Liberalis* is irrelevant. Tacitus' attitude towards Vespasian is distinctly favourable and reflects the debt which Agricola owed to the emperor.

[247] Cf. Levick 1999, 258. It is quite likely that Vespasian relied heavily on Titus, his consular colleague, cf. Suet. *Titus* 6.1. Jones 1984, 150 noted that *it would not* be unreasonable to assume that in this, the last year of Vespasian's reign, Titus was even more closely involved with military planning and had fully approved of Agricola's plans. See Appendix 3.

[248] Hanson 1991b, 1753; Dio 66.20.3.

[249] See Appendix 3. Titus assumed the title of *Augustus* within a week of his father's death, and the fifteenth imperatorial acclamation sometime between 9 September AD 79 and 1 January AD 80 (cf. Smith 1926, 95). Dio (66.20.3) does not link this acclamation to a *victory*, as Buttrey 1980, 25 suggests. Tacitus makes no mention of any victory in AD 79. But Dio's language (66.20.1) in the statement that Agricola in AD 79 *ravaged all the enemy's territory there* corresponds with Tacitus' *vastatis usque ad Taum nationibus* (*had ravaged nations as far as the Tay, Agr*. 22.1), repeated by *percucurrerat* (*had overrun, Agr*. 23.1), to describe incursions made beyond the isthmus. If Dio is accurate, Agricola's advance to the Tay was in response to aggression by the tribes of southern Scotland, since it is likely that *the war which had broken out again* refers to a recrudescence of problems which Agricola's predecessors had failed to resolve. I believe that we have an 'ebb and flow' situation here with the both Romans and Caledonians seizing and losing the initiative. The Romans, however, must have controlled the sea for some years before Agricola took office, and consequently the Fife peninsula, the home of the Venicones, may well have been targeted by Roman marines in advance of a full-scale invasion. If Vespasian's initial policy in AD 69-70 was total conquest, any way of achieving that aim, whether by devastation or treaty, was acceptable. There were evidently two wars in the Lowlands, no doubt punctuated by acts of aggression, spread out over a period of some ten years, the first one being the 'spill over' from the Brigantian war (AD 69-71) which may well have been prolonged by Venutius (there is no reference to him being captured or killed) among the peoples of southern Scotland, in the same way as Caratacus had prolonged the resistance among those of Wales. The second war, which Tacitus refers to as *expeditiones*, appears to have been initiated (if Dio is to be understood) by the Britons, and was punished by destruction. Tacitus' attribution of Scottish initiatives to Agricola may well disguise the reality that Bolanus and Cerialis had led the first incursions into the area (cf. D.J.

reflect what was an established fact, namely that Caledonia had received the unwelcome attention of Agricola's marines in the principate of Vespasian. The reference to *forests* is a repetition of Pliny's account of earlier campaigns and anticipates four years of Agricola's struggle against natural obstacles. Bolanus may well have inflicted the initial wounds before Agricola delivered the *coup de grâce*.[250] It would be strange for the poet to describe Vespasian's career and to omit (*pace* Momigliano) any reference to events occurring during his principate. Like Agricola, Silius owed much to Vespasian—who was prepared to overlook his dubious activities under Nero (Plin. *Ep.* 3.7.3).

The language of Silius requires close scrutiny. What did the poet mean by *hinc pater ignotam donabit vincere Thylen*?[251] Neither Momigliano nor Wijsman made any attempt to offer an explanation for *donabit vincere*. It cannot refer to the Claudian invasion, since Vespasian at that time was in no position to make a gift of Thule, a gift which must be interpreted before any other argument can be entertained. Few translators have bothered to come to grips with the Latin. It does not state or mean that Vespasian will conquer Thule. Thule will be presented by him for conquest. But presented to whom? In a series of translations, what is not there is assumed: by Duff, *shall give Rome victory over Thule*;[252] by Evans, *will allow (Rome) to conquer unknown Thule*;[253] and by Stover, *will give Rome conquest over unknown Thule*.[254] Yet Silius' text has no reference to Rome. Still, these translators at least recognise that *donabit* requires a recipient. The versions of Miniconi and Devallet and of Braund regrettably ignore *donabit* altogether, while Watt (preferring Momigliano's dating), rightly dismissing the unattested *denabit*(?) of Delz, conjectures *durabit* (*will last*) which is totally unnecessary.[255] The verb, as it stands, implies a legacy from Vespasian to his sons, which can only occur when he is *princeps*. Spaltenstein says that *'Donabit' is ambiguous, as if Silius was suggesting that Vespasian was merely laying the groundwork for these victories*.[256] What else was Vespasian doing but paving the way for his heirs?

None of the extant MSS of Silius Italicus is earlier than the 15th century, and if we accept the equally valid reading *huic* (*to this*), found in three of them,[257] then we have a worthy recipient: the pronoun refers to the *bellatrix gens*, the Flavian dynasty, Titus and Domitian, who will inherit their father's policy and complete the conquest of Britain, reaching the ends of the earth in the process.[258] *Hinc* was

---

Breeze 1996, 34). In that case, there already existed a blueprint for campaigning: that would facilitate and accelerate Agricola's campaigns.

[250] So E. Birley, 1953, 46: *It was the latter* [sc. Bolanus] *who set the ball rolling*. See Appendix 4.

[251] It should be made clear that only Silius, not *Flavian poets*, as Levick loosely puts it, 1999, 16, is responsible for this line.

[252] Duff 1934, 159. This mistake has recently been resurrected by Woolliscroft/Hoffmann 2006, 197. Nowhere does Silius say that Vespasian *achieved victory over previously unknown Thule*. The failure to note that the Latin refers to Vespasian's *legacy* leads, at 188 f., to spurious conclusions.

[253] Evans 2003, 257. She follows the reading *hinc* and consequently fails to establish a connexion, assuming a reference to Vespasian in Claudius' invasion (n.14), adding *though the conquest of the far north is much more appropriate to Agricola's victory after Vespasian's death*. A question of having your cake and eating it.

[254] Stover 2006, 36. Cf. also Levick 1999, 16: *nor yet conquer Thule or even lead an army against the Caledonian forests*. This is linked with Josephus' exaggerated claim for the role Vespasian played in the Claudian invasion. The true significance of *Caledonius* as being fact rather than exaggeration has been missed. What should have been noted is the link with Cerialis and Agricola. Who else was involved in the *Caledonian forests*?

[255] Miniconi/Devallet 1979, tom.1, 93; Braund 1996, 149; Watt 1988, 172.

[256] Spaltenstein 1990, tom 2.249: *'donabit' est ambigu, comme si Silius suggérait que Vespasien ne fit que préparer ces victoires*.

[257] F, G, Ξ (ed. Delz). These MSS, as may be seen from Delz's *stemma*, have as much validity as the rest, if not more. Curiously this reading does not appear among the variants in the edition of Miniconi/ Devallet. Drakenborch 1717, 174 points out in his notes the optional reading *huic pater*, but unfortunately submitted to the judgement of N. Heinsius whose authority in Latin poetry was always regarded as gospel.

[258] The glorification of the *warrior family* is a poor imitation of Virgil's panegyric on the *gens Iulia*, cf. *Aen.*1.287 and 6.781. Silius proceeds from the rustic origins of the *gens Flavia* in Sabine territory to beyond the Ocean and into the furthest limits of the known world. This arrangement creates the illusion of how far and how quickly Flavian domination had extended. Salway 1993, 117 refers to the triumphal arch set up at Richborough to commemorate the completion of the conquest: *Domitian would have had every incentive to mark as publicly as possible that it was under his auspices that the enormously prestigious expansion of Roman domination across the Ocean..., so strongly associated with his own family, had been brought to a successful conclusion in his reign*. This monument was a visual reminder to navigators who would see it in the distance. Sauer 2002, 344 draws a parallel with Augustus' *Tropaeum Alpium* at Monaco, and notes that *if in the 80s the majority of travellers entered and left Britannia via Richborough, then it made ultimate sense to build a monument there*.

adopted only because it appears several times earlier in Jupiter's speech (*Pun.* 3. 585, 586, 587, 593), where it means *next,* but it sits awkwardly in the panegyric, where it occurs nowhere else.[259] *Huic* with reference to Domitian occurs later (*Pun.* 3. 612, 619). The text may now be translated as

to this (family) the father shall present unknown Thule for conquest.

What could more striking than the product of humble Sabine Cures offering to his family the ends of the earth where no Roman had gone before? When else, but as *princeps*, when his sons were of military age, would Vespasian entrust them with the responsibility of completing his conquests? It can hardly refer to the Claudian era when Titus was only a few years old and Domitian not yet born. Silius and Juvenal are referring to the culmination of the Caledonian campaign, with Agricola's fleet conquering the Orkneys and reaching Shetland, terrifying the *minima contentos nocte Britannos* before the long nights set in.

It is natural for any eulogy on Domitian to exaggerate his successes in the north and the east where he was personally involved. References to campaigns in the west are more subtle and reflect his policy-making. His strategy, perhaps through the agency of Abascantus, should be seen behind Agricola's last two campaigns in Caledonia (AD 82-83) and the voyage to Shetland, hitherto *unknown* to any Romans, which could stand comparison with Alexander's fleet reaching the eastern limits of conquest.[260] Vespasian's legates faced an arduous task; Pliny noted that Roman armies had virtually reached the Caledonian forests c.AD 71, and Silius' *trahet* is apt. The difficulties faced by Agricola's army in the forests and mountains are stressed by Tacitus (*Agr.* 25.1).[261] They represent the weariness of an army struggling *almost against nature itself* (*Agr.* 33.2, *paene adversus ipsam rerum naturam*), just as Agricola's marines had to contend with the *adversities of storms and waves* (25.1, *tempestatum ac fluctuum adversa*). It is the Flavian dynasty, *bellatrix gens*, beginning with Vespasian (*primus*), which is responsible for armies being hauled into the Caledonian forests,[262] and for sending the fleet to *conquer unknown Thule.*

Valerius Flaccus in his tribute to Vespasian (*Arg.* 1.7-21) was writing about Caledonia before Statius and Silius, and this explains why Thule is not mentioned by him in connexion with Caledonia, whereas the connexion is mentioned or implied by the two later poets. In Silius' case there is one instance (*Pun.* 17.417) where Caledonia must be equated with Thule, a condensed indication that Agricola's campaigns of AD 79-83 began in the former and ended in the latter. But the poet is not generalising about Britain. He is referring to Scotland. Wijsman assumed that this reference in Silius' seventeenth book was derived from Caesar and his *essedarii (charioteers)*.[263] But any reference to *covinni (chariots)* at this date must surely derive from the battle of Mons Graupius, where the *covinnarii (charioteers)*, contrary to the view of editors, did *not* flee, but participated in the battle, as

---

[259] The reading may have been influenced by *inque* in the next line.

[260] Ogilvie 1967, 33, especially with reference to Oceanus and Thetis (*Diod.* 17.104). The theories of Fabre and Dion that Pytheas had received a commission from Alexander, whose apparent ambitions for conquest in the west were cut short by his untimely death, might gain some support if the Alexander-Pytheas-Agricola connexion is accepted.

[261] *Agr.* 25.1, *silvarum ac montium profunda* (*the depths of forests and ravines*); 26.2, *nisi paludes ac silvae fugientes texissent* (*if the swamps and forests had not sheltered the fugitives*); 33.5, *evasisse silvas* (*to have emerged from forests*); 34.2, *silvas saltusque penetrantibus* (*penetrating the forests and ravines*). Agricola's troops insisted: *penetrandam Caledoniam* (*Agr.* 27.1, *that Caledonia should be penetrated*). Evans 2003, 257 rather unfortunately tries to build a whole case on the verb *penetrare*, citing numerous examples of the verb (262 n.23) to support the use of sexual vocabulary in the *Agricola*. To apply modern views of sexuality to Tacitus is doomed to failure. As Adams 1987, 151 points out, '*penetrare*' does *not* occur in a sexual sense in the Classical period. This applies equally to her misinterpretation of *patientiae*.

[262] Hanson/Macinnes 1980, 102 make valid points on the nature of the terrain facing Agricola, but are incorrect in stating that Silius Italicus' reference to Caledonian forests was written *before* Agricola's campaigns. The Flavian connexion with the Caledonian forest is secured by the activities of Cerialis, as inferred by Pliny.

[263] Wijsman 1998, 319, citing Sil. *Pun.* 17.417-7, *caerulus haud aliter cum dimicat incola Thyles/ agmina falcigero circumvenit arta covinno* (*just so the blue-painted native of Thule, when he fights, drives around the close-packed ranks in his scythe-bearing chariot*). The *arta agmina* are Tacitus' *densa agmina* (*Agr.* 36.3). Caesar does not specifically mention that *essedarii* used *scythed* chariots. In fact the description he gives (*BG* 4.33) would make any scythe attachment positively life-threatening to the drivers running along the pole. For the differences between *essedarii* and *covinnarii*, cf. Couissin 1932, 102.

the codex clearly shows.[264] Silius' account confirms this. Till knew that Silius' description followed the publication of the *Agricola* in AD 98.[265] It was topical.[266] It is in the light of Silius' phraseology in his last book that Statius' references to the actions of Vettius Bolanus in Thule (*Silv.* 5.2.55-56) and the *Caledonian plains* (*Silv.* 5.2.142) should be assessed.[267]

Silius' panegyric was written some twenty-five years after Vespasian's death, yet paradoxically foretold the emperor's past career, which Silius was able to do in retrospect. By contrast, Valerius Flaccus' more restrained dedication, contentiously assumed to have been composed during the emperor's lifetime, can understandably make no future predictions for Vespasian's career. It was all but over—apart from his posthumous role as a star in the firmament (*Arg.* 1.16-17).[268] The emperor was now living on borrowed time.[269] It is Vespasian's *past* which is lauded, and that from a present viewpoint (*nunc*, line 20). But how far back in the past? My belief is that we are dealing with events which were recent and still ongoing. The prologue has always roused controversy in terms of its content and dating and has generated and continues to generate a mass of dubious literature which has nothing new to add.[270] But three lines merit comment in the light of my previous suggestions:

> *tuque o, pelagi cui maior aperti*
> *fama, Caledonius postquam tua carbasa vexit*
> *Oceanus Phrygios prius indignatus Iulos…*
> *Arg.* 1.8-10

And you, whose glory is greater for having opened up the sea, after the Caledonian ocean had borne your sails, the ocean which had previously raged against the Phrygian Iuli…

Whatever position scholars may adopt in a much debated theme, no one can possibly doubt that

---

[264] *Agr.* 36.3, *equitum turmae fugere* (*the squadrons of cavalry fled*) is clear enough (cf. Burn 1953a, 154; Lund 1981, 84). The British cavalry fled, and the *covinnarii* became involved in the infantry action. They were not *driven off*, as Burn 1969, 57 (contradicting his previous belief) and B. Dobson 1981, 10 suggest, and their alleged flight appears to have occurred before they were actually involved in the battle. Laederich's version (2001, 351 *nos escadrons de cavalerie, après avoir mis en déroute les chars montés, se joignirent au combat des fantassins*) is nonsense. Where does it say *our* squadrons ? It is hardly likely that Silius would use a simile suggestive of failure in order to describe a triumphant Masinissa.

[265] Till 1944, 249: *man kann vielleicht Tacitus' Agricola, der im Jahre 98 veröffentlicht wurde, als Ausgangspunkt für Silius' Schilderung annehmen.*

[266] Martial (*Epig.* 10.44.1) talks of his aged friend Quintus Ovidius leaving the comfort of his Sabine farm to visit *Caledonios Britannos*. There may be touch of irony here. But *Caledonios* was topical, and Martial's tenth book was published in the same year as the *Agricola*. The Flavian involvement in northern Britain was as much a topic for satirists as it was for the epic poets. For the relationship between Martial and Ovidius, cf. Kleywegt 1998, 270-272.

[267] Statius' treatment of Bolanus' activities in Scotland is discussed in Appendix 4. Claudian (*III Cons. Hon.* 53-56), describing the campaigns of Count Theodosius in northern Britain, refers to *ratibus impervia Thule* (*Thule inaccessible to ships*, ignoring Agricola's achievement), *Pictos* and the conquest of *the Hyperborean waves*. Wijsman's theory, 1998, 323, that Thule in this instance is equated with Britain generally, instead of the far north of Britain, cannot be correct, and Rutilius Namatianus (*De red.* 499-501), whom he quotes, clearly distinguishes *Thule* from the *ferox Britannus*.

[268] Val. Fl. *Arg.* 1.16-17 *lucebis ab omni/ parte poli* (*you will shine from every part of the sky*). This is the poet's rather limp comparison with the comet which appeared in 44 BC, following Caesar's death. This is referred to by Virgil (*Ecl* 9.47) as *Caesaris astrum* (*Caesar's star*) and by Horace (*Carm.*1.12.46) as *Iulium sidus* (*the Julian star*). But there may be some substance to Valerius' suggestion. The comet which appeared in 44 BC represented the departure of Caesar's spirit, which would ultimately be translated among the gods. Valerius would certainly have been aware of the comet, described by Suetonius (*Vesp.*23.4) and Dio/Xiphilinus (66.17.2-3), which appeared in the spring of AD 79— confirmed in Korean records—and was visible for twenty days. This was supposed to predict Vespasian's death, cf. Ramsay 2006, 162. This may well have given Valerius in hindsight the idea of a spiritual link between the comet, a bright star and a translated Vespasian.

[269] It was not gout, but a slight fever (Dio 66.17.1) which led to Vespasian's death. It is quite clear, however, from Suetonius (*Vesp.*24), that from the time when he was *temptatus… motiunculis levibus* (*attacked by a slight bowel disorder*) to the time when he died from more serious intestinal problems (dysentery), a number of weeks had elapsed. During these weeks he had been able to travel from Campania to Rome and from there to his Sabine homeland, to carry on his duties as emperor. I suggest that it is precisely during this period of his declining health that he received news of Agricola's successful naval operations in the Tay, and that Valerius Flaccus composed his dedication.

[270] Details of earlier contributions to the controversy on dating may be found in Scaffai 1994, 2368-2373 (particularly Ussani's groundwork). See also Taylor 1994, 214 and Liberman 1997, xviii-xxiii. A concise account of the dating problems may be found in Stern 1974, 1.502-3. Stern unfortunately follows the ubiquitous Momigliano in the treatment of *Caledonius* and so misses the point completely.

Caledonia was topical when Valerius wrote his prologue. The assumption that the poet's use of *Caledonius* is a reference to Vespasian's role in the Claudian invasion has generally held sway.[271] But how correct is this assumption? The first point to examine is the significance of *tua*. How could the ships be described as Vespasian's? They were either the ships of Claudius who initiated the expedition or of Plautius who led it.[272] If they are Vespasian's ships, then the initiator was Vespasian, i.e. as *princeps*. The second point is the meaning of *Iulos*. Does it refer to Julius Caesar and the problems he faced in the English Channel?[273] In that case why is it plural? The plural can hardly refer, as Lefèvre suggests, to Caesar and his troops.[274] Surely they could not all claim Trojan ancestry? Or does it refer to the problems faced collectively by both Caesar and his Julio-Claudian successors, as Burmann suggested[275] and Stover reiterated?[276] Terwogt made the point that Vespasian had achieved success where Julius Caesar and his successors had failed.[277] So a distinction should be made between the Julio-Claudian and later Flavian achievements. It is generally assumed that the *Iulis* of Silius refers to the *gens Iulia* (*Julian family*) in general, and not simply to Caesar. The fact that both poets use the word in eulogistic contexts would suggest that the meanings should be identical.[278] If Silius borrowed the term from Valerius (mutual borrowing between Valerius, Statius and Silius has always been recognised[279]), then its use in the latter has been generally misconstrued and reflects Oceanic problems posed not only to Caesar, but also to other Julio-Claudians.

Vespasian then belongs to a later era of Oceanic exploration and conquest. Peters perceptively suggested a reference to the campaigns of Cerialis, based on *Agr.* 17.[280] This was rejected by Smallwood, without good reason.[281] Although there is nothing in Tacitus to associate maritime activities with Cerialis, whose role in Britain is deliberately understated, there can be little doubt that he used his fleet, perhaps from bases in the Solway Firth, and on the Tyne, for northward exploration.[282] It is very likely that the Roman administration was focused on events in Britain, albeit

---

[271] Blomfield 1916, 22; Mozley 1934, 2; Momigliano 1950, 52; Lefèvre 1971, 52; Strand 1972, 29; Taylor 1994, 217; Lang 2003, 316; Kleywegt 2005, 14; Nauta 2005, 27; Galli 2007, 40. Benferhat 2004 refers to *Vespasian's expedition to Britannia* as if he initiated it.

[272] Stover 2006, 36 f. n.61, in trying to promote the role of Vespasian in the Claudian expedition, falls into his own trap by stating that *it was Claudius, not Vespasian, who claimed the glory by celebrating victory in Britain with a triumph, commemorating his naval success by setting up a 'corona navalis' on the gate of his Palatine house.* Never were truer words spoken. All the more reason for Valerius Flaccus to be referring to current events; the *gens Flavia* had surpassed the achievements of the *gens Iulia* in the Northern Ocean, but in the Flavian era.

[273] Thus Mozley 1934, 2.

[274] Lefèvre 1971, 53.

[275] Burmann 1724, 7. Flavian propaganda would emphasise Julius Caesar's failure in Britain (*Agr.* 13.1), and the wrecking of his fleet would be seen as the Ocean's revenge for Caesar's pilfering of its pearls (cf. Suet. *Caes.,* 47; Plin, *HN* 9.116. Augustus' *consilium* (*policy, Agr.* 13.2), for Augustus did not finish off what Caesar had started and the Flavians would look at the excuses with some scepticism. Gaius' brief excursion into the Channel and back (Dio 59.25.2), which Malloch 2001, 554 saw as *symbolic of Gaius having extended his imperium over the sea* would be interpreted otherwise by Flavian apologists and would be represented as *mal de mer* and a failure to conquer the Ocean, hardly compensated by a collection of sea shells (Suet. *Gaius* 46; Dio 59.25.2). Hind 2003, 272-4 expands on the idea of pearls as *spoils of the Ocean,* but how many shells would you have to pick before you find a single pearl? Claudius' expedition, like Caesar's, found itself driven off course in the Channel (Dio 60.19.4). None of the Julio-Claudians was enamoured of *Oceanus*, and vice versa. All this should be set against the triumph over the *Caledonius Oceanus* by Vespasian's navy under his legates. The conquest of the Ocean (*victus Oceanus, Agr.* 25.1) by Agricola's marines, who bragged about it in AD 82, had been ongoing since AD 70.

[276] Stover 2006, 37: *Claudius is implicitly grouped among the 'Phrygii Iulii'* (sic) *who in fact are said to have failed to accomplish what Vespasian is credited with having done.* Stover unfortunately associates Vespasian here with the events of AD 43, when they really belong to the Flavian era. See Appendix 5.

[277] Terwogt 1898, 9-10.

[278] It is surprising that Kleywegt 2005, 14 gives examples of the plural use of *Iuli*, but fails to cite the obvious parallel from Silius.

[279] Summers 1894, 18-31; Getty 1936, 61; Matier 1983 79. Steele 1930, 328 suggested that they may have heard each other's recitations.

[280] Peters 1890, 10. His idea follows on from Bernays 1861, 12 and was taken up by Preiswerk 1934, 435.

[281] Smallwood 1962, 171.

[282] That Cerialis established a fort at Carlisle c. AD 73 is now confirmed by dendro-chronology, Frere 1990, 320, and supported by the numismatic evidence, Shotter 2001, 21-29. Naval operations through the Solway Firth towards Galloway and beyond would not be unreasonable. Pliny in a well-known sentence (*HN* 4.102, mistranslated by Rackham) writes: xxx *prope iam annis notitiam eius* (sc.*Britanniae*) *Romanis armis non ultra vicinitatem silvae Calidoniae propagantibus* (*in almost thirty years now Roman arms have been spreading knowledge of Britain as far as the neighbourhood of the Calidonian forest.* This can only refer to the period of expansion from the Claudian invasion to Pliny's own time. Dilke 1985,

without over-publicising the fact, especially as the Judaean War no longer made headlines. So involvement in the west throughout the 70s until the accession of Titus was building up to a climax. Peters' suggestion is valid, as it marks the beginning of naval operations which spanned a decade and capped Vespasian's principate with Agricola's invasion of Caledonia in AD 79. But Peters doesn't take into account the intricacies of the Silian parallel which continue where Valerius left off.[283] Thule was still four years away when Valerius wrote his address to Vespasian. Silius fills the gap. In the space of a dozen years the Ocean had carried Vespasian's navy from the Humber to the Tay, then through his successors to Thule and all the way round Scotland to the Clyde.[284] The irony is that the emperor did not live long enough to see his initiatives brought to fruition and that armchair critics have given them less than due credit.

Attempts to explain *Caledonius* have been far from convincing. Once it was supposed to be merely a case of *flattery* and *exaggeration*, later the label was *metonymy*: all feeble excuses for the failure to dig deep enough.[285] In the period when Silius and Valerius were writing, the word *Caledonius* would have reflected Flavian policy in Scotland between AD 79-83.[286] Agricola was resurrected by commentators as a reference point, a part of the exaggeration, and never given any credit, which in fact is precisely what the Flavian poets wanted. They had no intention of mentioning Agricola. Epic poems deal with emperors, not their employees. That is why the coinage always shows the *emperor* in military dress, never any legate on his own: *the quality of a good general was the monopoly of the emperor* (*Agr.* 39.2, *ducis boni imperatoriam virtutem esse*).

Only rarely does one come across a chink of light, and Soubiran deserves all credit for his recent observations on the role of Vespasian's governors in Britain.[287] Moreda likewise points out that *the*

69, following Rackham's impossible *about thirty years ago* (not, *pace* Hanson, *possible linguistically*), erroneously assigns Pliny's reference to the Claudian era, and then accuses Pliny of *lack of serious study*. Bianchetti 1998, 143 is even more unfortunate in her observation that *the reference seems to be to the expedition of Claudius in 43, when the "unexplored forest of Scotland" was not reached by the Roman army. The true and proper Caledonia was only reached by Agrippa* (sic) *in 83*. Quite clearly her eye strayed to the next paragraph (103) which begins with *Agrippa* (and we criticise Dark Age scribes?). But this does not excuse Magnani 2002, 169 from actually repeating this *lapsus oculi*. Roseman 1994, 88 f., like Rackham and Dilke, mistranslates as *it is almost thirty years now since acquaintance with (Britain) was extended by Roman arms...*, and talks of exaggeration in relation to the Claudian conquest. I see no exaggeration on Pliny's part and nothing that would preclude the presence of Roman troops near the Caledonian Forest. Pliny's contentious statement is as loud as Tacitus' silence on the matter. The *Historia Naturalis* was dedicated to Titus in AD 77. But this does not help us over the date of the reference, which could have been inserted either at the time when Book 4 was written, or added later, as the dedication was, in order to include the latest information. A date c. AD 70-71, however, is in keeping with *in almost thirty years*, and would tie in with Statius' references to Bolanus' activities (assuming the poet is correct) in the *Caledonian plains*. The location has always been open to question (cf. Rivet/Smith 1979, 290; Hanson 1991a 56). If Bolanus was operating in the Lowlands, then there is no good reason why Cerialis should not have capitalised on this by pushing up to the isthmus or even beyond. Agricola would not have achieved so much in his third campaign and been able to establish forts in the Lowlands (*Agr.* 22.1), if his predecessors had not already prepared the ground, cf. Nesselhauf 1952, 222ff; Levick 1999, 59. B. Dobson's attribution, 1981, 7, of Agricola's successful push to the lack of pugnacity of the Lowland tribes may well be correct—if they had already experienced the might of the Roman army.

[283] Tanner 1991, 2715 assumed that the two references from the poets *could equally apply to Agricola's activities under Domitian*. But Valerius is referring in his prologue to recent events which cannot postdate the death of Vespasian. Otherwise he would surely have referred to Thule. Silius' panegyric was written in the 90s. The common factors in both poets are Caledonia and Vespasian as the initiator. Tanner was correct in referring to Agricola.

[284] The political consequences of Roman control of the Ocean and the eastern seaboard may be seen in the willingness of the Parisi and Votadini to adopt a pro-Roman stance. The Venicones learnt to their cost the consequences of resistance. Any arrangements made by the Romans to protect the land frontiers of these tribes required permanent garrisons. But control of the sea was always unassailable and reassuring. The effect on hostile tribes of the presence of the Roman fleet is well documented by Tacitus (*Agr.* 25.1-2, 29.2).

[285] Flattery and exaggeration: cf. Taylor 1994, 217 n.37. Levick 1999, 18 is surprised that Valerius should link the conquest of the Isle of Wight with *Caledonian Ocean*. So am I. Metonymy: Caviglia 1999, 125. To this collection of irrelevant epithets we may add the noun *magnification*, Stern 1974, 1. 505.

[286] Lefèvre 1971, 9 was incorrect in translating *Caledonius* as *British*. This misconception is due to the misdating of Agricola's governorship. Unfortunately the suggestion has been taken up by others, with no sound evidence to support it. See Appendix 5.

[287] He writes of Vespasian's successes in Britain as *less perhaps his own...than those of his legates, Cerialis, Frontinus and Agricola after he attained the principate*, Soubiran 2002, 10, then makes a perceptive observation (202) which should have been followed up, *the Roman marines played their part in it*. By contrast, Lang 2003, 317 deserves all criticism for claiming that Cerialis, Frontinus and Agricola were involved in *non-naval operations* (*nicht-nautischen Aktionen*).

term 'Caledonius' puts the poem at the turn of the year 80 through the reference to Vespasian's operations in Scotland and the North Sea, precisely when Agricola entered Caledonia.[288] He was a year out, but he was right otherwise. The tide of history had moved on. Köstlin had suggested a link between *Caledonius* and the campaigns of Agricola, but mistakenly applied the reference to the later campaigns initiated by Domitian in AD 81.[289] Smallwood, without acknowledging Köstlin's contribution, also suggested *topicality,* a reference to Agricola's invasion of Caledonia, but harking back to the Claudian era. She claims that *Valerius clearly intends to flatter Vespasian by the exaggeration 'Caledonius'.*[290] This point was later echoed by Wijsman.[291] But it would have been intolerable for Valerius to exaggerate the emperor's achievements when their reality was startling enough, and new limits were being reached and breached. In AD 79 the ailing emperor would be cheered by the reality of Agricola's progress, since Agricola had taken more decisive steps than any of his predecessors in teaching the Caledonians that stubborn resistance would eventually lead to a scorched earth policy.[292] Tacitus knew how much Agricola was indebted to Vespasian's initiatives and didn't need to broadcast the fact that the emperor had given Agricola "the green light" to reach the end of the island. Smallwood uses the concept of topicality to date the dedication to c.AD 80, on the basis that Agricola reached the Tay at that time. The fact that he got there in AD 79 completely demolishes her argument. She was right about topicality, but how can a dedication to Vespasian possibly fall within the principate of Titus? Lefèvre likewise, wrongly assuming that Agricola's entry into Caledonia occurred in AD 80 and therefore *after* the death of Vespasian, objects to Smallwood's topicality, and claims that *Caledonia* may be merely a poetical paraphrase for Britain.[293] He cites Lucan's *Caledonii Britanni* as a parallel, without realising that this phrase must refer to *northern* Britain, probably Scotland.[294] He was not the last of the lemmings.

Syme and Strand, albeit differing in their views as to when the dedication was inserted into the epic, agree that it was made to a living, rather than to a deceased, Vespasian.[295] I would support Taylor's view that it was composed in the principate of Vespasian,[296] and also Strand's contention for a starting date of c.AD 75/76,[297] but only for the commencement of the narrative. I believe the dedication to be a later insertion, but not Domitianic, as Syme suggests, and I would not support Liberman's *fictitious framework for a prophecy* in a dedication to a living emperor.[298] I propose a compromise, that the dedication was made to a *dying* man who was soon to become a celestial luminary. A date of AD 79 (Syme: c. AD 78), perhaps in the early weeks of June,[299] when the report of Agricola's successful

---

[288] Moreda 2000, 25.
[289] Köstlin 1889, 651. He dated the campaigns between 81-85. He is unaware of the 79 campaign, initiated by Vespasian. The link between *Caledonius* and Agricola's penetration of Scotland has lately been resurrected by Moreda 2000, 25. This must be correct, although I do not accept his theory of a dedication made to a deceased emperor, which, as Strand 1972, 31 f. emphasised, would be *an enigmatic and unnatural act...unique in Roman literature.* Once again the failure to appreciate the revised dating of Agricola's governorship, by putting the incursion into Caledonia in AD 80, instead of AD 79 has deprived Vespasian of the satisfaction of Agricola's success.
[290] Smallwood 1962, 171. Caviglia 1999, 12 notes Smallwood's reference to topicality, but insists on claiming it as *l'enfatizzazione propagandistica* for Vespasian's campaign under Plautius, whose British expedition is equally misapplied by Taylor 1994, 217. D'Espèrey 1986, 3072 refers to *le surnom excessif de 'Caledonius'*. There is nothing here that cannot be explained by simple truths.
[291] Wijsman 1998, 217 n.37. Where does one draw the line between *flattery* and *homage*? D'Espèrey 1986, 3073 says that Vespasian *would not openly reject this sort of homage*. She stresses that Valerius isn't *poete courtisan*. This being the case, there would be no need for him to flatter or pay homage to the emperor. There is a big difference between projecting Vespasian among the stars (which could never be proved or disproved) and referring to his imperial directives which were historical fact. There was never any need for the contents of the prologue to go beyond the parameters of the Flavian era.
[292] Whittington/Edwards 1993 produce palynological evidence for Agricolan devastation in Fife. See Appendix 3.
[293] Lefèvre 1971, 52. Spaltenstein 2002, 29 agrees that *Iulos* refers to Julius Caesar, Augustus and Gaius, but ignores Claudius who is part of the same family. This is inconsistent with his reference to Sil. Pun. 3.595 which he quite rightly interprets as the Julio-Claudians.
[294] Spaltenstein 2002, 29 repeats this misconception. See Appendix 5.
[295] Syme 1929, 137; Strand 1972, 34. Wilkinson 1957, vi made a valid point that *it is hard to believe that if Book 1 was published under Domitian he would have been content to be ignominiously sandwiched between two appeals to his father.* Kleywegt 1986, 321; 2005, 19 brings up the same point from a different angle.
[296] Taylor 1994, 215.
[297] Bernays 1861,12 suggests a date of 74/5 on the basis of Cerialis' operations.
[298] Liberman 1997, xxiii *dédicace fictive à l'empereur vivant.*
[299] None of the commentators on the dedicatory prologue of book 1 seems to be aware of the numismatic evidence for dating

naval operations had reached Rome, would not be inappropriate, and the adjective *Caledonius* would not be a *metonymy* or an *exaggeration*, not *irresponsible*, as Momigliano suggested, not an *extremely unusual indication*, as Lefèvre would have it,[300] not a *synecdoche*, as Río Torres-Murciano suggests,[301] and not as a piece of flattery, as others have proposed,[302] but an important record of a decade of amphibious advance beyond the Humber, culminating in Agricola crossing the Forth-Clyde isthmus into Fife, which he would have reached during his third campaigning season of AD 79. In this context may be seen the significance of Braund's perceptive observation that *Vespasian's appointee Agricola had not only sailed the Caledonian Ocean, but also examined Thule, though his final conquest of Caledonia occurred in the early years of Domitian himself.*[303] Braund does not make it clear whether he thinks that Vespasian was alive or not at the time of Agricola's initial operations. It is incredible that in the ten years following his book no one took his suggestions seriously, while editions of Valerius Flaccus and reviews of the same followed closely on each other like lemmings. Tanner, citing both Valerius Flaccus and Silius, points out that *the two references from poetry could equally refer to Agricola's activities.*[304] He was correct on that point. His only mistake was to relate them to the principate of Domitian. I hope that D'Espèrey's pessimism (*arguments are lacking to pinpoint the moment in Vespasian's reign when the prologue was written*[305]) will give way to some optimism.

As in Silius, Vespasian is seen as the initiator (cf. *primus, aperti*) of the Caledonian campaign, the only difference being that Silius produces a *vaticinium ex eventu* (*prophecy following the event*), while Valerius is merely giving a lesson in history which caps the decade of Vespasian's principate. Failure correctly to interpret *pelagi...maior aperti fama* may lie at the root of the problem. How is *maior* to be interpreted? Terwogt suggested that Vespasian's glory was *greater* than Jason's.[306] But there is no need for any Jason/Vespasian comparison within the parameters of the dedication. There is a connexion between Jason, Augustus and Agricola, namely a desire to go further than anyone previously. Jason sailed east into the unknown. So did Augustus' fleet under the command of Tiberius.[307] Agricola's expedition reached *unknown Thule*. To suggest a comparison between a British campaign of AD 43 and the Argonautic expedition is pointless.[308] Jason was venturing into the unknown, Vespasian had been instructed to follow a beaten path. The rivalry between the Julian and Flavian families to conquer the Ocean reaches its peak here. Vespasian's fame was enhanced, as Wilkinson pointed out, by the opening up of the northern seas.[309] His *legati* had revealed what the *Iuli* had not, and his ships had triumphed over an Ocean which had frustrated his Julian predecessors. No wonder that his reputation, which was already great, had now become greater. Kleywegt was correct in his observation that *maior* refers to *the implied superiority to Caesar's former, less successful attempts.*[310]

Vespasian's role in Agricola's Caledonian campaign, despite the clues offered by Harold Mattingly. See Appendix 3. The year 79 for Vespasianic policy is given no consideration at all, despite the fact that the date of the dedication, the earliest coinage of Titus and Agricola's third campaigning season should all be set in that year. The latest effusions of material on Book 1 of Valerius Flaccus still resurrect the ghost of Claudius. Zissos 2006 criticises Kleywegt 2005, 13 for imprecision in linking Vespasian to Jason. He supports a reference to the Claudian expedition, describes *pelagi...aperti* as a gross exaggeration (Caesar's expedition being earlier) and says that the expedition was *implausibly credited to Vespasian who was not commander*. The last point would be correct, if it referred to AD 43—which is not the case. The failure to associate *Caledonius* with the principate of Vespasian is a major lapse (see Appendix 5). Why would Vespasian, who had now ruled for ten years and was patriarch of a new dynasty, want to be given a supporting role for the old dynasty, which he was aiming to surpass ?

[300] Lefèvre 1971, 52 *außerst seltene Bezeichnung*.
[301] Río Torres-Murciano 2005, 89.
[302] Smallwood 1962, 171; Taylor 1994, 217 n.37; Wijsman 1998, 319; Stover 2006, 236.
[303] Braund 1996, 150. He is correct in interpreting *dispecta est*, but I fail to understand why he translates it later (158) as *viewed*.
[304] Tanner 1991, 2715.
[305] D'Espèrey 1986, 3075.
[306] Terwogt 1898, 10. This view was followed by Lefèvre 1971, 9 and Braund 1996, 150.
[307] See n. 2 above.
[308] D'Espèrey, *ibid*. Likewise Kleywegt 2005, 13 describes as *obvious* the parallel between Vespasian and Jason *opening the sea*. The point has been missed.
[309] Wilkinson 1957, 59.
[310] Kleywegt 2005, 14.

It was only *after* Vespasian became *princeps* that the *magni duces, egregii exercitus* (*Agr.* 17.1 *great generals, outstanding armies*) produced the successes which enhanced the emperor's credit for initiating them. The *opening up of the sea* cannot refer to Vespasian crossing the English Channel, which had already been *opened up* by Julius Caesar, if not by previous generations of cross-Channel traders. But the concept of *opening up* is paralleled by Tacitus' comment: *tertius expeditionum annus* (AD 79) *novas gentes aperuit, vastatis usque ad Taum...nationibus* (*Agr.* 22.1, *the third year of campaigning revealed new peoples and native populations were ravaged as far as the Tay*).[311] Perhaps the reference to *revealing new peoples* should be treated with caution; but there is no doubt a distinction here, between *new peoples* and the *hitherto unknown* ones pacified in the fifth season (*ignotas ad id tempus*, *Agr.* 24.1).[312] And what of the Orkneys, also described as *hitherto unknown*, and which Agricola is explicitly said to have *discovered* as well as *pacified* (*incognitas ad id tempus insulas, quas Orcadas vocant, invenit domuitque*, *Agr.* 10.4)? According to a much later writer, the chronicler Eutropius, they had already submitted to Rome forty years before this, back in AD 43: Claudius *added to the empire certain islands beyond the Britains in the Ocean, called the Orchades* (*quasdam insulas etiam ultra Britannias in Oceano positas imperio Romano addidit, quae appellantur Orchades*, 7.13.3). Has Tacitus actually lied this time, or at least exaggerated? Lund made a point of attributing initiatives to Agricola.[313] But by following Tacitus too closely he merely highlighted the propaganda instead of questioning it. The hard work in the north had been done possibly by Bolanus and probably by Cerialis. Valerius Flaccus would have known the truth. Unlike Statius after him he had no need to exaggerate. Can the claim for Agricola be explained as retaliation against those who foisted their own candidates into the limelight with dubious justification? But as far as the Orkney islands are concerned, there may be another explanation, reserved for separate discussion.[314]

To return to the third season: the mention of an estuary is important in terms of Oceanus, and it is here that Agricola's fleet would operate. Hanson noted the Tay estuary as a *striking topographical feature...particularly if the fleet had been employed to scout ahead*.[315] References in Valerius Flaccus to Caledonia, ships and Ocean, a suggested date of AD 79 augmented by the numismatic evidence from June of that year,[316] can mean only one thing: that Agricola's fleet, still under the auspices of Vespasian, was transporting marines to pave the way for the army's later arrival, reopening, perhaps, rather than opening, the waterways around the Fife peninsula.[317] Ogilvie makes a clear distinction between the role of the fleet in earlier campaigns and its terrorising role in the sixth campaign.[318] I see no such distinction. The sight of an armada in any campaign was an awe-inspiring novelty. Smallwood's insistence that no ships under Vespasian's command went anywhere near Caledonia is correct only in so far as it cannot apply to Vespasian as a legionary legate under Claudius.[319] But it does apply to Vespasian as emperor. Who else but Vespasian initiated the policy for his governors to embark on the conquest of Caledonia? The recognition of their achievements in tributes to the emperor who had sponsored them should be seen as poetical embellishment, not as flattery.

---

[311] See Appendix 3.
[312] Cf. E. Birley 1953, 16.
[313] Lund 1980, 275-282.
[314] See Appendix 4.
[315] Hanson 1991a, 84.
[316] See Appendix 3.
[317] Wijsman 1988, 319, following Ehler's chronology (AD 71-79, cf. Liberman 1997, xxiii) for the composition of the *Argonautica*, says that *time would not have allowed the author to have known the splendid results of Agricola*. Not so. This claim is obviously based on the old dating for Agricola's governorship, AD 78-84, which puts the death of Vespasian *before* Agricola's raids into Caledonian territory.
[318] Ogilvie 1967, 239. Martin 1992, 12 has missed the point on the fleet's terror tactics. He says that it was sent ahead to plunder in order *to establish and defend coastal supply bases in default of secure land lines of communication*. A theory cannot be built on half a quotation. In any case, where does Tacitus say this?
[319] Smallwood 1962, 171. The notion that Vespasian entered Caledonian waters in the 40s is still believed in by Galimberti 1996, and the whole issue of the references to Vespasian in the works of Valerius Flaccus and Silius Italicus has been dredged up again by Río Torres-Murciano 2005, 89 n.61. See Appendix 5. He does not even mention AD 79, but restricts himself to the straitjacket of AD 43 and consequently misses the target. The rejection of Smallwood's theory that *Caledonius* has a connexion with Agricola's campaigns is ill-conceived. Vespasian and Titus were very much committed to furthering Agricola's campaigns—as Valerius Flaccus knew.

The Ocean extends the length of Britain, and the Ocean which *indignatus Iulos* is merely a continuation of the North Sea, into which the Forth and Tay flow. Even Lucan could link the Ocean with the Caledonians in the north and the tide-battered shores of Richborough in the south. Why Vespasian's fame had become *greater* is simply, as we saw in Silius, that the Caledonian campaign, in which the Romans had advanced further than under previous regimes, was the military highlight of his principate and, as Miniconi and Devallet aptly put it, *son règne fut marqué par la soumission des Ecossais*.[320] The poets were correct in drawing attention to the military initiatives in Vespasian's principate since they were in the process of being brought to fruition, and thereby newsworthy.

---

[320] Miniconi/Devallet 1979, 158: *his reign was marked by the submission of the Scots* (sic). Spaltenstein 1987, vol.1, 259-50 is incorrect in stating that Agricola's *first* contact with the Caledonians was in AD 83, four years after the death of Vespasian. Agricola had penetrated Caledonia as far as the Tay in AD 79. Hanson 1977-8, 143; 1991a, 84 f. tentatively associates the camps at Abernethy and Dunning with this campaign.

CONCLUSION

The purpose of this book was primarily to promote the idea of a Roman naval presence in Shetland, specifically in a harbour sufficiently noteworthy to merit the attention of Tacitus, to identify the Thule of Pytheas as the Thule of Tacitus, i.e. Shetland, accessible because of its reasonable proximity to Caledonia, and to explain how Caledonia fits into the context of the late first century poetic tradition. These objectives can only be attained by a re-appraisal of the relevant literary sources, the Greek and Roman geographers for locating and identifying Thule, and the late Silver Age poets (all part and parcel of the same social and literary establishment) for alluding to the role of Agricola and his predecessors as Vespasian's agents. The route I have taken cannot be other than by textual analysis, even if my methods may upset the purists. Before any word can be properly interpreted, we have to decide whether it is a Silver Age production or a Dark Age blunder. If it is an error, how did it come about? You cannot impose your own preference without a full explanation.

The worst enemy of the truth is tradition. If people really believe that Thule is Iceland or Norway you will never convince them otherwise, however rational your arguments are. In many of the books and articles I consulted Agricola was either peripheral, confused with someone else or was not even mentioned, while Pytheas was either given more credit than he deserved or none at all. The old explorer provided ample ammunition for scatterbrained theories from people who should have known better. The fragmented data allowed any amount of distortion, and the unenlightened will believe anything they read if you put it on their coffee tables. People would rather be comfortable with an illusion than uncomfortable with a reality, and to be faced with a sudden challenge to established belief is to confront the unacceptable. This is as applicable to literature and history as it is to religion. Replace the bible with the lexicon and ask yourself whether you can trust this accumulation of data. Dictionaries are only as good as the scholars who compile them and these can be wrong in their interpretations.

As for Tacitus and his biography of Agricola, we should be careful in references to conciseness or obscurity. His style of writing may well fall into that category. But obscurity in the presentation of historical events is far more damaging to historiography than questions of style. Whatever charges may be brought against him may well be based on some distortion of historical truth, and he had his reasons. But it would be wrong to look for fabrications behind every sentence and thereby run the risk of 'throwing out the baby with the bath water'. Archaeology undoubtedly has changed our perceptions and perspectives of events in northern Britain, but whatever damage may be done to Agricola's case may come from within as much as from without. Archaeology is only one side of the coin. Agricola has been given more credit than he deserved, and less credit than he deserved. Revisionism is only valid if it can determine *where*, *when* and *why*. Conclusions cannot be drawn without a sound knowledge of the historical context and a decent familiarity with the Latin language. The *Agricola* is not a work for amateurs to trifle with, and the absence or abuse of Latin among freelance writers can lead to conclusions which beggar belief. A chain is only as strong as its weakest link. English alone is inadequate in the context of Romano-British history. The interpretation and analysis of a Latin text requires a Latinist. You do not employ a plumber to mend a fuse-box.

Much that has been written here may be somewhat abstruse for the layman. For non-classicists I hope that the English versions have been a reasonable guide to the Latin and that they will help readers to make some headway into unfamiliar areas. For the classicists and ancient historians I have stated my case as clearly as I can. There will be many who may not agree with the points raised in this book, just as I disagree with the views of even more whose sensitivities I would not wish to offend. As an Englishman paddling in Scottish waters, I run the risk of stepping out of my depth. But Latin recognises no national boundaries and provides a suitable platform for reasoned debate. The palaeographical and philological arguments, proposed here, have been carefully weighed, not casually conjured up as a pretentious introduction by those who profess to know what they don't. The archaeological material on Scottish sites proved more helpful to me than some of the extravagant commentaries on Latin authors which I had to plough through. Eden was right when he referred to *the practice of using a commentary to obscure the little that is intended to serve the author by a lot which can serve only his bibliographers*. Archaeology had the merit of being frank rather than pretentious, down to earth rather than in the clouds. The need for inter-disciplinary co-operation has been stressed by others before. Archaeology streaks ahead, and it always will. The earth offers more opportunities than the text. Latin scholarship operates within ever shrinking parameters, as its disciples clutch at straws for innovation.

The numismatic evidence in support of my arguments features in Appendix 3. The relationship between numismatics and the Julio-Claudian/Flavian issues in Silver Age poetry offered new perspectives and the opportunity to re-examine the nature of dynastic propaganda. No one, as far as I am aware, has ever made any serious attempt to establish a link between the two. This, perhaps, is not surprising, since one side had its head buried in the sand, while the other merely scratched the surface. You need to build a bridge from both sides in order to span a gorge. The numismatist is generally uncomfortable with Latin poetry, while the classicist regards numismatics as an arcane science. The fact is that they complement each other.

I very much appreciate the contributions of Romano-Celtic scholars which I have found to be illuminating, informative and helpful. I never realised how far native place-names could be taken to reconstruct a derivation. But the application of Celtic philology for resolving the problems of Latin palaeography is tantamount to applying a sticking plaster to mend a broken leg. The leg still stays broken. A ninth century scribal error requires that we find out why and how the error occurred. You cannot build a toponymic theory on a word that does not exist. For the sceptics I have no doubt that the *Boresti* (see Appendix 1) will continue to thrive somewhere in the Scottish mists and some revisionist will eventually claim that they were immigrants from an Icelandic or Norwegian Thule. No one will object, because fiction is more entertaining and more digestible than fact, and a mystery must always remain a mystery.

Any evaluation of what I have suggested must take into account what others have written upon the same topic over the last five hundred years. Scholars have been going around in ever decreasing circles, with the inevitable consequences. The validity of hypotheses has fallen in proportion as their number has risen. As my comments have shown, there was more to question than to accept. I never thought of finding myself in this position, like a window-cleaner peering through the glass to see what he wasn't supposed to, while struggling to keep his balance on the top of the ladder. This is the first and last time I 'put my cards on the table', *without any apprehension*, as one septuagenarian Yorkshireman once put it, *of growing leaner by censures or plumper by commendations*. I have no intention of competing with those better qualified than myself. But I was disappointed with what I found. Research requires a return to the source, not a repetition of misconceptions. Far too much of the material which I came across consisted merely of old, worn out ideas, dressed up in new clothes. Sacred cows were being worshipped, when they should have been sent to the abattoir. Pretentious hypotheses were put forward by scholars with good intentions and poor judgement. It was never my original purpose to 'put the cat among the pigeons'. But some pigeons need to be shifted. Whatever changes I made to Latin texts were not made gratuitously, but to create sense out of nonsense, a good deal of which masquerades under the name of scholarship. My objective was to shed new light on an old theme, to go right back to the beginning, to examine the validity of some dubious textual readings, to generate further enquiry, to stimulate more intensive investigation into Flavian military policy and to give the inhabitants of Shetland an opportunity to claim that *ultima Thule* did on one occasion at least come within the ambit of Rome.

APPENDIX 1

THE *BORESTI* : THE CREATION OF A MYTH

in finis Borestorum exercitum deducit
　　　　　　　　　　　　　　　　Agr. 38.2

He led his army down into the territory of the Boresti

Michael Jarrett started an article on 'An Unnecessary War' by quoting Rivet: *One curious feature of Romano-British studies must be noted. This is the tendency, perhaps due to the intractable nature of the evidence, to create myths.*[321] It is much easier to create a myth than to unravel a mystery. As for *intractable* it is not quite clear what Rivet meant; in fact one wonders whether Rivet himself actually knew what he meant. A hand-grenade is intractable once you have pulled the pin. One can examine the *nature of the evidence* and evaluate it, but to imply that it cannot be handled, as if it were a hot potato, is to surrender before the battle starts. So let us examine an instance of *intractable nature* and see if we can handle it. In this case the evidence is the reference to an 'unnecessary' tribe known as the *Boresti*. As for its derivation, Rivet and his colleague Smith found it a 'hot potato': *none can be suggested.*[322] This should have provided a clue that all was not well.

At the end of the summer of AD 83 Agricola followed up his success at Mons Graupius with a show of strength both on land and sea. I have already explained my views on his naval ambitions. But where do the *Boresti* fit into the plans of the victorious army? In 1986 Ian Keillar produced for popular consumption an article entitled '*In Fines Borestorum*—To the Land of the *Boresti*'. In eager anticipation I sought answers to my questions: who were the *Boresti*, and where were they located? But answer came there none. They did not appear in any of the maps, which, as it turned out, was a sensible approach;[323] and, apart from the Mattingly and Handford translation of the sentence, there was nothing about the *Boresti*, who were presumably to be located in Moray. That the Romans were involved this far north is a certainty and has been subsequently confirmed, although a secure date for military installations has yet to be established. But who were these people? Two questions need to be answered. Firstly, why are the *Boresti* unattested in Ptolemy? Are we really to suppose, as suggested by Burn and again by Rivet and Smith, that they were a sub-division of one of the peoples which *do* appear on Ptolemy's map?[324] Mann and Breeze propose that the Boresti *certainly seem to have escaped his* [Ptolemy's] *notice.*[325] Earlier, Breeze had put it more dramatically: they *were the lost* (?) *tribe of Ptolemy.*[326] Such a solution is merely an *argumentum ex silentio,* but at least is better than to suppose that Tacitus mentioned them because they were the furthest known tribe on the mainland. This leads to my second question. Why would Tacitus bother to mention an insignificant people in a Caledonian context, where he normally generalises (*Agr.* 25.1)?[327] No other people of Scotland is mentioned from the moment Agricola crossed the Forth-Clyde isthmus. This is the *intractable nature* of the problem.

---

[321] Jarrett 1976, 145; Rivet 1958, 29.
[322] Rivet/Smith 1979, 272.
[323] Their location on the map in Jones/Mattingly 1990, 45 is an act of faith.
[324] Burn 1953a, 156; Rivet/Smith 1979, 272-273.
[325] Mann/Breeze 1987, 87. Their claim that Agricola had not penetrated north of the Moray Firth would be invalidated by my interpretation of the MS. Henderson 1985, 328 drew attention to Ptolemy's list of putative forts in Moray, *Tuesis* and *Pinnata Castra*, noting that *forts were invariably built in conquered territory in the year after the army had passed that way.*
[326] D.J. Breeze 1982, 31.
[327] *civitates trans Bodotriam sitas* (*the states situated across the Forth*), 25.3 *Caledoniam incolentes populi* (*the peoples inhabiting Caledonia*). Hanson 1991a, 120 asks why Tacitus would refer *only to the Caledonii in opposition to Rome* and explains this as *imprecision in matters geographical.* On this basis the *Boresti* are anomalous. If Tacitus was imprecise, then Agricola would simply have *taken his army down to the coast.* Burn 1969, 38 says that *Tacitus dexterously and deliberately avoids loading his narrative with unfamiliar names.* But he does not explain why Tacitus mentions the *Boresti*, expresses frustration with Ptolemy for not mentioning them and suggests (58) that the reason for the omission was quite simple: *the Boresti were probably a component of the far-flung Caledonians.*

Are the *Boresti* as much a myth as *Trucculensis portus*? Hanson noted that *the location of this tribe remains a mystery* and talks of a more northerly location, perhaps in Angus or in Moray,[328] while Breeze, half-correct, proposes that *their name may indicate that they were the people who lived at the end of the island*. But the *end of the island* lies in Caithness, not in Moray.[329] Henderson's suggestion that *Boresti* might be a *made-up geographical appellation and might fall out of use quickly* cannot be supported. Till paradoxically sited them *in southern Scotland, north of the Firth of Forth and Firth of Clyde*, while Levick firmly places them between the Tay and the Dee.[330] But no one is prepared to offer the obvious solution, that Tacitus never wrote *Borestorum* at all. We need to examine the possibility of textual corruption in a codex where proper names are shown, on more than one occasion, to be suspect. I believe that there is a transmission error here, and perhaps one of long standing. Had the correct form appeared in earlier MSS, it was likely to have been recorded by E^{2m}, who specialises in producing good quality doublets of dubious proper names.[331] Ogilvie noted that *E* was copied from *an exemplar which was either in 'scriptura continua' or did not have the division of words satisfactorily resolved*.[332] This was surely the cause of textual contamination: I suggest that *Borestorum* comprises *two* words and that we should read

in finis boreos totum exercitum deducit

He led his entire army down into the northern extremities

This is palaeographically sound and the corruption from *-t* to *-r* and the fusion of words is exactly paralleled at *Agr.* 27.2, where *E*'s meaningless *locatura* is corrected by E^2 to *loca tuta* (*places of safety*). The implication of such a correction is that we no longer have to look for a people that does not exist. I would suggest that the next edition of the *Tabula Imperii Romani: Britannia Septentrionalis* (*Map of the Roman Empire: Northern Britain*) should remove the questionable *Boresti* from the Moray coast,[333] and furthermore restore Shetland to its rightful place in Romano-British history.[334]

Just as Agricola split his army into three divisions in Caledonia (*Agr.* 25.4) in AD 82, so it was reunited the following year for what was virtually a triumphal procession northwards to the point where Caledonia ended. No more imposing or more demoralising sight could have greeted the enemy than the *full* might of Agricola's army, with the fleet dominating the coastal waters. This marked the *total* conquest of Britain (*tum primum [Britannia] perdomita est, then for the first time the conquest of Britain was completed, Agr* 10.1), a claim which only made sense if the Romans took hostages from the peoples living where the island actually ended, on the northernmost coast of Scotland.[335] Agricola had fulfilled what his army had demanded the previous year: *penetrandam Caledoniam inveniendumque tandem Britanniae terminum* (*Caledonia must be penetrated and the furthest limit of Britain found at last, Agr.* 27.1).[336] This interpretation would invalidate Hanson's observation that

---

[328] Hanson 1991a, 140. Yet his map (fig.15) locates them between the Dee and the Tay, parallel with the Vacomagi. He also states, 1991b, 1770: *it is particularly ironic that one of the few tribal names in the whole of Tacitus' narrative, the Boresti, is otherwise unattested*. There is nothing ironic here. The question should have been asked: *Why is it unattested?* The irony lies in accepting the possibility that such a 'tribe' existed and then bringing it into the scenario. Hanson's summary of all the possibilities is a pointless exercise, if textual corruption is ignored.
[329] D.J. Breeze 1990, 55.
[330] Henderson 1985, 331; Till 1979, 72 (*in Südschottland, nördlich vom Firth of Forth und Firth of Clyde*); Levick 1999, map 2. Hunter 2007, 8, writes of the 'Boresti', *if they are even a tribe*.
[331] *Togidumno* 14.1, *Boudicta* 16.1, *Taum* 22.1, *Trutulensem* 38.4.
[332] Ogilvie 1967, 86.
[333] Keppie 1988, 439, reviewing this map, points out that locating the Boresti on the southern shore of the Moray Firth is *not perhaps to everyone's satisfaction*. Far better for any location to be ignored completely.
[334] Rivet in *TIR* 1987, viii regretfully informs us: *We have not been able to take in the Shetlands, which were evidently sighted* (sic) *by Agricola's fleet and which Tacitus...and after him, Ptolemy...took to be Thule* (surely erroneously, since they were probably the '*Haemodae*' *of Mela...and the* '*Acmodae*' *of Pliny*). I beg to differ on all counts here.
[335] Keppie 1989, 61, commenting on the victory at Mons Graupius, aptly described the moment as *the best opportunity of carrying through the conquest* of the island to its logical end (cf. Robertson 1975, 5). The concept of total conquest is reinforced by the taking of hostages in the northern extremities.
[336] It is somewhat ironic that Henderson 1985, 330 claims that the Boresti merited special attention because they inhabited the *terminus Britanniae* or *finis terrarum* (*lands' end*). There is no doubt that tribes inhabited Caithness, as Ptolemy shows, but

Tacitus makes no claim for Agricola reaching the end of the island.[337] Likewise, a march northwards would negate Keppie's suggestion that *Agricola's descent into the territory of the Boresti could refer to a southwards march towards Aberdeen or Stonehaven.*[338] It is in reaching the northern limits of the island, as much as in its circumnavigation, that we find *the final expression of total conquest.*[339]

I believe that Tacitus' *northern extremities* lie in Caithness. What we have is a Tacitean generalisation: after all, what would have been the point of introducing an insignificant 'tribe' which, like the supposed *Trucculensis portus*, would have been of no historical relevance to *an audience accustomed to discourse and lacking maps*?[340] Tacitus could supply names when he chose to: the second part of the *Germania* focuses on the *institutions and practices of the individual peoples* (*singularium gentium instituta ritusque*, 27.2), a good five dozen of which are named—with details on their location. But the *Agricola* is a monograph whose focal point is a personality.[341] Too many names of peoples would have been a distraction. Only thirteen British geographical names occur in the whole of the *Agricola*, in the text printed by modern editors: a region, *Caledonia* (10.3, 11.2, 25.3, 27.1, 31.4);[342] four states or 'tribes', *Silures* (11.2, 17.2), *Brigantes* (17.1, 31.4), *Ordovices* (18.1, 2) and *Boresti* (38.2); three islands or groups of islands, *Orcades*, *Thule* (10.4) and *Mona* (14.3, 18.3); three estuaries, *Taus* (22.1), *Bodotria* (23, 25.1, 3) and *Clota* (23); the site of the final battle, *Mons Graupius* (29.2); and the harbour, '*Trucculensis' portus* (38.4)—which has already been shown above to conceal a second reference to *T(h)ule*. If we cannot locate the *Boresti*, can we expect Tacitus' readership to have fared better? It seems highly probable that this name can also be eliminated.

It may be argued that the standard word for *northern* in Tacitus is *septentrionalis* and that *boreus* is a rare usage. But only two examples of the former (*Agr.* 10.2, *Germ.* 1.2) should not militate against the acceptability of the latter. *Meridianus* and *australis* are equally acceptable among Latin writers for *southern*. It was not impossible for *boreus* to be used by an historian to provide relative bearings. Like Tacitus, Ammianus uses *septentrionalis* twice (27.10.9, 31.10.21), but in a geographical digression describing the *Persidis extremitates* (*the extremities of Persia*) he refers to *boreum latus* (*the north side,* 23.6.74).[343] Classical sources distinguish between *septentrionalis Oceanus* (*North Sea*, Tac. *Germ.* 1.2) and *Oceanus Hyperboreus* (*Ocean beyond the North*, Ptol. *Geog.* 2.2).[344] Greek is much

---

they were not fictional.

[337] Hanson 1979, 26.

[338] Keppie 1980, 84.

[339] Braund 1996, 171.

[340] Ogilvie 1967, 32. cf. Hanson 1991b, 1747, who writes that *it is customary by way of explanation to point out that Tacitus' audience of upper class Romans would have been bored by the use of too many strange sounding names*. It is precisely because of Tacitus' deliberate avoidance of geographical trivia that the emendations of Richmond, *Anavam primum*, and of Oniga *Novium primum* (*Agr.*25.1) for *prima nave* are really non-starters, although Richmond's suggestion still has its supporters, cf. Wellesley 1969, 267; Murgia 1978, 161-162. Likewise, Maxwell's suggestion of *Tamium*, 1984, 221 f., based on *E*'s unfavoured *Tanaum* (*Agr.* 22.1), cannot be supported, especially as Maxwell himself points out that *the character of the Agricola does not lead us to believe that he was concerned with such topographical precision*. Henderson 1985, 319 was correct in his assumption that geographical details would bore or distract Tacitus' readers. But in that case why would he have mentioned the *Boresti*?

[341] Gorrichon 1974, 196 drew attention to the emphasis on Agricola rather than on the island when she described the geographical imprecisions in Tacitus' account; somewhat ironic in view of the fact that she resurrects the long discarded *Mont-Grampian* and assumes that *Tanaum* (certainly inferior to *Taum*) refers to the Tyne, which de Saint-Denis (following Furneaux) believed to be the geographical limit of Agricola's third campaign. Ogilvie 1967, 31 was correct in his view that *geographical information in the 'Agricola' is largely incidental*. It is surprising that Rutledge 2000, 92 n.48 believes that such information *is fundamental to the Agricola's ultimate purpose*.

[342] Contrary to what is sometimes stated or implied, Tacitus nowhere uses the term *Caledonii* to refer to the inhabitants of *Caledonia*, the land beyond the Firth-Clyde isthmus

[343] It is quite possible that Ammianus borrowed this adjective from Tacitus. In a recent thoroughly detailed survey, Viansino 2004, 124 f. produces *ninety-three* examples of Ammianus' vocabulary which echo that in the *Agricola*. Blockley 1973, 67 attributes Ammianus' verbal borrowings from Tacitus to *narrow, stylistic purposes*. This need not be the case with *individual* words such as *boreum/boreos*, rare in prose writers. For more evidence for Ammianus' reading of Tacitus, cf. Barnes 1998, 194 f.

[344] A link between *Boresti* and the Hyperboreans was suggested by Holder 1896, 1.490 and supported by Henderson 1985, 330, with reference to *Boreas* and the adjectival form *Boreus*. Ogilvie 1967, 282 and Burn 1969, 58 discounted any connexion with modern Forres, an option which Frere 1987, 97 and Robertson 1976, 7 leave open. The dismissal of the '*Boresti*'-Forres link is not, as Grant 2007, 110 states, my *main objection* to the myth. Etymological links in this instance are irrelevant. If a 'tribe' is the delusion of Dark-Age thinking, there is no sense in perpetuating the link in the present century by

more flexible than Latin in defining geographical bearings. Strabo uses such words as *more northerly* (*boreioteroi, Geog.* 2.1.18) and refers to Thule as *the most northerly* of the British isles (*boreiotaten, Geog.* 2.5.8), far more precise than the un-geographical *ultima* (*furthest*) of Virgil, Pliny and Solinus. Had such adjectival forms existed in Latin they would have been used. Dionysius Periegetes, writing in the second century, refers to the Mysi as *the more northerly of the Thracians* (*boreioteroi Threikon, Orb. Descr.* 322). Significantly enough Priscian, in his fifth-century Latin paraphrase of Dionysius, writes *Mysi Thracum boreis in finibus orti* (*the Mysi originating in the northern borders of the Thracians, Perieg.* 789).[345] What Priscian has done is to emphasise the noun *fines* (*limits, ends, extremities*) rather than the adjective. The problem caused by the absence of superlative directional adjectives in Latin is solved by switching the emphasis from the adjective to the noun and selecting a noun containing a superlative sense (*furthest point, extremity*) and applying to it the word *northern*. The Greek word for *extremity* is *akron*. Polybius in a geographical digression (*Hist.* 1.42.2) uses the plural form *akra* in reference to the *extremities* of Greece, and Strabo (*Geogr.* 2.5.15) employs the same word for *the extremities of the inhabited world*. One may compare Tacitus' *priorum exercituum terminos, finem Britanniae* (*the limits reached by previous armies, the boundary of Britain, Agr.* 33.3) and *nos terrarum ...extremos* (*us, the furthest people in the world, Agr.* 30.3). Consequently the *farthest points north* (i.e. *northern extremities*) would be *boreia akra* (*fines borei*). Tacitus has converted a Greek expression into a latinised form. In reference to Ptolemy's map Ogilvie stressed *the Roman origin of the entire body of information* and noted the failure *to transpose into Greek the Latin terminal endings of the three northern capes* (Dunnet Head, Duncansby Head, Noss Head).[346] It is true that Ptolemy has transliterated many Latin names. But natural features which had existed long before the presence of the Romans in the area may have originally been given Greek names from earlier explorations and surveys (such as those in which Pytheas and Demetrius of Tarsus had participated).[347] Ogilvie's choice of words, *northern capes,* is a direct, if unconscious, rendering of *boreia akra*, which may have been the collective name given by Greek explorers to the Caithness coastline, from Wick to Thurso. This area could well be Tacitus' *fines borei*. It is worth noting that Ptolemy (*Geogr.* 2.2) uses *boreion akron* for *Bloody Foreland* in Donegal, clearly not evidence for transliteration from Latin.

---

inventing a link. Other suggestions, which reflect, as Maxwell, 1989, 70, aptly put it, *the ingenuity of generations of scholars and amateur philologists,* include Rhys 1904, 283 f., who proposed a connexion with the Late Latin *floresta*, Whatmore 1913, 215, who conjured up a link with Loch Ericht, Pitblado 1936, 108, who thought there was a connexion through 'phonetic change' with *Brossi*, equivalent to *Ross* or *Rossia*, the ancient name for Fifeshire, O'Rahilly 1946, 529, who imagined a corruption of *Voretii* (*dwellers by the Forth*?) and Walters 1899, 109, whose fantasies produced a connexion with the *Borussi* from Prussia. More recently A. Breeze 2005 put forward a suggestion of a link with *roresti* (dropping the unCeltic initial *B-*), indicating *run*. All these suggestions are speculative, and lead away from the solution rather than towards it. Hübner 1897, 731 had the sense to refrain from any identification. Once the myth had been accepted as reality, the scramble to locate this Iron-Age Brigadoon gathered pace. Anderson 1922, 141 blindly follows Furneaux 1898, 149 with the comment, *they were between the battle and his winter quarters,* confusing the meaning of *deducit* with that of *reducit*. Fraser 2005, 115, likewise citing the Latin *deducit* and mistranslating it as *led back*, produces a whole paragraph on the 'Boresti', *the northernmost of the peoples made subject to Rome*, which unfortunately takes him in the wrong direction. Laederich 2001,353 offers us an incorrect French version, *ramena*. His note (354 n.32) on the 'Boresti' and *portus Trucculensis* is superficial and treads well worn ground. Hind 1985, 15, unsure which MS reading to prefer, covers every possibility with the sense of *on his way back and down*. But even diehard traditionalists locate the phantom 'tribe' north, not south, of Mons Graupius. Kamm 2004, 87 refers to the surrender of the 'Boresti' because *they had not participated in the battle* and locates them in Moray, while Legg 1983, 77 informs us that *Agricola later received the formal surrender of the territory of the Boresti*. Grant *ibid.* has opted to retain the MS reading, with no good reason. How can an alleged Scottish 'tribe', which would certainly have been recorded by Ptolemy, mysteriously appear in the *Agricola*, which is not a repository for trivia ? Any 'tribe' which appears in the *Agricola* should reappear in Ptolemy. The parallel cited in support of scribal error shows how the mind of the copyist worked. No amount of toponymic papering is going to fill the crack left by textual corruption.

[345] Since *boreus* is an unusual word, the combination of this adjective with the appropriate form of *finis* seems too much of a coincidence to be fortuitous. It is possible that Priscian read and remembered the *Agricola*. This would not be surprising, since geography features in both authors. Avienus translates Dionysius more freely, *borean subit altior agro/ Moesus* (*Descript.Orb.Terr.* 462, *the Moesian further up in his land faces the north*).

[346] Ogilvie 1967, 45.

[347] Demetrius' imperial expedition of inquiry and survey (cf. Burn 1953a, 114 f.; 1969, 53 f.; Ogilvie 1967, 32 f.; Braund 1996, 12), which may also have been involved, as Wainwright 1962, 66 suggested, in gathering military intelligence, would have produced a report written in Greek. It is worth noting the dedication set up at York (*RIB* 662, 663), written in Greek by Scribonius Demetrius, surely to be identified with Plutarch's Demetrius (*De Def. Orac.* 410A, 434C), whose visit to York coincided with that of Agricola (cf. *RIB, Addenda and Corrigenda* 771).

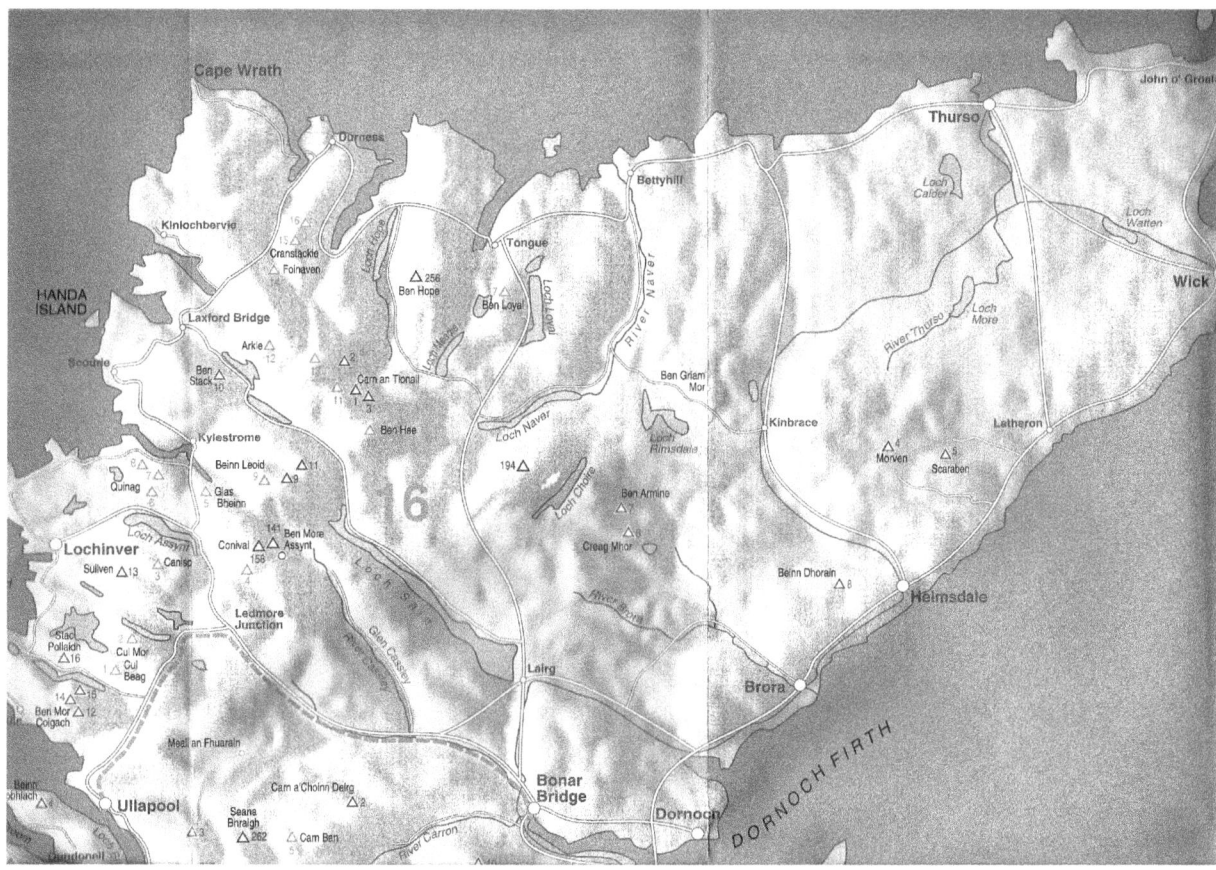

Fines Borei: **the area north of the Dornoch Firth, map courtesy of Harvey Maps, www.harveymaps.co.uk**

There is no doubt that *deducit* suggests that Agricola was taking his troops down from higher ground onto the coastal plains (the likeliest location would be the plains beyond Wick and Thurso) to link up with his fleet, perhaps in Sinclair's Bay, a convenient point for the beginning of its circumnavigation.[348] The peoples who gave hostages would, on the basis of Strang's co-ordinates, be Ptolemy's broch-dwelling *Smertae* and *Lugi*, doubtless known to Agricola, but of no significance to Tacitus.[349] The taking of hostages suggests a virtual capitulation in the face of a land and sea cordon. This need not be seen as a major operation. The thousands who had fled from Mons Graupius posed no further threat, and were out of the reckoning (*neque usquam conglobari hostes compertum*, it was discovered that the enemy were not massing at any point, *Agr.* 38.2). The opportunity for Agricola to reach the *terminus Britanniae* without interference was too good to be missed. This is where *perdomita Britannia* becomes a reality.

Possible locations for the site of Mons Graupius are well documented.[350] A march down to the coast of Caithness might well follow a battle there. A.R. Birley was right to support Henderson's argument in favour of the far north as the site of the battle.[351] Equally, he was correct to draw attention to the words

---

[348] Henderson 1985, 331 f. quite aptly pointed out that *it almost a necessity for the fleet to have begun the voyage from a point quite near the Orkneys*.

[349] Strang 1997, 27, fig.11b.

[350] Crawford 1949, 130-133; Burn 1953b, 127-133; 1968, 316; 1969, 56; Richmond 1958, 51 f.; Ogilvie 1967, 65, 182; St. Joseph 1978, 279-285; Henderson 1984, 28; Keppie 1980, 79-88; Maxwell 1989, 58 f.; 1990, 72-123; Jones/Mattingly 1990, 76 f.; Hanson 1991a, 129-137; Jones 1993, 225 n.44; Fletcher 1999, 4. I had originally been seduced by St. Joseph's location, Mt Bennachie. But the very large adjacent Roman camp at Durno might well be Severan.

[351] A.R. Birley 1999, 85, following Henderson 1984, 28. Birley's point (88) that the *aestuaria* (*Agr.* 33.5) could comprise the Moray and Dornoch Firths has much to commend it. The density of brochs north of the Dornoch Firth (cf. Jones/Mattingly 1990, 62) would suggest a considerable source of manpower for resistance against Agricola and a good enough reason why a final confrontation to defend the last remaining settlements should have occurred somewhere nearby. Frere's suggestion, 1987, 94, that the broch-builders may have been friendly to Rome would be invalidated by the taking of hostages (*Agr.*38.2)

The plateau of Scaraben looking east towards the North Sea, photo courtesy of Peter Standing, www.geograph.org.uk

used by Calgacus, *nulla iam ultra gens, nisi fluctus et saxa* (*Agr.* 30.3, *there is no nation beyond us now, only waves and rocks*) and by Agricola, *in ipso terrarum ac naturae fine* (*Agr.* 33.6, *at the very place where the world and nature end*).[352] The rhetoric put into the mouth of Calgacus comprises

---

in the northern extremities. Richmond 1958, 51 noted that the broch area *must have supplied a substantial part of the native force*. Nearly a hundred brochs so far discovered in the Shetlands imply close cultural and, perhaps, strategic links with the Orkneys and the Scottish mainland. Ogilvie 1967, 33 was misguided in relying on Solinus as proof that the Orkneys were deserted. The evidence from Clickhimin in the Shetlands suggests a tradition of maritime activity (Hamilton 1968, 78 f.) which may have extended to the Scottish mainland. One can understand Agricola's need, despite Tacitus' silence, to sever the links and stop the Orkneys and Shetlands becoming, as Anglesey once did, a *sanctuary for refugees* (*Ann.* 14.29.3, *receptaculum perfugarum*). I see nothing to support Wainwright's theory, 1962, 65, of *hostile relations between the seafaring people and the mainland fort-dwellers*, which he has conjured up out of the alleged Claudian *clientela*. A.R. Birley's argument, 1999, 90, that the *Boresti* should be located in Caithness supports my case for *the extreme north* (*fines borei*). Burn 1953a, 156 located the coast of the '*Boresti*' as *well to the north* without committing himself to a positive location beyond Moray which the *terminus Britanniae* must surely imply. Richmond's comment, 1958, 52, that *the Latin account indicates that after the battle Agricola did not advance farther* can only be supported if he follows E^{2m}'s *reducit*, which all editors reject. D.J. Breeze 190, 55 writes: *the lack of place-names in Ptolemy's Geography north and west of the Great Glen suggests that Agricola did not penetrate into these areas and that therefore the battle of Mons Graupius was not fought beyond Inverness. No place-names means no army presence*. This need not be so, since the *lack of place-names* need not preclude the existence of marching camps, indicative of penetration beyond Moray. Has anyone really looked for them? Maxwell 2004, 78 likewise assumes that *the limit of Roman conquest and campaigning by land is indicated by Ptolemy*. Since when is Ptolemy a guide for campaigning? Ian Keillar informs me that in the early 80s he had an aerial photo of a rectangular crop-mark near Berriedale in Caithness. He had been shown this by the regional archaeologist, who commented: 'It looks Roman, but it can't be. It's too far north'. Keillar gave the photograph to Barri Jones, but unfortunately it has not been traced after the latter's death. If this site proved to be a Flavian marching camp (or a Severan one, following Agricola's line), any suggestion that the Romans never got beyond the Moray Firth would have to be seriously reconsidered. Berriedale is close to the conspicuous Scaraben with its three distinct summits. This perhaps should be listed among possible sites for Mons Graupius.

[352] Burn 1953a, 150 writes: *fairly near the sea*. The tendency of commentators to infer rhetorical exaggeration ignores the fact that the reality does not require distortion. Gsell's assertion, 1894, 170 n.5, that *it is impossible to draw any geographical indications from Tacitus' speeches*, fails to grasp the personal experiences of Agricola in Britain, as relayed from father-in-law to son-in-law. Hanson's reasons (1991a, 129) to question Calgacus' reliability in locating the battle close by the sea are

factual detail which Tacitus could easily have derived from his father-in-law.[353] Agricola knew exactly where he was, and his remark that *finem Britanniae...castris et armis tenemus* (*Agr.* 33.3 *we hold the boundary of Britain with arms and encampments*) is surely an indication that marching camps should be sought much further north.[354] The northern extremities of *Britannia* lie in Caithness, not in Moray. Tacitus knew this because Agricola's fleet had proved so. Keillar's identification of forts at Thomshill and Easter Galcantray, would testify to a permanent or semi-permanent occupation in Moray much further north than Stracathro, the long considered limit of Flavian occupation.[355] If forts can be located further north, then so can marching camps. If the battle of Mons Graupius and Agricola's subsequent descent to the plain occurred where I suggest, it gives support to Tacitus' statements that Agricola's forces had reached the *finem Britanniae* and that total conquest had been achieved (*Hist.* 1.2.1).[356] It is somewhat ironic that Agricola, the paragon of modesty, is being pushed by Tacitus to rival the

---

groundless. Tacitus knew the details; Calgacus in this instance is merely his mouthpiece. The need to retain close contact with the fleet must surely indicate a reasonable proximity to the coast.

[353] Grimal 1990, 68-71, on the basis of Tacitus' vocabulary, assumes that Tacitus was serving in Agricola's army during the Mons Graupius campaign and was an eye-witness to all that happened. But his idea that Tacitus was with Agricola as *proquaestor* is alas, quite impossible: quaestors and proquaestors served with proconsuls, not with imperial legates. There is no evidence that Tacitus was in Britain during the principate of Domitian. All the same, despite the claims of Mann/Breeze 1987, 85 and Hanson 1991a, 23 that Tacitus did not visit Britain, a good case for him having had a military tribunate under Agricola, during the reigns of Vespasian and perhaps briefly of Titus too, has been made by A.R. Birley 1999, ix and 2000, 235.

[354] So Rutledge 2000, 78. Hanson's translation, 1991a, 129, *we hold with arms and forts*, does not meet the definition of *castra* as laid down by Ogilvie 1967, 198, who assigns *castra* to the legionary fortresses and *castella* (forts) to smaller units. Why must we subscribe to Ogilvie's insistence that *castra* should be rendered by *fortress*, not *camp*? Which Latin word do we use for camp? What legionary fortress ever graced the *finem Britanniae*? Which governor would station his finest troops in Caithness? I believe that in this example *castra* means *marching camps* (so Robertson 1975, 7). This is implied by the use of *in agmine* (*on the march*) in the next sentence. When the Romans set up camp in hostile territory it is an indication, however temporary, of conquest. It was the marching camp (*castra*) of the Ninth legion which was attacked by the Caledonians in the sixth campaigning season (*Agr.* 6.1).

[355] Keillar 1996, 8 f. This has now been expanded into a book (Keillar 2005). Gregory 2001, 177-222 reports the excavations carried out by Jones and Daniels on the Moray coast. Compelling arguments had been put forward by Jones for quingenary forts at Thomshill and Easter Galcantray (disputed by Hanson/Slater 1991, 70) and a possible camp at Balnageith (cf. *Britannia* 1991, 226 and plate 25). Gregory noted (214): *Both Daniels and Jones, and their co-worker Keillar, were convinced that these sites were potentially forts or camps of Flavian date, associated with Agricolan activity in north-east Scotland. This interpretation, if correct, would suggest that the traditional picture of the Agricolan advance....requires radical consideration.* Gregory adds (210) that *Findhorn Bay offered a sheltered harbour to accommodate fleet activity possibly associated with the Agricolan advance.* Edwards/Ralston 2003, 198 deny that there are any distinctive morphological features to suggest Roman forts. The aerial photographs from Boyndie and Balnageith suggest Roman installations.

[356] *perdomita Britannia*, still emphasised nearly twenty-five years after the event. Dorey 1969, 7 notes that the archaeological evidence proves that *the Roman claim 'Britannia perdomita' was no idle boast*. This may be somewhat premature until the evidence is found in Caithness, but I am happy to take Tacitus' claims at face value. Shotter 2004a, 6 offers the ingenious idea that the words *perdomita Britannia* might have been used in a secondary inscription added by Domitian to the Richborough Monument, which, he suggests, might have been originally erected under Vespasian to honour Claudius. He bases his argument on a fragment bearing the letters *PE*. But is the lettering large enough to have come from the main dedication? See Birley 2005, 93 and notes. Furthermore, *perdomita* is a literary usage and there is no epigraphic or numismatic evidence to support its official use. Martin 1994, 45 suggests that *perdomita* probably came to Tacitus from his father-in-law. The simple form *domita* would be acceptable and is attested in Augustus' *Res Gestae* (5.27). Tacitus elsewhere uses *subacta* (*Agr.* 33.3), which is also on a sestertius of Marcus Aurelius for AD 172 (*Germania subacta, RIC* 3. 294. no.1021); and *subactis* occurs in *CIL* 6.1014. We find *Iudaea devicta* (*BMC* 2.62, no.27) on the coinage of Vespasian. Nonetheless, Shotter may not be far off the mark. I can visualise a monument erected by Domitian, bearing an inscription such as *Britannia subacta, Britannia devicta* or *Britannia in potestatem populi Romani redacta*. What Claudius had started, Domitian finished. I am puzzled by the suggestion of Jones, 1993, 58, that Domitian *was severely disillusioned by his failure to complete the conquest of Britain in 82, as Agricola had promised*. I see nothing in Tacitus about any promise to Domitian. According to Whitmarsh 2006, 319, *the rhetorical construction of Agricola as the conqueror of the world's limits is, or can be read as, provocatively subverted*. I see no *rhetorical construction* here. When did the reality ever require embellishment? Did not Tacitus himself say: *quae priores nondum comperta eloquentia percoluere rerum fide tradentur* (*Agr.* 10.1, *what my predecessors rounded off with fine words before they had yet learnt about it will be recorded with factual truth*)? Since when is the truth a *subversion*? D.J. Breeze 1988 devotes an entire article to the reasons why the Romans failed to conquer Britain. Braund 1996, 158 disagrees: *it is idle to object that Agricola's conquest was not complete*. Braund is right—Tacitus' statement is quite clear: *Britain has been found and conquered*. The Romans already occupied the northern limits with encampments and subsequently took hostages from peoples in that area. Southern says, 1975, 11, that the total conquest *may now be seen to have been, in a sense, true*, a view endorsed by Jones/Mattingly 1990, 77, likewise Maxwell 2004, 88: *the material evidence thoroughly supports his* (*sc.* Agricola's) *claim for the completeness of the conquest*.

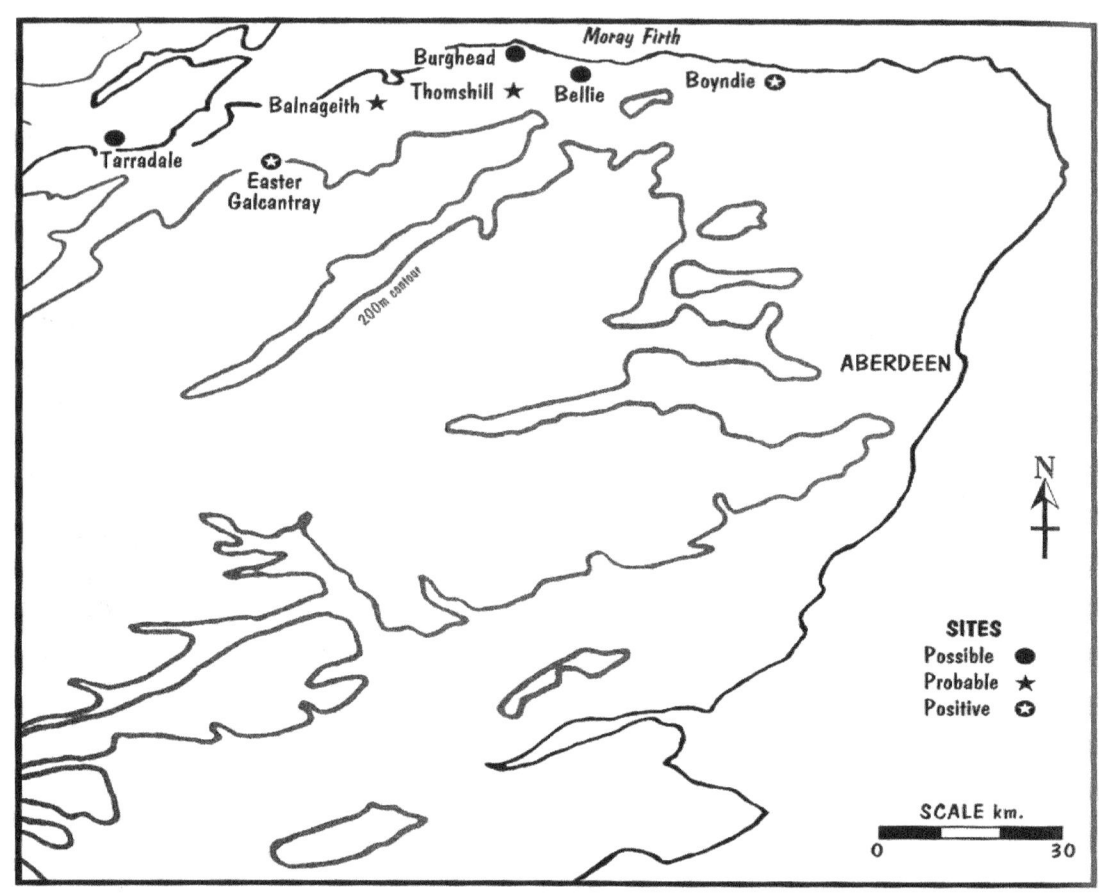

Map of north-east Scotland, showing possible and probable sites, from *The Romans in Moray*, courtesy of Ian Keillar

Crop-mark at Balnageith, photo by E.D.B. Jones, courtesy of Ian Keillar

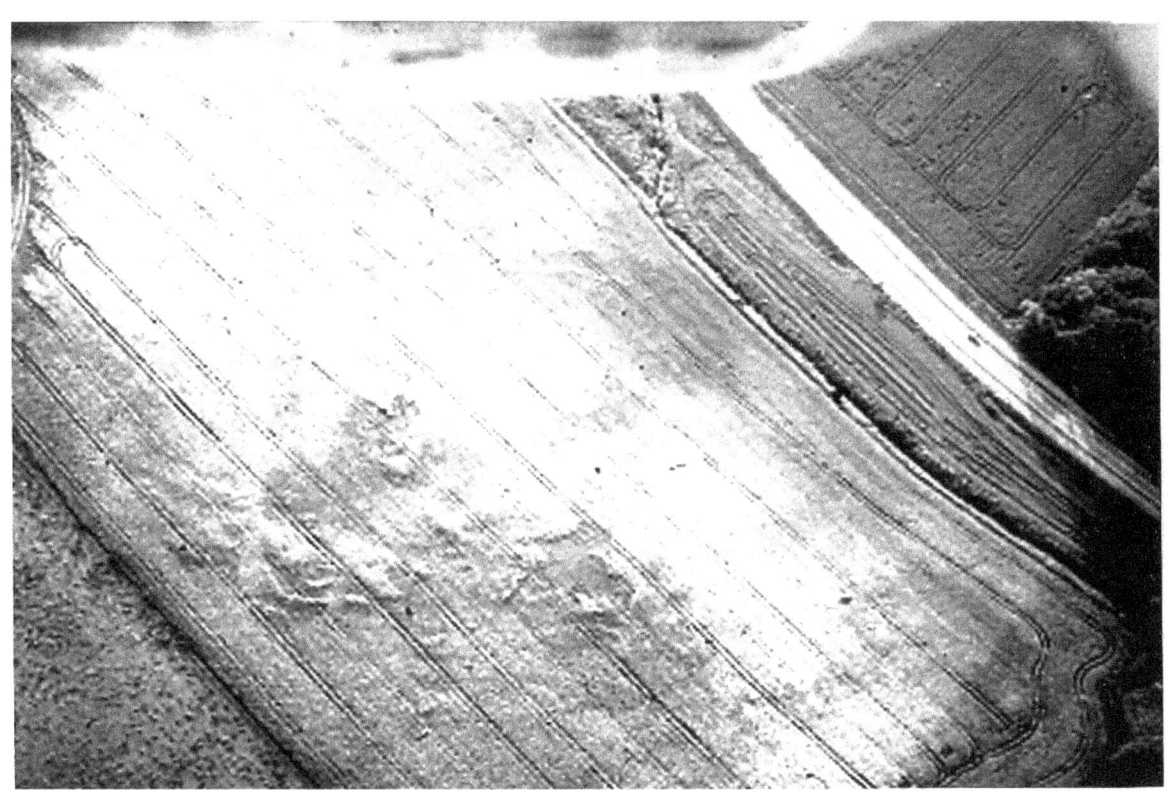

Crop-mark at Boyndie, photo by E.D.B. Jones, courtesy of Ian Keillar

West ditch of installation at Easter Galcantray, photo courtesy of Ian Keillar

achievements of the egoistic Alexander, who was seized by *cupido visendi Oceanum adeundique terminos mundi* (Curt. *HA.* 9.9.1 *a desire to look upon the Ocean and face the limits of the world*).[357] No Roman army had ever before reached the northern extremities of Britain, just as no Roman navy had ever before reached Thule. In terms of exploration and conquest it would be reasonable to claim that Agricola and Alexander had reached the furthest limits in their respective parts of the world.[358]

---

[357] Bosworth 2004, 554-557 notes distinct similarities between Agricola/Calgacus and Alexander/Darius on the eve of Gaugamela as recorded by Quintus Curtius. But care should be exercised in distinguishing between the ambitions of both commanders and their characters. Fabre 1975, 44 noted a theory that Alexander was aware of the explorations of Pytheas, and that after the exploits of Nearchus he dreamed of conquering the British Isles and even Thule. But Fabre regarded this hypothesis as *extremely risky*. Dion 1977, 209 cites Seneca, *Ben.* 7.2.5 for the activities of Onesicritus (*praemissus explorator*), Alexander's pilot, in the western ocean.

[358] Ogilvie 1967, 33, noting the dedications to Oceanus and Thetis.

APPENDIX 2

A PROBLEM OF IDENTIFICATION or *PIE IN THE SKYE*?

Eutropius (7.13.3) apparently tells us that Claudius *added the Orkneys to the Roman empire*. Müller charged him with *wishful fantasy*,[359] while Bird states that *Eutropius' claim seems improbable*.[360] But neither stopped to consider where such an odd reference might have originated. Armit, in order to put the Orkneys in a *southern* context, suggests close links *perhaps through marriage or military alliance* between 'kings of Orkney' and tribes far to the south.[361] Wainwright claims that *chieftains of the Orkneys made formal submission to Claudius*.[362] The phrase *chieftains of the Orkneys* is very vague, and there is no record of this in Eutropius. Some might suppose that their names appeared on the Arch of Claudius at Rome. Line 8 of its inscription was fancifully restored by the antiquarian Gauges de Gozze to read *gentesq(ue) e[xtremarum Orchadum]* (*and the nations of the furthest Orkneys*).[363] The Orcadians probably would not even have known what was happening in the remote south, or even if they did, they would be little concerned. This possibility is no more plausible than Stevens' theory that *some adventurous sea-captain put into Camulodunum and made submission to Rome in the name of his people*.[364] The Caledonians, according to Calgacus (*Agr.* 30.2-3), had been confident that their remoteness would protect them from Roman domination, as it had done for forty years—I have no doubt that Agricola's interrogation of prisoners-of-war elicited such sentiments. But to assume that a delegation came all the way from Orkney to surrender to Claudius beggars belief.

Fitzpatrick links the discovery of a specific type of *amphora* sherd at the Broch of Gurness with a Claudian *clientela*.[365] This is a very tenuous thread on which to hang such a theory.[366] The sherd could have reached Orkney by way of trade through many hands. The evaluation of the literary evidence in support of this theory is based on a misinterpretation of the Latin, relying too much on Momigliano, while there was no adequate argument to counter Maxwell. I see no grounds for believing that *the panegyrics provide inferential support for the Claudian submission of the Orkney Islands*. Tacitus and Juvenal knew who was responsible for the conquest of the Orkneys and I do not believe *they had at the back of their minds this earlier claim of annexation*.[367] Braund believes that a Claudian contact was Flavian propaganda.[368] But it is hard to see why the Flavian dynasty would wish to boost the credentials of its predecessor.[369] It is certainly impossible to accept Galimberti's theory of Vespasian's presence in the Orkneys (as stated earlier).

Any link between the Orkneys and Claudius is, rather, the consequence of confusion between sources. This can be explained by textual analysis and comparison. Eutropius made a mistake, and the error-prone Orosius and the others who followed him fell into the same trap. Eutropius produced two separate accounts, one referring to Claudius, the other to Vespasian, when in fact the submission of *Vectis* (Wight), which he has taken from Suetonius, should bridge the roles of emperor and *legatus legionis* (*legionary commander*). It is worth noting that Eutropius ascribes to Vespasian the initiative for the *Vectis* episode, without mentioning Claudius being in Britain, whereas Suetonius (*Vesp.* 42)

---

[359] Müller 1883, 104.
[360] Bird 1993, 113.
[361] Armit 1998, 104.
[362] Wainwright 1962, 65.
[363] Cited by Barrett 1991, 11 f., cf. his n. 40 for details of the publication of De Gozze's transcription. For the modern text see *CIL* VI 920+add.=*ILS* 216=*CIL* VI 40416. *Extremae Orchades* fits into the same category as *Ultima Thule*, a literary usage and unlikely to feature in an official inscription.
[364] Stevens 1951, 8; cf. Burn 1969, 39: *conceivably some traders in northern products may have made some profession of obedience*. Why would they want to do this?
[365] Fitzpatrick 1989, 24-33. See also previous note.
[366] The Roman brooch found at Norwick in Unst in 2003 could never be used as evidence for a client relationship between Shetland and Rome. It would have passed through many hands before it reached its final destination.
[367] Stevens, op.cit.
[368] Braund 1996, 150, 195.
[369] In the Silver Age writers Claudius should be seen as the means to an end, namely the rise of Vespasian. There is no parity. Tacitus (*Agr.*13.3) puts it well. Claudius is the sponsor, a figurehead, no more. His achievement lies in the selection of Vespasian. The Julio-Claudians get short shrift.

makes the crucial qualification, *partly under the leadership of Claudius*. It is plausible to infer that Eutropius, following two different sources, one for each emperor (his source for Claudius also produces a reference to Cn. Sentius Saturninus, not found elsewhere in a British context), has produced two different versions of the same event, the surrender of the Isle of Wight. Consequently any surrender of the Orkneys is false. Stevens tried to establish a link between Claudius and the Orkneys via Pomponius Mela on the basis that he is the first to mention the *Orcades*, whereas *Diodorus and Strabo knew nothing about them*.[370] But the fact that the two Greeks do not mention these islands is no evidence for ignorance. *Orcades* is a Greek word and probably derives, like *Thule*, from Pytheas; it was available. Suetonius made no mention of *Vectis* in his *Life of Claudius*, preferring to reserve it for Vespasian, and no mention at all of the *Orcades*—always *topical* in Flavian writers—whose remoteness would surely have merited a reference in the biographer and in Cassius Dio and most probably in Seneca's *Divi Claudii Apotheosis per satiram* (*Satire on the Deification of the late Claudius*). Suetonius and Orosius were correct in referring to only one instance of surrender (not surprising since the latter drew on, and frequently corrupted, the former). Historical reality and common sense must tell us that the reduction of the Isle of Wight is the natural consequence of campaigning in southern England, and that to link Claudius with the Orkneys is extreme.

So how did *Vectis* come to be confused with the *Orcades*? The answer may lie in Agricola's conquest of those islands, a detailed report of which would have included the names of all the islands between the Caithness coast and Mainland, Orkney. Tacitus was not interested in recording geographical trivia. But such details found their way to Marinus, and from him to Ptolemy. I believe that *Vectis* is the name given to one of these islands and was so recorded by Ptolemy, whose text was subjected to numerous alterations before it reached the hands of the Ravenna Cosmographer and the scribes of the 13th and 14th centuries. Ptolemy's name for Wight is *Ouektis* (*Geogr.* 2.3.14). But between Ptolemy's reference to *Orcas* promontory and the *Orcades* islands we find the mysterious *Sketis*, the reading of the X manuscript (*Vaticanus Graecus* 191), which is assumed to be the Isle of Skye. It is evidently so identified in the *Ravenna Cosmography*, whose sequence of islands defies any explanation. Yet Pliny does not mention Skye in his list of the Western Isles between Ireland and Britain (*NH*. 4.103 *Riginia, Vectis* (?), *Silumnus, Andros*) and it has never been explained how a man who knew Vespasian well could have located *Vectis* in the Irish Sea.[371] The *Ravenna Cosmography* lists *Vectis* before *Malaca* (Mull?). It seems reasonable to assume that there was an island called *Vectis* located in the north. Its *precise* location is problematic. The reading of Ptolemy in the U manuscript (*Vaticanus Urbinas Graecus* 82) and in most MSS is *Okitis*. U was unknown to Müller, but Fischer claimed that it was the most reliable of all the MSS; Rivet and Smith conjure it up whenever it suits their purpose. but admit that *there is still no general agreement on the correct text*, and to complicate matters they prefer *Scitis*, a variant found in three Florentine MSS (corruption from *O* to sigma *C*, a common error in earlier uncial lettering), presumably because it comes closer to its alleged derivative, Skye.[372] But there is another possibility. A similar composite of the readings in *X* and *U* produces *Oketis* (restoration of sigma *C* to *O*), which is virtually a *metathesis* of *Ouektis*. Metathetical distortions are common in Ptolemy, *especially where there is a 'k' or 'g' in the name concerned*.[373] So *ket* becomes *ekt*. The result is that we have *two* islands called 'Wight', a familiar one in the south and a duplicate in the north.[374] The northern version would appear to be Pliny's Irish Sea *Vectis* (the proper Latin name for Skye?). Ptolemy's northern *Ouektis*, whether or not it is Skye with a distorted location,[375] or some other island (Stroma?) off Caithness, was assumed by later historians to be one of the Orkneys because it was sandwiched by Ptolemy between *Orcas* and *Orcades*. Whatever variants we find in the medieval MSS of Ptolemy, it is plausible that the original reading is *Ouektis*, that Ptolemy located it near *Orcas promontory* and that this is what Eutropius' unnamed source assumed to be part of the

---

[370] Stevens, op.cit.
[371] According to Roseman 1994, 89, *Pliny has evidently made a careless error in moving it into the Irish Sea*.
[372] Rivet/Smith 1979, 129, 452.
[373] Schutte 1917, 22; he cites *urg > rug, ukl >luk*.
[374] Vossius 1658, 255 goes one better and offers us three: one that gives its name to the present Isle of Wight, one in the Irish Sea and the third which Ptolemy lists as *Oketis*. At least he is perceptive enough to suggest a correction to *Ouiktis*, i.e. *Ictis*. He was not far off the mark.
[375] *By a strange mistake,* writes Thomas 1875, 206, *the name of this island has wandered far away to an island off the north end of Scotland*.

Orkneys. Duplications are common enough in Ptolemy (eg. *Camulodunum*, *Coria*, *Alauna*, *Derventio*, *Dumnonii*, etc.). Agricola's marines could not have overrun Skye, since Skye is bigger than *Thule* or any of the Orkneys, and Tacitus would have mentioned any invasion of the Hebrides. Stroma was almost certainly overrun, but is not mentioned by Tacitus (because it was categorised among the *Orcades)*, as was Swona, likewise situated in the Pentland Firth. Yet Stroma would be known to Agricola and may well be my suggested *Vectis*. In that case *Dumna* needs to be re-examined, especially since Pliny, as I maintain, puts it in a *Scandinavian* setting, where Stichtenoth prefers to locate it.[376]

---

[376] Thomas 1875, 224 identifies Dumna as Stroma; Stichtenoth 1959, 84.

APPENDIX 3

THE COINAGE OF TITUS AND AGRICOLA'S CALEDONIAN CAMPAIGN OF AD 79

tertius expeditionum annus novas gentes aperuit, vastatis usque ad Taum
(*aestuario nomen est*) *nationibus.*

*The third year of campaigning revealed new peoples, and nations were
laid waste as far as the Tay* (*that is the name of the estuary*)

Tacitus *Agricola* 22.1

This is not the place to question Tacitus' claims about *new peoples*, when the archaeological and literary evidence suggests that Bolanus or Cerialis were there nearly a decade earlier, nor to dispute with Woolliscroft and Hoffmann the meaning of *Taus*. The palaeographical evidence for that question is patently obvious.[377] Nor need one here attribute any imperatorial acclamation for Vespasian to any success that Agricola's predecessors may have achieved in Britain.

While his legates continued to extend the western frontiers, the emperor was still celebrating his victory in Judaea with protracted commemorative coins issued years after the event. Although these may have been intended to keep Flavian successes in the public eye, they would have had no more lasting impact than *Britannia* on a modern British coin in reminding its users of the glories of the British Empire. Coins are for spending, not studying. The novelty soon wears off.[378] This is a Flavian 'ego-trip'. One assumes that the purpose of the *Judaea capta* series was to impress the *senatus* rather than the *populus Romanus*, who would look for the more obvious benefits of victory, such as the construction of the Flavian Amphitheatre. As already pointed out, Vespasian needed to end his career with a military success on the other side of the empire. A building project might eventually satisfy the needs of the *plebs*, but glory and triumph were achieved on the battlefield, not on a building-site. The body may have been failing, but the driving ambition was still there, as were the generals who would fulfil it before the end of the decade.

Scholars have been left with no room for manoeuvre by the erroneous dating of Agricola's third campaign to AD 80, when Vespasian was already dead, instead of AD 79, when his joint initiative with Titus (*see below*) promoted an advance into Caledonia. This later chronology was given respectability by Ogilvie and Richmond.[379] Unfortunately it is still supported in more recent times.[380]

---

[377] Woolliscroft/Hoffmann 2006, 176. Anderson 1922,lvi unfortunately preferred the reading *Tanaum*, which he assumed to be the Tyne, and consequently will be remembered for his pompous declaration that *an advance to the Tay is wholly out of the question*. Laederich 2001, 336 prefers *Tanaum* without being aware of the marginal variant or Ptolemy's reading. He does not commit himself to a translation, merely stating that *La Tay.... un véritable estuaire* seems *trop éloignée*. Rather than assuming that the error arose through confusion with *Tanais* (the Russian *Don*), we might consider the addition of the extra syllable *-an* as attributable to scribal carelessness. Till 1943, 53 cites the MS *Nah-an-arvali* for *Naharvali* at *Germania* 43.2. A summary of the various interpretations may be found in Hanson 1991b,1743. With the MS offering two options there was no need for Maxwell 1984, 222 to conjure up a third (cf. n.340) for a different location, especially after writing, *the case for identification with the Tay appears to be very strong, since the explicit reference to an estuary and the form of the name itself combine with military considerations to narrow the choice considerably.*

[378] The classic instance of this is the pretentious £2 coin depicting the stages of technological advance from Celtic art to the internet. *Homo Britannicus* is neither aware nor interested, except in so far as it can buy him a pint of beer. Are we to assume that *homo Romanus* was any different?

[379] Ogilvie 1967, 230. He should have examined Anderson's arguments more carefully and noted his final comment, 1922, 173: *On the whole...the difficulties are perhaps not sufficiently serious to justify the rejection of the date* (for the commencement of Agricola's governorship) *suggested by the narrative of Tacitus, AD 77*. Burn 1969, 50 is convinced that *the year was pretty certainly 78*. This has a knock-on effect, *swept north in AD 80...to carry Roman arms to the Firth of Tay*. Consequently, when Domitian becomes emperor in AD 81, Burn is at a loss to explain why Agricola was *left for another year*. In fact the year 80 was spent in consolidation. Burn is followed by D.J. Breeze 1978, 24: *The advance of Agricola in AD 80 was an unprovoked act of Roman imperialism associated with Titus*. One year of misdating can lead to false conclusions. He wisely revised his views ten years later, 1988, 16. Jones/Mattingly 1990, 74 offer timetables for both

The numerous articles and dissertations which base their theories on the old dating should now be discarded. The difference of just one year has meant that the possibility of a successful British campaign in AD 79 has seldom been part of the literary tradition, and never part of the numismatic tradition. The Judaean commemorative issues have had such a hold over the traditionalists, as have the romance and tragedy of the *Bellum Iudaicum* (*Jewish War*), that it was anathema to look in any other direction. The website of the Jewish Museum in New York illustrates its own specimen of the Titus denarius (*described below*), not only giving it the wrong date ('78 CE') which, in the historical context, is unacceptable and misleading, but also, as I maintain, the wrong country, *Iudaea capta* (*Judaea captured*).[381] There is no such legend on the coin—yet Reifenberg states unequivocally that the reverse type is *a captive Jew kneeling under a trophy*.[382] It might be asked on what criteria he based the nationality of the captive. Yet all these misinterpretations are understandable in the light of the knowledge currently available. There is a fine line between patriotism and parochialism; but objectivity is always the loser.

The Judaean war was not forgotten by Titus, but I believe that AD 79 marks a watershed in the transitional period from stagnation to rejuvenation. The focus was gradually changing from east to west and now needed to be concentrated on new areas, where successes, albeit not as spectacular as those in the east, could be guaranteed. The Flavians had been in power for a decade and the *bellatrix gens* needed to reconstruct its image and boost its prestige. The oft trumpeted *Judaea capta* was beginning to wear a bit thin by the late 70s and its propaganda value would have had little effect except to rub salt into the wounds of Jewish prisoners working on mammoth building programmes in Rome. A successful dynasty cannot rely entirely on its past. But Britain was a different proposition entirely, far enough away for governors to absorb minor reverses, but fragmented enough to break down.[383] It was a convenient theatre for any regime in search of a new image. Cerialis and Frontinus had paved the way for Agricola. What better way for the ageing emperor to mark the tenth anniversary of power than by celebrating successes in Britain with a new coinage issue in the name of the one who he knew was soon to take his place?[384] It would not be surprising for British operations to be recognised numismatically. What is surprising is that they played second fiddle to Judaea for nearly a decade, during which Vespasian's own son-in-law, Cerialis, had achieved a measure of success in Britain.[385] Perhaps blood was thicker than marriage.

Judaea, like Britannia, is always represented iconographically as a *woman*, whether the coin has a legend or not, but suddenly we are confronted with specimens of a Vespasian denarius from the mint in Rome, issued for Titus as Caesar (*BMC* 2.46 nos. 258-9) in AD 79, with a kneeling *male* captive, in front of a trophy which, as Jane Cody describes in such admirable detail, appears to be identifiable

---

chronologies, when one would have sufficed, but recognise the sense of the earlier one: *the major policy changes can be better explained in terms of changes of emperor.*

[380] Cody 2003, 110; Kamm 2004, 70; Fraser 2005, 51; Allen 2007, 190; McCullough 2007, 58. Most recently of all Grant 2007, 91 writes: *The forward policy seemed to have ended in AD 79 with the death of Vespasian*. This view would be invalid, if, as I suggest, Vespasian was still alive when Agricola's marines reached the Tay by the middle of May. The numismatic iconography is crucial here. Grant's reference (96) to a monument for Vespasian at Arthur's O'on would support this view. *Perhaps victory was imminent* may be closer to the truth.

[381] The website *Jerusalem Through Coins* illustrates a 'captive' reverse type issued by Titus as emperor and dated to 80-81 CE. The reverse appears to read TRP VII COS VII. This combination would date, at the latest, to March of 78, and cannot be applied to Titus as *princeps*. Either the coin has been incorrectly or indistinctly engraved or it is a forgery. I suspend judgement. In any case it has no connexion with Jerusalem.

[382] Reifenberg 1953, 14

[383] *singuli pugnant, universi vincuntur* (*Agr.*12.2, *they fight individually, and are beaten collectively.*

[384] Vespasian was acclaimed emperor in Alexandria by his troops on 1 July AD 69 (Tac. *Hist.*2.79.1). Although he died a week before the tenth anniversary of his acclamation, Romans regularly began to celebrate *decennalia* at the beginning of the tenth year. there would have been arrangements in advance to celebrate it. The army had put Vespasian in power, and the army would enhance his image with successes in Britain under Agricola.

[385] For Cerialis as son-in-law of Vespasian see e.g. Birley 2005, 64, 65 f. Caruana 1997, 48, pointing out Cerialis' progress in the north as anticipating Agricola's presence in the area, states that *we should be wary of accepting that the 3rd and 4th seasons...were also extending the limits of the province. Were new forts built on the Tay in year 3?* I do not deny pre-Agricolan activity in the region, but maintain that it was short-lived and ineffective. Why else did war break out again in the area, and why the scorched-earth policy, if not to signal Agricola's intentions? Why no special coinage issues for AD 72-3? Cerialis was doing a 'holding job'. It was to Agricola that Vespasian entrusted the total conquest of the north.

with Britanno-Celtic weaponry. She writes, *these new types have a helmet and cuirass, crossed spears on the left and round shield on the right, instead of the oblong and round shields on the undecorated stem of the Judaea Capta coins.*[386] Trophies reflect a military tradition associated with a particular nation, and a closer look at the Judaean trophies might have provided Cody with further criteria.

A summary of the evidence points to Vespasian as being the initiator of the policy for Agricola's Caledonian campaign during that year which saw its completion under Titus. I believe that the male *captive* reverse was deliberately selected by Vespasian to prove that after ten years of power the *gens Flavia* could match, indeed surpass, the military successes of the *gens Iulia* in western Europe. The design is clearly taken from the coinage issued by Julius Caesar to commemorate his Gallic triumphs.

A   B

**A. Denarius of Julius Caesar, *BMCRR* 2.39. No.9; *RRC* 1. 467. 452 nos.4-5 issued in 48-47BC.
Photo courtesy of CNG Coins, www.cngcoins.com**

**B. Denarius of Titus as Caesar, *BMC* 2.46. No.258, issued under Vespasian
about mid-June AD 79.
Photo courtesy of Andreas Pangerl, www.romancoins.info**

But Caesar had 'failed' in Britain. The emperor is claiming what Tacitus expresses so eloquently about Caesar's failure: *Britanniam...potest videri ostendisse posteris, non tradidisse* (*Agr.* 13.1, *he can be seen to have pointed Britain out, not to have handed it over, to posterity*). This statement cuts even deeper. Caesar had left nothing for Augustus. Vespasian passes on a legacy to Titus. This is why there is such poignancy in the numismatic imagery of Vespasian issuing a 'Caledonian' prototype in the name of Titus. Could anything more appropriate reflect the close cooperation between father and son in their plans for the conquest of northern Britain? The Flavian family will succeed where the Julian family had failed. Caesar may have won a victory in Gaul and, by adopting Octavian, may have precipitated the move towards a new dynasty, but he could never issue a coinage showing the portrait of his successor. The iconography reflects both the closeness of the *gens Flavia* and its competitive nature, a rivalry to be found not only in Tacitus, but in contemporary poetry, cf. the prologue of Valerius Flaccus (*Arg.* 1.8-9) described earlier (ch. 5).

---

[386] Cody 2003, 11.

German prisoners-of-war beneath a trophy from a scene on the lower section of the *Gemma Augustea*. Note the brimmed Celtic helmet which was adopted by the Roman legionaries.

Ogilvie suggests that the short British shields (*brevia caetra*) were rectangular, as on the Antonine distance-slab from Bridgeness.[387] But circular versions appear on the British triumphal coins of Claudius. It is strange that Ogilvie refers to Herodian's description of *circular* shields (*Hist.* 3.14.8), since these are there described as *narrow*, not *circular*. Different shapes may indicate local variations. Cody draws attention to both the round and the rectangular shields on the DE BRITANN (*Victory over the Britons*) issues of Claudius (*BMC* 1.168, no.29), noting that the Romans often did not discriminate between Gauls and Britons, cf. *Agr.* 10.2.[388] This may be the case, but two different styles of Celtic weaponry may reflect tribal rather than *ethnic* differences. An *oval*-shaped shield is found on the denarius of Caesar (*BMCRR* 2.39 nos.59-60, see illustration above).

Herodian's statement (*ibid.*) that the Caledonians did not wear breastplates may be correct, but only insofar as it refers to the rank and file, since Statius, referring to Bolanus' activities in the Caledonian plains, alleges (*Silv.* 5.2.149) that the governor *seized a breastplate from a British king*.[389] His trophy, including *the gifts and weapons*, which *he dedicated to the gods* (*Silv.* 5.2.147), was gained in the same area where Agricola was now operating, and would provide the pattern for the 'trophy' coinage of AD 79. So the captive on the coin should represent a tribal prince, stripped of all dignity.

The trophy which appears on the 'legitimate' Judaean *aurei* and *denarii* always contains *greaves* below the apron.[390] Engravers, even in western mints such as Lugdunum and Tarraco would be aware that Judaea had been ruled by Hellenistic kings and was part of the culture going back to Alexander the Great, who had annexed Judaea to his Macedonian empire in 332 BC. Greaves (*ocreae*) were part of the defensive armour used by the Macedonians and Seleucids during the era of the Maccabean revolt, which broke out at about the same time as Rome's Third Macedonian War. A denarius, issued

---

[387] Ogilvie 1967, 274, and plate VII.
[388] Cody 2003, 11.
[389] This is discussed in Appendix 4.
[390] This is a very distinctive feature on the Jewish trophy and clearly symbolic. We find crossed greaves on the *Divus Augustus Vespasianus* denarii of Titus and on the base metal issues of Titus Caesar and Domitian from Caesarea Maritima (*RPC* 2. pt.1, 317, no.2313; 316, no.2304) which commemorate the same events.

in 62 BC (*RRC* 1.441 no.415), commemorates the victory of Aemilius Paullus over Perseus at Pydna in 168 BC. The reverse shows a trophy, complete with greaves, Paullus on the right, a bound Perseus and his sons on the left.[391]

Denarius of Julius Caesar with double-captive reverse (described in text)

The Jewish military 'manual', the so called Hebrew 'War Scroll',[392] refers to greaves as part of the armour which the *Sons of Light* (the Israelites) are to employ in their eschatological war against the *Kittim*.[393] The engravers are
simply following guidelines originating from Judaeo-Hellenistic traditions.

During the first Jewish War Hellenistic armour should not be confused with its Roman counterparts.[394] Greaves do not appear on the 'Celtic' trophy of Titus. The Caledonians fought bare-legged. Leg-guards would in any case merely hamper warriors whom Agricola describes as *fugacissimi* (*Agr.* 34.1, *the greatest runaways*).

All the evidence supports the case for the male captive being a northern Briton rather than a Jew. I

---

[391] Greaves are listed among the captured weapons in Plutarch's *Life of AemiliusPaulus* 32.

[392] 1*QM*. Treves 1958, 419 says that *the many precise details, some of which have parallels in contemporary Hellenistic and Roman tactics and organisation...give it the appearance of a plan for a real war to be waged in the author's days*. The weaponry contains elements of both cultures (cf. Polyb. *Hist.* 6.25.3ff) and the organisation and ritual suggest a considerable Jewish input. The scroll presents a scenario for a 'Holy War' based on a fusion of the best of contemporary strategies, but the fabulous equipment seems more appropriate to the parade ground.

[393] The Kittim are the *Sons of Darkness*, and could be taken as portending the Romans. The scroll, according to Golb 1995, 126 f. originated in Jerusalem and in its earliest form may date from the time of the Maccabean revolt against Antiochus IV. It would have been edited and reinterpreted by subsequent generations as the template for combating the Romans. The Book of Daniel was composed at about the same time and refers to the Kittim. The Habakkuk Commentary, probably contemporary with the revolt of AD 66, interprets Daniel's Kittim as the same as the Kittim who *make sacrifice to their standards,* i.e. the Roman troops of Vespasian (Driver,1965, 211-214, cf. Jos. *BJ.* 6.6.403, Plin. *HN* 13.23). So the Seleucids are identified with the Romans two centuries later. This would not be unusual. The *Sons of Darkness* in Jewish culture could refer to the Spanish Inquisition, the Nazis or the tsarist *pogromshchiki.* If the 'manual' is followed to the letter, the Jews will be armed in Hellenistic fashion, with the cavalry wearing greaves, breastplates and helmets, and carrying shields and spears, precisely what we find on the trophy. It is unlikely that the Zealots would have contemplated the reality of forming an army in this way, but there is no reason why their generals should not have made some concession to tradition by wearing greaves as well as other items of defensive armour. This feature would distinguish them in battle, making them a target for the Romans and providing a fitting adornment for a trophy.

[394] It is worth noting that on the larger flans of the *Iudaea capta* sestertii, where there is greater scope and variation of composition the helmets are distinctly Hellenistic, resembling those worn by Mars. The suggestion that these are helmets of Roman officers may be dismissed, since in some instances the general or the goddess *Victory* is depicted with a foot resting on one.

believe that this issue should be dated to the final days of Vespasian's principate, when news of Agricola's progress in the Caledonian campaign was beginning to reach Rome and the first successes were being recorded. This is why exactly the same reverse and legend occur on the earliest issues of Titus, which appeared during the week following his father's death: TR P VIII COS VII (*BMC* 2.223, nos.1-3, 23/24 June-1 July).

**Denarius of Titus as Augustus (*BMC* 2.223.no.1) issued 24 June - 1 July AD 79.
Illustrated in the Wikipedia entry on Titus.**

These earliest issues of Titus, both as Caesar and Augustus, reflect the results of joint planning between Vespasian and Titus on the progress of the British campaign in the north. Levick observes that *this summer Titus alone took credit for Agricola's success, becoming 'imperator' for the fifteenth time.*[395] This title was assumed after 8 September, when the campaign had been under way for months. The reverse of these coins, as Cody notes, *merely alludes to Titus' support of the campaign under his father's authority and to his own endorsement of Agricola's command once he himself became emperor.*[396] This becomes operational from 24 June. Cody has dwelt only on the numismatic aspects which, although convincing in themselves, need to be supported by the literary allusions to Vespasian's initiatives in Silius Italicus (*Pun.* 3.597)[397] and Valerius Flaccus (*Arg.*1.8-9), whose reference to *Caledonius Oceanus* in the prologue should be dated to 79. This fits in well with the activities of Agricola's fleet in the Tay estuary where, perhaps as early as the beginning of May, the initial reconnaissance and landing of the marines would 'soften up' the local population before the army got there later.[398]

---

[395] Levick 1999, 159. Breeze 1988, 16 likewise thinks that after Vespasian's death *there was no time for a change in policy that year.* He goes astray in his statement that *80 was the first year that Titus' actions could be recognised.* The numismatic and literary evidence suggests otherwise.

[396] Cody 2003, 11. It is worth noting that the issues of Titus as Augustus far outnumber those issued by Vespasian for Titus, a clear indication that time was running out for the father. Further research should examine the proportions involved as well as die patterns.

[397] Cf. A.R.Birley 2005, 92.

[398] If we assume some plundering raids in southern Scotland in 78, (cf. A.R. Birley 2005, 80), the enemy will have already been 'softened up'. Two altars to Neptune (with dolphin and trident, *RIB* 1319) and *Oceanus* (with anchor, *RIB* 1320), dedicated by the Sixth Legion, have been found in the River Tyne, an indication that *Oceanus* would protect shipping in the estuary. A denarius of Hadrian (*BMC* 3.257 no.127) shows a reverse of Oceanus with anchor and dolphin, which in the view of Mattingly 1930, cxxxii, *clearly marks the way of Hadrian to Britain.* Since *Oceanus* is clearly indicated by the anchor, which must relate to ships, it is likely that the ongoing operations of Agricola's marines in the Clyde-Forth area during AD 80-82 are recorded by a series of *aurei* and *denarii*, issued by Titus (*BMC* 2.234 no.71) and Domitian (*BMC* 2.297 no.3) and showing a dolphin and anchor reverse. These reverses are not recorded at any other time during the Flavian period and would confirm that Domitian was in favour of continuing his brother's policy. This would demolish Sear's observation (1986) that *Agricola's spectacular successes in northern Britain in the opening years of the reign* (of Domitian) *were totally ignored.* For the role and impact of Agricola's navy in AD 81-82 cf. *Agr.* 24-25.

 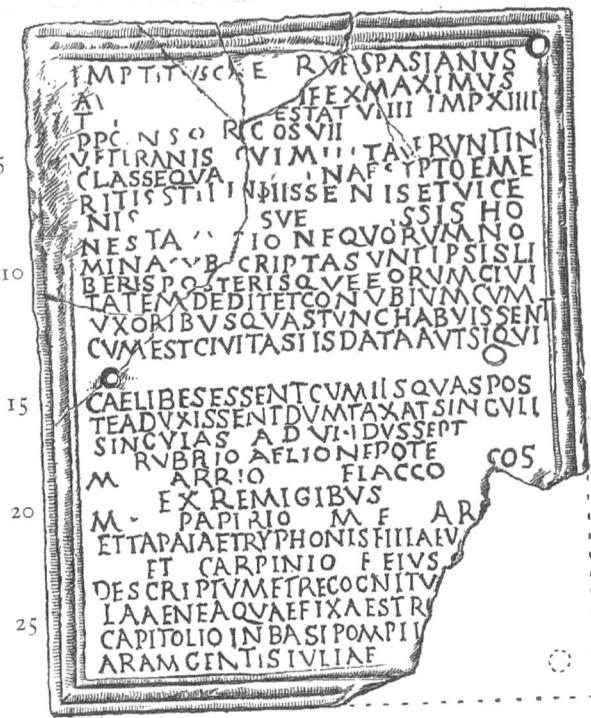

Roman Military Diploma from Egypt (*CIL*.16.24) from AD79. References in line 3 to the 14th acclamation of Titus, and in line 17 to *the 6th day before the Ides of September*. ie 8th Sept, provide supporting evidence for the earliest possible date for the next acclamation attested in Dio (*RH* 66.20.3).

These issues then pave the way for the two series of *captive* reverses, with imperatorial acclamations, for Titus, who can now claim sole responsibility for military successes after a convenient period of filial *pietas*. The first series reverse legend is TR P VIIII IMP XIIII COS VII[399] and should date from 1 July to, at least, 8 September.[400] The second series reverse legend, confirmed by Cassius Dio/Xiphilinus (66.20.3), is TR P VIIII IMP XV COS VII and covers the rest of the year.[401] Since IMP XIIII is attested epigraphically for the first quarter of 79,[402] when Vespasian was still alive, it may be based on the Agricolan campaign of 78,[403] when the governor was operating in the north. This would not affect the reverse. The Romans would not distinguish between the peoples of northern Britain. The fact that Dio actually records for a success in Britain a specific date, which appears on specific coins with reverses not hitherto found during the Principate, should have alerted numismatists to taking a positive stance rather than vacillating. The evidence is clear enough.

A new series of acclamations was not started when Titus became emperor.[404] He had already accumulated an impressive number, and it was only a question of adding to them. In 79 there would have been considerable advances through the Scottish Lowlands, with ensuing devastation and fort-

---

[399] *BMC* 2.224. no.5. There was a short-lived intermediate series without *IMP XIIII* which post-dates 1 July (Mattingly 1930, *BMC* 2.lxxi). The interruption of the 14th acclamation may be attributed to respect for the late emperor. The gold issues of the 'male captive' reverse type commence with this acclamation.
[400] Cf. A.R. Birley, 2005, 83n.
[401] *BMC* 2.223. unref. Not *crossed swords*, as suggested, but crossed spears.
[402] *CIL* 2. 2477. I don't quite follow Buttrey's reasons (1980, 7) for a 14th acclamation from July 78 where he equates it with Vespasian's 20th acclamation. The latter was effective up to mid-March 79.
[403] The 13th acclamation, about which Buttrey 1980, 24 is not sure whether it is applicable to 77 or 78, would not result from Agricola's campaign in Wales in 77, since Tacitus (*Agr*.18) makes it quite clear that Agricola did not send laurelled dispatches. It was on these that the senate would authorise an imperial acclamation. Millar notes, 2003, vol.2, 172, that the attack on the Ordovices would indicate that end-of-campaign reports were normal, adding that, if Dio is correct, Titus also would receive such a report. As Millar uses the later dating for the governorship, thus putting the Ordovican campaign in 78, any acclamation during that year could not refer to that specific campaign, for the reasons set out above.
[404] Jones 1984, 115.

building right up to the Forth, culminating possibly in the autumn with the rout of the peoples in the Fife area. This would be the likely theatre of operations where, as Dio states (66.20.1), *war had broken out again*. For these operations the senate awarded a 15th acclamation for Titus. One wonders about the cause of the hostilities, the role of the Venicones and the function of the Gask *limes*, if it was operational at that time. The Venicones could hardly be allies, as Hanson suggests, if Agricola 'ravaged their lands'.[405] David Mattingly is sure that these people *were under supervision. Indeed the prime evidence of Roman campaigns shows that their territory was repeatedly targeted.*[406] Kamm assumes that the Venicones are the *novas gentes*.[407] In terms of devastation he lays stress on the *lands* rather than the people, thereby contradicting his subsequent hypothesis of living off the land: the lands were torched. The evidence of a scorched earth policy by Agricola comes from the pollen analysis carried out at Black Loch in Fife by Whittington and Edwards. They suggest that *given the ravaging nature of those incursions it is most probable that the initiation and even persistence of the agricultural decline stem from that event.*[408] The verb *vastare* should be treated with caution. With *nationes* as its object it also implies heavy loss of life (cf. Tac. *Ann.* 14.38, *quodque nationum...igne atque ferro vastatur*, i.e.'with fire and sword').[409] Calgacus' *solitudinem faciunt* (*Agr.* 30.5, *they create a desolation*) also includes depopulation. One is reminded of the aftermath of Mons Graupius, *vastum ubique silentium* (*Agr.*38.2, *the silence of desolation everywhere*). The possible effects of Agricola's invasion on the economy and political structure of the indigenous population are set out by Armit.[410]

One assumes that Dio had access to official records in Rome or to a source now lost, but he was, as is generally the case, careless in his interpretation of the *Agricola*; he misread Agricola's two invasions across the Forth (79 and 82) as one, thereby transferring the events of the latter year (including the Usipian mutiny) to the former and giving revisionists a field day.

There is curiously no reference in the *Agricola* to Titus. But we would not expect any allusion there to an imperatorial acclamation. It should be remembered that in 77 Agricola did not broadcast his successes, *ne laureatis quidem gesta prosecutus est* (Tac. *Agr.*18.6). The fact that *he did not even use laurel-wreathed dispatches to announce his achievements* may have been appreciated by Vespasian who could read between the lines. At the same time, only an officially accredited success would give him real satisfaction. Yet they were still *achievements,* the implication by Tacitus being that they were *bene gesta*, 'successes', for which imperatorial acclamations were justified.[411] The devastation of enemy tribes with the resultant acquisition of prisoners would be considered *bene gesta* by an emperor who had done exactly the same in Judaea. It did not require a decisive victory to merit an acclamation and the official view in Rome was entitled to magnify events which the governor himself underplayed. In the battle between *modestia* and *gloria* there could be only one winner.

Harold Mattingly observes that *the exact occasions of the two victories which brought Titus these acclamations are not known, but they were both probably British.*[412] I agree with his *two* victories, one of which should be dated to 78/9 and be shared with Vespasian (*IMP XX*), but *victories* may be an overstatement for *bene gesta*. As for *probably,* read *surely.* Does not Dio confirm this? Where else but in Britain at this time could Titus, who had served there himself as a military tribune during Nero's principate and who was well acquainted with Agricola, merit such acclamations? Mattingly further adds: *in the coinage of AD 80 the two captives probably symbolise a victory in Britain...though the*

---

[405] Hanson 1987, 157. Shotter 2004b, 23: *perhaps friends of Rome*.
[406] D. J. Mattingly 2006, 151.
[407] Kamm 2004, 70.
[408] Whittington/Edwards 1993, 14 f., 20.
[409] The point of *vastatis* is noted by Southern 1996, 373. But she relates it to the economic, rather than humanitarian, consequences.
[410] Armit 2003, 132.
[411] The validity of imperatorial acclamations is open to question. They cannot all be accounted for by victories. Both Vespasian and Titus are accorded five separate acclamations in 76. It might be asked for what.
[412] H. Mattingly 1930, lxxi. With the earlier dating of Agricola's governorship now confirmed, Mattingly's attribution of imperatorial acclamations to specific campaigns in Britain needs to be put forward by one year.

Jewish victory was not forgotten.[413] There are problems involving this issue. The *aureus* shows a trophy without the greaves and would relate to the Caledonian campaign. The *denarii* with greaves[414] would continue the Judaean series, as Mattingly suggests, and may commemorate the tenth anniversary of Titus' siege of Jerusalem. With a male and female captive on either side of a trophy, the design is unique in first-century coinage. It should be noted that this type, like the Julius Caesar 'trophy/captive' issue also derives from a *gens Iulia* prototype of male/female/trophy, issued c. 48 BC to commemorate Caesar's victories in the Gallic Wars. Such trophy issues reflect the conscious need of the Flavian family to establish at least parity with its Julian predecessors. Superiority cannot be reflected in coinage issues, only in the eulogistic literature.

Denarius of Julius Caesar, issued in 47-48BC (*BMCRR* 2.3959; *RRC* 1.479. 468 nos. 1-2) to commemorate his Gallic victories

Aaureus of Titus as Augustus, issued AD80 (*BMC* 2.230 no.36). courtesy of CNG Coins, www.cngcoins.com

---

[413] H. Mattingly 1930, lxxii; *BMC* 2.230. no. 36.
[414] Engravers would be working on both the 'Caledonian' and the 'Judaean' series roughly simultaneously. The *aureus* claims priority in commemorating new victories in the west. It would be difficult for engravers to decide the parameters within which to formulate the design of the reverse. The solitary male prisoner on the Vespasianic issue of 79 has long hair, while the issues of Titus as Augustus show both long hair and the cap, associated with eastern captives. What we have is a transition from 'Judaean' to 'Caledonian' style.

The conclusion to be reached is that the *denarii* of Vespasian and Titus, dating from the middle of 79 and having a reverse showing a kneeling male captive next to a distinctive Celtic-type trophy, are derived from Republican prototypes and commemorate events in northern Britain, not in Judaea. Had there been any Judaean connexion, these coins, like the *Judaea capta* series, would have appeared much earlier. But they do not appear on any imperial coinage before the middle of 79. If Agricola began his offensive in southern Scotland in April/May of 79, British prisoners and hostages would have been mentioned in official dispatches to Rome in June and throughout the summer right up to September and beyond. The numismatic and literary package collectively must surely dispose of any lingering idea that the commencement of Agricola's governorship can be dated to 78.[415]

---

[415] Berard in his paper on troop movements, 1994, 235, still prefers the old dating on the basis that *we don't know exactly the date of Agricola's consulship*. But that is no longer an essential requirement if we work back from AD 79. Saddington 1991,1738 informs us that *precision cannot be arrived at with the evidence available at present*. This depends on whether all the evidence is thoroughly examined in the first place.

APPENDIX 4

VETTIUS BOLANUS IN THE NORTH: *FACT OR FICTION* ?

It is unfortunate that whatever successes Bolanus achieved in Britain were interrupted by the Civil War and subsequently overshadowed by the after-glow of Vespasian's triumphs in Judaea. The degree of success is debatable and the literary evidence for it is polarised by the contrasting views of Statius and Tacitus. There are five points to note:

1. Statius' account of Bolanus glorifies his achievements to the point of *hyperbole*.
2. Statius alludes indirectly to Agricola's success in Britain.
3. Tacitus' account of Bolanus' operations in Britain is less than positive.
4. Both authors cannot be right.
5. The reasons for such a divergence in the accounts may be sought either in policy differences between Bolanus and Agricola or in personal differences between Agricola and Statius.

Statius' flattering 'reminiscence' to Crispinus, Bolanus' son (*Silv.* 5.2.140), as delivered by an imaginary Caledonian, merits close scrutiny: *magno tellus frenata parenti* (*the land reined in by your great father*).[416] Taken together with the phrase *suetus dare iura parens* (*Silv.* 5.2.144, *your father used to deal out justice*),[417] these expressions appear to show a common source, Ilioneus' appeal to Dido,[418] *iustitiaque dedit gentis frenare superbos* (Virg. *Aen.* 1.524, *[Jupiter] has granted you to rein in proud nations with justice*).[419] Ilioneus shares the same longevity (*maximus*) as Statius' Caledonian and no doubt has shared the same unpleasant experiences which Virgil stresses and Statius cunningly disguises.[420] Age commands respect, whoever the speaker. A borrowed poetical allusion, however, does little to enhance Bolanus' reputation (*hyperbole* could equally diminish it). Rather, it illustrates an addiction to a poetical tradition, just as noticeable in Silius Italicus, where any Virgilian echo was expected to get a round of applause. Crispinus might appreciate Statius' panegyric, but the unbiased *cognoscenti*, aware of Statius' sycophancy and tendency to exaggeration, would hardly be impressed. The metaphorical *frenata* is far less than Tacitus' *perdomita* (*completely subdued*), and Statius, if he had really wished to exaggerate, could easily have replaced it with *devicta*, which has the same meaning, but did not suit a poetical context where metaphorical language is more effective. *Reins* (*frena*) are used to control a boisterous horse, in this case *ferox provincia* (*a fierce province*). But the horse was not completely broken in (*perdomita*),[421] merely, according to Statius, controlled (*frenata*), whereas Tacitus clearly implies a lack of control, *nec Bolanus...agitavit Britanniam disciplina* (*Agr.* 16.5, *Bolanus did not bring Britain into line by imposing discipline*).[422] The metaphor is maintained

---

[416] *magno...parenti*. Tacitus does not think so: Bolanus is not listed among the *magni duces* (*Agr.*17.1). There is other evidence to suggest that the historian is out to set the record right.

[417] *iura dare* is common in poetry. Gibson 2006, 247 cites Virg. *Aen.* 8.670, *Georg.* 4.561-2; Hor. *Carm.* 3.3.43-4. *iura* represents the civil law as part of Bolanus' dealings with the native population

[418] Statius' Virgilian links are more evident and widespread in the *Thebaid*, cf. Ganiban 2006.

[419] Dido had to deal with hostile Numidians and Gaetulians on her borders in much the same way as Bolanus had to deal with northern Britons. The route she takes is far different from that prescribed by Virgil for Rome's destiny—cf. *debellare superbos* (*Aen.* 6.853, *to crush the arrogant*). The irony, of course, is that from the native viewpoint it is the Romans who are arrogant (*quorum superbiam frustra...effugias* (*Agr.* 30.3, *whose arrogance you would escape from in vain*).

[420] The destruction of Troy and devastation of Caledonia (though the latter Agricolan).

[421] The verb *subigere* is used similarly for *breaking in* or *taming* an animal or even difficult soil. This is why the participle *subacta* is so apt in reference to fierce countries being subdued.

[422] Laederich 2001, 325 comes close to the correct sense, *Vettius Bolanus....ne traita pas la Bretagne avec la discipline qu'il aurait fallu* (*did not handle Britain with the discipline required*). Ogilvie's translation, 1967, 204, regurgitated once again from Anderson, '*harassed Britain by keeping his army in training*' does not make sense. One assumes first of all that he means *did not harass*. But why the allusion to harassment? The last thing you do when a province is *ferox* is to harass it, any more than you would provoke a rabid dog. *Disciplina* is what you require when *controlling* a province, not harassment. This accords quite well with what Tacitus says in *Agr.* 8.1 where the emphasis is on *being in charge* (*praeerat*) and *too gently* (*placidius*). A 'bucking bronco' needs to know who is in charge and it requires tougher, not more gentle, handling, as anyone who has watched an American Wild West rodeo understands. Furthermore I do not see any allusion to *keeping his army in training* . What does that mean anyway? A classroom teacher uses discipline to bring the children into line, not to harass

with the verb *agitare* (*to ride, handle, control*). A wild (*ferox*) horse can only be broken in, after being made to conform, by the man in the saddle. In maritime metaphors the reins are replaced by the rudder. In both circumstances the metaphors relate to government or control over unruly elements. This takes the form either of military coercion or the application of fair judicial procedures (*iura dare*), the latter usually following the former. What we have from Statius is a poorly disguised admission that Bolanus had pursued a policy of containment (i.e. limited control) rather than expansion, just as Didius Gallus *parta a prioribus continuit* (*Agr.* 14.2, *held what his predecessors had secured*). It was not a quest for glory or greatness, whatever flowery words Statius uses, but necessity that took Bolanus into the *Caledonian plains* (*Silv.* 5.2.142).[423] It was desperation, damage limitation, the need to stop the tribes of Lowland Scotland from supporting the fractious Brigantes. What Didius' *predecessors had secured* could apply equally to Bolanus. I cannot see how Bolanus could have launched a *permanent* move forward, while Venutius was still loose.[424] The Brigantian problem would never go away unless the whole of Scotland came under Roman control. The arguments put forward by scholars that Scotland had nothing to offer the Romans should take in the wider picture, not be based too closely on the arguments proposed by Calgacus. Tacitus knew full well what the strategy for Caledonia was: ultimate conquest; the only frontier was the Ocean. That too would be challenged and beaten.

No doubt Bolanus would have been happy to have posthumous glory, but without the exaggerations. Whatever creditable progress he makes comes crashing down with an outrageous claim by Statius,

> *quantusque negatam*
> *fluctibus occiduis fessoque Hyperione Thulen*
> *intrarit, mandata ferens...*
>
> *Silv.* 5.2.54-56[425]

---

them. The point that Tacitus is making is that while the Civil War was ongoing, Bolanus did not want to curb the unruly tribes by behaving as a martinet, especially as his manpower was now stretched He knew that the Britons would take advantage of the situation. His reluctance to interfere was interpreted as *inertia*. Tacitus appears to be guilty of double standards. He accuses Bolanus of *inertia* when the province is *ferox*. He accuses Trebellius of the same failing when the Britons are settling down to *seductive vices*. Governors are damned, whatever the Britons do. At least Ogilvie had the common sense not to repeat Anderson's comment about an *ironical expression*. One is reminded that the Britons, as Tacitus neatly puts it (*Agr.* 13.2), were *iam domiti ut pareant, nondum ut serviant* (*broken in to obedience, not yet to slavery*). The original meaning of the verb *domare* is *to break in, to tame* (an animal). The language is once more metaphorical. For the uses of *agitare* in both senses, *to ride* and *to control*, cf. OLD sect. 2 & 13, p.85. The phrase *agitatio terrae* (Col. *RR* 2.2.6. *The working of the land*) implies the ultimate taming or breaking in of the land, cf. Virg. *Georg.* 1.125 and previous note. For *gubernator* meaning rider, cf. Enn. *Ann.*445. For the metaphorical use of reins with *disciplina*, cf. Cic. *Rep.*2.58.

[423] What is fact and what is fiction is difficult to determine under the umbrella of poetic licence. Despite the embroidered language there appear to be elements of truth (cf. E. Birley 1953, 13; B. Dobson 1981, 4). Ogilvie's observations, 1967,156, on the extent of Bolanus' activities should be treated with caution. The disparagement of Bolanus has a long tradition, going back to Gibbon. For the fullest details of Bolanus in Britain, cf. A.R. Birley 1999, 68; 2005, 57-62. For pre-Agricolan involvement in Scotland, cf. Woodhead 1947-8, 56; Hanson 1979, 16 f., 1991a, 55 f. For the most perceptive comments and predictions, cf. E. Birley 1953,13 f.,40f. Evans 2003, 259 is somewhat premature in her assertion that Bolanus *never even got close to Scotland*. Gibson 2006, 247 likewise suggests a*n exotic exaggeration..* Unfortunately he follows Ogilvie/Richmond too closely on the extent of Bolanus'campaigns. Laederich 2001, 326 writes that *it seems hardly likely that Caledonia could have been reached*. Reliance on outdated commentaries can be a walk through a minefield. Pre-Agricolan penetration of Scotland was to become a fact rather than a fancy, even if Bolanus himself was not involved. Perhaps Cerialis has a better claim than his predecessor. Any attempt to minimise Bolanus' theatre of operations in Britain should be held back while the jury is still out.

[424] The story of Venutius, consort—and subsequently ex-consort—of Cartimandua, queen of the Brigantes, and the problems he caused the Romans are recorded by Tacitus (*Hist.* 3.44-45).

[425] Here I follow the text of Gibson, although not without reservations. In the standard text we find *negantem* and *fesso usque Hyperione*. The idea of Thule *resisting the western waves* sounds like a woman refusing her favours to an aggressive suitor. But it does make sense despite Gibson's reference to a *sluggish sea*. A suitor's aggression is only manifest in contact with his lover, not when he is miles away from her. Likewise a *sluggish sea* is only aroused by contact with the coast. The likelihood is that *fluctibus* and *Hyperione* are both in the ablative case. As a pair they support each other. Yet the replacement of a valid MS reading *negantem* is risky unless an exceptionally strong case can be made and suitable parallels adduced for MS corruption. I have my doubts. Furthermore, by changing the participle from active to passive you actually change the meaning of the verb. You can say *resisting*, but not *having been resisted*. The double elision is a technical disaster, and *usque* with *quant -usque* in the previous line is extremely harsh, apart from the fact that, as Gibson explains, 2006, 210, about *usque*, there is no parallel for its use as a *modifier of an adjectival phrase such as 'fesso Hyperione'*. The elimination

What a great man he was, bearing the emperor's instructions, to enter
Thule that had been denied by western waves and weary Hyperion

The reference to *weary Hyperion* (the sun) is clearly an echo of Pytheas, where Thule is described as the place *where the sun has its bed*.[426] But in composing these lines Statius clearly had in mind what he had written earlier (*Silv.* 5.1.88-89) about the implied surrender of Caledonia in AD 83. Note the similarity: *quantus/quantum*, verb moods, *intrarit/cesserit*,[427] synonyms, *fluctibus/gurgite* and the position and inaccessibility of *Thulen/Thule*. By regressing a quarter of a century to the governorship of Bolanus he produces a stanza which is highly dubious and at the same time disturbing. The curious similarity, between Bolanus entering Thule on Vespasian's instructions,[428] and Agricola's fleet reaching Thule on Domitian's instructions, raises the question of major distortion.[429] Statius composed this poem c. AD 95, a decade after official reports of Agricola's final campaign were in the public domain. Tacitus' *hactenus iussum* (*their orders took them this far*) clearly represents the official *mandata* and may well echo the basis of such a military report which Statius could have used and manipulated for his own ends.[430] The simple fact is that Agricola had been dead two years and was no

---

of *usque* means that the two ablatives *fluctibus occiduis* and *Hyperione* are instrumental and closely linked as a pair. Thule, says Gibson, had been denied to others (no reference to these in the text) by the *darkness and western seas* (*mare pigrum*?) which created a barrier to those who would reach it. Gibson is labouring to make his point. I can see where he is going. But what does *denied by the western seas* mean? If anything, it would be the *voyager* who would be denied, not his destination. Gibson might have cited Tacitus' *victus Oceanus* as an instance where resistance has been overcome. *Negatam* furthermore, according to Gibson, *gives point to quantus and intrarit, emphasising the difficult character of the voyage*. Despite the fact that there never was such a voyage and consequently no difficulty, the reasoning behind the textual changes sways me. Gibson's suggestions are logical. He dislikes the idea of *fluctibus occiduis/ fesso Hyperione* as ablatives absolute. He also admits that *this is a passage where complete certainty seems unobtainable*. This observation is rather an anticlimax after such an effort to plead his case, like a defence lawyer giving up on his client. The question of Thule being *denied* or *denying* in the context of Bolanus, *hyperbole* or otherwise, does not excuse Statius from suppressing the truth that Thule had *not* been denied to Agricola, as is implied in *Silv.* 5.1.89. By AD 95 everyone would have known the truth and it no longer 'made the front pages'. It would not be politic for Statius to resurrect the story, when events in eastern Europe were causing greater concern to Domitian. This is why Bolanus is a convenient hook on which the poet can hang his coat. Bolanus did not reach Thule, but Agricola's men did. But the poet has his own agenda. Gibson might have offered reasons for Bolanus being in Thule in the first place. It certainly does not refer to Britain, as pointed out earlier. To describe it as *hyperbole* and then link it to Silius' *reference to Vespasian's time in Britain* is to miss the point completely. It is awkward enough to take Crispinus back a quarter of a century. To take him back half a century is pointless. If it is *hyperbole* (rather a downright deliberate distortion), then the later comments on Bolanus in the Caledonian plains would fall into the same category. But I think there is some truth here.

[426] Geminus (citing Pytheas) 6, Fr.8, ultimately derived from Homer (*Od.* 1.24).

[427] Gibson notes, 2006, 111, a *double-entendre* with *cesserit*, the ends of the earth have not only surrendered, but retreated as Roman power extends still further. This could also apply to Statius' treatment of Bolanus. Just as 'he entered Thule', so Thule 'retreated'.

[428] *mandata* were the official orders from the emperor's secretariat controlled by the *ab epistulis*, cf. the role of Abascantus *magnum late dimittere in orbem / Romulei mandata ducis* (*to broadcast to the world at large the commands of the Roman prince* (Stat. *Silv*.5.1.86-87). For a discussion of *mandata* and other forms of communication between emperor and governors, cf. Millar 1982, 8 ff. The fact that Statius establishes a link between Vespasian, Bolanus and Thule automatically eliminates any connexion between Thule and the Claudian invasion. Silius shows more sense in casting Vespasian as the first of the Flavians to become involved in the total conquest of Britain, culminating in the Thule episode. Once Valerius Flaccus enters the melting pot the Flavian connexion with Scotland emerges and the *gens Iulia* becomes history. It is a pity that scholars still insist on introducing Claudius into an undoubtedly Flavian context. It is like attributing the D-Day invasion of 1944 to Lord Kitchener.

[429] There are curious contradictions in the imagery of Domitian as presented in Tacitus and as seen objectively. One might ask why Domitian would allow Agricola to achieve fame by reaching the western limit of the world. He might bathe in the reflected glory. It does tie in with Agricola's unusual length of governorship and the erection of the Richborough Monument. One might argue that the further away from Rome Agricola was, the less of a threat he would pose to the emperor. But this is not the impression that Tacitus gives. If Agricola perishes *at the very place where the world and nature ends* (*Agr.*33.6), it will be *his* decision, not the emperor's, and he will die for the Roman empire, not for Domitian. Thule is the ultimate challenge, and even if Agricola does not go there himself, he can add it to his *res gestae* (*achievements*). It is even possible that Domitian authorised the expedition with the proviso that Agricola was *not* to risk his life. But Tacitus would never admit to such.

[430] There would, in fact, have been no need for Statius to search for documentation; the achievement was famous in its own right and by now general knowledge. Perhaps after a decade Thule had lost its mystery, as I suggested earlier, and people were not too concerned about who got there first. Since Neil Armstrong landed on the moon in 1969, has it ever made the headlines? After the withdrawal of troops from Britain in AD 87, public interest at this time would have switched to the

longer around to state his case, while those who survived him held back through fear. The honest truth could never survive against a background of flatterers and informers. Agricola's retirement from the political scene and his own modest lifestyle, coupled with the inglorious achievements of Domitian's generals, gave Statius, ever ready to oblige the emperor and his entourage, the opportunity to misrepresent the past in order to bury the present. The *longaevus trucis incola terrae* (*Silv.* 5.2.143, *the aged native of a fierce land*) is more than a mentor to Crispinus. He is a nostalgic reminder of Roman glories which were notably absent during Domitian's reign. What Statius cunningly conceals is that the same old man would have witnessed Agricola's triumphs in northern Britain which were more impressive than those of Bolanus.[431] It would have been easy for Statius to treat Agricola's British successes as if they had never occurred. Perhaps he anticipated the approval of Domitian's intimates. What the poet had never intended in his flattery of Abascantus was for people to see the reality behind the façade. Triumphs in distant lands can always be traced back whatever the extent of the obfuscation.

There may be a hint of antipathy towards Agricola and his background in Statius' exaggerated description of Crispinus' ancestry, *no inglorious line of ancestors produced you from plebeian stock* (*Silv.* 5.2.15-16). This disguises the fact that Bolanus was the first of his family to hold a consulship; the distinguished lineage may have been on the mother's side.[432] But whom does the poet have in mind when he disparages equestrians with the boast that Crispinus is not *sanguine cretus turmali* (17-18, *sprung from equestrian blood*)? Although Agricola's father was a senator, his background was equestrian. One may compare Crispinus, <u>not</u> *obscurum proavis* (*undistinguished by your great-grandfathers*), with Tacitus' proud statement that both Agricola's grandfathers had been imperial procurators, which represented *equestris nobilitas* (*Agr.* 4.1, *the equestrian nobility*). Was Tacitus attempting to redress the balance? Statius is stressing a difference in *class*, and whether or not he is being a snob, a sycophant or a downright liar is immaterial; the written word would enable people to read into it whatever they wanted. A comparison between the grandfathers of Bolanus and Agricola would not be out of place in a context where one former governor is glorified at the expense of the other, and the fact that Crispinus had obtained a military tribunate at a much earlier age than Agricola would allow Statius the opportunity to take the comparison right back to its roots. Agricola and Statius were contemporaries, Agricola being the older, and although both men had different backgrounds, the likelihood is that influential people in Domitian's circle would have known them both.[433] It is even possible that Agricola may inadvertently have slighted Statius, or one might imagine Abascantus discussing with his staff confidential issues relating to Agricola's governorship—memoranda have a habit of springing leaks, especially when bad news is involved.[434] Whether the paths of the poet and the general ever crossed is debatable, but it is more probable that Statius was familiar with Agricola's achievements than vice versa. It is easier to digest genuine campaign details from the *Acta Diurna* than to choke on fictional scenarios from the *Thebaid*. The success at Mons Graupius would receive no notice among the poets who inflated Domitian's frontier campaigns to almost mythological

---

Danube.

[431] Bernstein 2007, 190 gives an interesting analysis of the relationship between Crispinus, Bolanus and the *anonymous Caledonian, whose configuration as a gentle and admiring preceptor obscures political realities, such as the possibility of native dissatisfaction with imperial rule.* This is a valid point and should be compared with Calgacus' tirade against Roman imperialism. Simply because Crispinus is a teenage orphan with no one to advise him is no reason for Statius to conjure up a Caledonian *deus ex machina* who was more likely to loathe the Romans for burning his land and enslaving his family.

[432] Cf. Gibson 2006, 182 who notes the vagueness of *tuorum* in *praecedente tuorum/agmine* (20-21, *preceded by the throng of your family*), and suggests that this is due to the need to suppress the mother's criminality, *if Crispinus' claims to distinguished ancestry did depend on his mother's lineage.* The alternative he offers is that Bolanus' antecedents had been senators, *but had not risen as high as the consulship.* Statius obviously had inside information, but his statement is too vague to admit of any conclusive interpretation.

[433] There was a certain degree of polarisation in Domitianic society. White 1975, 300 observes that *the society to which the Silvae were addressed had even less in common with Pliny's circle.* Tacitus and Pliny were good friends, but we do not know what views they shared on Statius and his patrons.

[434] Statius' wife, Claudia, was a very close friend of Priscilla, the wife of Abascantus. Priscilla had been very much involved in promoting her husband's career before the emperor. It would be interesting to know how much official business was taken home and discussed in bed. It is difficult to determine into which category of freedmen Tacitus puts Abascantus. Is he one of the *optimus quisque libertorum amore et fide, Agr.*41.4, *the best of the freedmen whose love and loyalty [spurred on the emperor]*? Or is he one of the *pessimi malignitate et livore* , (ibid.) *the worst whose spite and jealousy [towards Agricola...]*? If the latter, the ill-feeling would transmit itself to Statius.

proportions. Flattery and fiction replaced fact. One might easily classify Statius among those whom Tacitus describes as *pessimum inimicorum genus, laudantes* (*Agr.* 41.2, *the worst type of enemy, flatterers.*) They not only fawned on Domitian up until his demise in AD 96, but on anyone else whose friendship and patronage might give them a foothold on the social ladder.

Nobody, bar Tacitus, would comment on Statius resurrecting the dead at the expense of Agricola. For the Silver Age poets Agricola simply does not exist. He is merely a cog in the imperial mechanism, a name that means nothing except to his family, an official to be discarded and forgotten. Bolanus is exhumed as Vespasian's first governor of Britain, and dressed up as a successful one at that. Tacitus' riposte comes three years later when it was safe to speak freely. Poetic licence is now seen in its worst form. Bolanus, like Agricola, is no longer around to tell the truth; Crispinus had not even been born when Agricola assumed the governorship.[435] A quarter of a century had elapsed since the events which Statius alleges. It is not my intention to discredit Statius in all he says. It would be easy to accuse him of exaggeration because some of his potentially true statements have been expanded into that category. Poetic licence is the biggest insurance policy against potential criticism. But if Statius even in one instance attributes to Bolanus what should have been attributed to Agricola, what credence can we give to his other statements where both men were operating in the same area? Hopefully the archaeologists will provide us with some of the answers.

What does emerge among the Silver Age poets is that activities in Caledonia and the northern isles are seen as part of an ongoing campaign. This is balanced by the more realistic account we find in Tacitus. There is no more likelihood of Bolanus campaigning in Shetland than there is of a Shetlander (*incola Thyles,* Sil. *Pun.* 17. 417, *native of Thule*) driving a chariot at Mons Graupius—or an Orcadian sea-captain landing in Essex. It is in the light of Silius' phraseology here that Bolanus' activities should be assessed. Compare *incola Thyles* with Statius' *trucis incola terrae*.[436] Both poets are referring to the same barbarians and are describing the areas which covered Brigantia and southern Scotland. Where Silius has credited Vespasian, perhaps justifiably, with the achievements of Agricola whom, in the current political climate, the poet will not mention by name, Statius has transferred some of Agricola's achievements, with no justification, to the *res gestae* (*history*) of the *gens Vettia* (ie. the family of Bolanus). This is ironic, since, by alluding to the link between Domitian, Abascantus and the surrender of Caledonia, Statius has unconsciously acknowledged the role of Agricola. Flavian sycophants, like Martial, always inflated Domitian's operations against the Chatti or the Dacians.[437] They never directly mentioned the campaign in Britain.[438] No client with ambition would wish to compromise his position by highlighting successes in Britain—which in any case was so far away that good news could be easily suppressed if it conflicted with bad news from Germany or Dacia. This is why Tacitus is so determined to show the other side of the coin.

For a balanced picture of Bolanus we need to set Statius' account of his successes against Tacitus' criticisms (*Agr.* 8.1, 16.5) of his apparent inadequacies. Both writers are separate strands of the same

---

[435] By mishap, De la Bédoyère 2003, 80 claims that Crispinus served in his father's army during the war in Britain—which took place ten years before his birth. Instead of going back to the original source he followed Shotter's unfortunate observation, 1994, 22, that *a son of Vettius Bolanus...was involved in the establishment of forts.* Ironically, Shotter later adds, *if Statius' remarks about Bolanus' son are to be taken seriously* (28)—perhaps he confused Bolanus with Ostorius Scapula, whose son served under him in Britain (Tac. *Ann.* 12.31.4). Dalby 2000, 100 is equally at fault with his *bold young Roman, soon perhaps to take part in Agricola's northern adventure in Caledonia in the 80s.* An infant is hardly of an age to participate in a campaign, but at least he was alive at the time. Evans 2003, 258 states that *Britain looks like a lucky province for Crispinus' debut.* The fact that his father served there should not lead to this assumption about his son's destination, *lucky* or otherwise.

[436] The correspondence between the adjectives in *trucis terrae* and *feroci provincia* is reminiscent of the balance between *fama trux* and *fama ferox* (cf. above, ch. 4).

[437] Statius won the prize at the Alban Games of AD 90 for his now lost poems on Domitian's victories against the Germans and Dacians (*Silv.*4.2.66-67).

[438] Martial (*Epig.* 6.61.3-4) cites lines from the poet Pompullus which refer to the Usipians as being *fickle* and dissatisfied with Roman authority. This suggests the episode of the Usipian mutiny. It was bad news and would reflect adversely on Agricola's governorship. Martial was aware of the event; it was famous. Bad news always makes good reading and Domitian might privately have a good laugh at Agricola's expense, even if publicly it was another blow for imperial pride that Germans were causing aggravation from a different direction.

thread which leads to the emperor, hypocrisy.[439] Statius relies on a *nexus* of influential friends to scrape a living, and his flattery disguises a decent, albeit, misguided, talent.[440] His ultimate aim is to impress Domitian. Tacitus, like Agricola, is a career politician whose progress thrives under the emperor, while others die for speaking out against the regime.[441] Yet he is quite ready to denounce him on his demise.[442] It is hard to determine whether the poet or the historian deserves the greater censure. They were both opportunists. But which of the two is the most convincing writer? Statius can shelter under the umbrella of poetic licence, but there is no hiding-place for Tacitus. We learn as much from his silence as we do from his statements. The fact that Tacitus was closer to Agricola than Statius to Bolanus is more likely to raise doubts than to inspire confidence in the poet as a source. There is a difference between a son-in-law and a sycophant, and the truth lies somewhere between the two.

Tacitus, in his usual style, blends his contrasts in such a way that you are led to think the worst. Bolanus will always be remembered because of *inertia*[443] and lack of *auctoritas*, not because he was *innocens*.[444] Whatever had prompted Tacitus to suggest a weakness in the administration of a distinguished general, whether to redress the balance or to get his revenge, was unlikely to go down well with the *gens Vettia*, and it would be interesting to know how Crispinus, himself on the verge of a distinguished military career, would have reacted to such aspersions on his father's governorship.[445]

---

[439] Bastomsky 1985, 393 refers to Agricola's *hypocrisy in co-operation with a despised regime*. Dorey 1969, 6 suggests that *Tacitus distorted the account of events in chapters 39-44* to avert criticism, to present Agricola as a victim of Domitian rather than as a beneficiary of his favours. The policy of carrying out one's duty while avoiding confrontation is as applicable to Tacitus as it is to Agricola, cf. Martin 1994, 47.

[440] Dominik believes that the *Thebaid* contains cryptic messages unfavourable to Domitian, and in regard to the *Silvae* he says, 1994, 141, *the expressions of admiration and support for Domitian are so adulatory as to suggest their insincerity to a modern observer*. I think that he is right. Statius was an opportunist and a hypocrite, and the regime encouraged flattery

[441] Tacitus criticises those who *ambitiosa morte inclaruerunt* (*Agr.* 42.4 *achieved fame by an ostentatious death*) without any benefit to the state. What was it that irritated Tacitus? Was it their fame, their pretentiousness or their 'useless' gesture? There is an irony here. *Ambitiosus* can also mean *eager for glory*. It was *glory* that spurred Agricola on (cf. *Agr.* 5.3, 8.2, 3; 33.6, 41.1). At least the victims of the regime were honest.

[442] There is a certain irony in Agricola being destined for future recollection, and Domitian being officially erased from public records (*damnatio memoriae*). The curious fact is that Domitian, whether good or bad, features prominently in contemporary literature, whereas Agricola does not even rate a mention. Why no echo of him in Pliny or Suetonius? It is almost as if Agricola has been shunted into a separate compartment, shielded by Tacitus from the infections of a corrupt society and subsequently resurrected as a role model for would-be soldier-statesmen. It is equally ironical that if Agricola had been a notorious flop as a general he might have acquired notoriety in writers such as Juvenal. What is lacking is an objective source. If Tacitus' biography had not existed, and if Statius had written a panegyric on Agricola instead of Bolanus, would we have believed him ? There can be little doubt that Tacitus' comments on Bolanus were in consequence of the publication of the *Silvae* (A.R. Birley 1975, 154 n.95). Laederich 2001, 325 refers to Tacitus' description of Bolanus as *cruel* and a *présentation déformée*. He cites the latter's good qualities as listed in Statius without being aware that any poetic exaggeration is also a *présentation déformée*. Tacitus is not simply boosting the credentials of his father-in-law; he is restoring the balance. Statius' readership went beyond the circle of Pliny and Tacitus to the heart of the court. Once the old regime had been swept away, literary society would be receptive to balanced judgements. Tacitus' blinkered eulogy does not make him a bad historian any more than Statius' flattery makes him a bad poet. Posterity is the best judge. We remember Agricola the man, *posteritati narratus* (*Agr.* 46.4 *his story has been told for posterity*), but Statius had the same ambitions for Melior's tree (*Silv.*2.3.63, *ingenti forsan victura sub aevo* (*destined perchance to live for centuries*). In this instance posterity has made its judgement on both writers. How many people today read about Melior's tree ?

[443] Tacitus uses the word *inertia* later on (*Agr.* 41.3) in comparing Agricola's vigour, determination and expertise with the failure of the generals on the Danube frontier. But their *inertia* is coupled with terror. Tacitus never accuses Bolanus of being afraid. Statius' description suggests quite the opposite.

[444] Shotter 2004b, 23 quite rightly points out that the duration of his command until 71 *must suggest that his actions were regarded, at the least, as satisfactory*. A positive role for Bolanus should be assumed. Gorrichon 1974, 178, for once, was correct, *Vettius Bolanus fut peut-être moins inactif que ne le prétend Tacite*.

[445] The Vettii had sustained a dreadful period, during which Crispinus' mother had been condemned to death by Domitian for attempting to poison her son, possibly over an inheritance. The last thing they needed was posthumous aspersions on the abilities of the father. Perhaps this is why Tacitus mitigates his criticisms with phrases such as *innocens...et nullis delictis invisus* (*Agr.*16.5, *innocent and with no offences to make him hated*), which ironically contrasts with his wife. Whatever his military capabilities, his character was intact. Crispinus held a military tribunate at the unusually early age of 16. He has been identified with C. Clodius Crispinus, *consul ordinarius* in AD 113, probably having changed his *nomen* after adoption by a Clodius (thus A.R. Birley 1981, 65 n. 24, approved by Salomies 1992, 154). His older brother, Marcus, was consul in AD 111 The *gens Vettia* had a tradition of public service right through to the fifth century, cf. Kahlos 2002.

There is a distinct difference between the accounts of Bolanus in the *Agricola* and in the *Histories*. In the latter there is no criticism and no reference at all to Bolanus in the Cartimandua affair. The *Histories* were published c. AD 105 and it is quite conceivable that Tacitus may have mellowed by then. Perhaps Crispinus had erased the stain by an energetic career under Trajan. As for Tacitus' biography it is understandable to hoist Agricola on the shoulders of others. Their track records unfortunately have no one to offer any form of assessment to counter Tacitus' arguments. Consequently any allegation of *incuria vel intolerantia priorum* (*Agr*.20.1, *the indifference or intolerance of his predecessors*) becomes a fact. The concept of writing history *sine ira et studio* (*without anger and partiality*, *Ann*.1.1) does not mean that you cannot indulge in a little misrepresentation and is as valid in AD 98 as it was twenty years later. It should be remembered that this new freedom of speech did not restrict criticism solely to the emperor and his entourage. Everyone was now fair game, especially the dead, and people have long memories. With Bolanus, Statius and Domitian all departed no one would object if Tacitus was economical with the truth, especially when his literary predecessors had distorted or exaggerated it. It was simply a way of trumping Statius, and I doubt whether the *beatissimum saeculum* (*Agr*. 3.1, *the most fortunate age*) would look back on the poet with any sympathy. Yet poetic licence does not mean that Statius would totally misrepresent the military achievements of a deceased general. Tacitus may be deliberately overcompensating in his effort to set the balance right. Any assessment faces a dilemma. If Bolanus is misrepresented by the historian, there is a good chance that Trebellius before him and Cerialis after him are also given less credit than is due; unfortunately there were no poets to sing their praises. But if Bolanus is exaggerated by Statius, then Agricola's achievements go unrewarded.

One may assume that Tacitus was familiar with the contents of the *Silvae*,[446] and although Agricola had been dead five years by the time his biography was published there is no reason why the deceased should still not have his say. The speech which Tacitus composed for him at Mons Graupius contains one interesting comment: *finem Britanniae non fama nec rumore sed castris et armis tenemus* (*Agr*. 33.3, *our occupation of Britain's furthest limit is not unfounded talk or hot air; we hold it with arms and encampments*). *Fama* and *rumore* could well be a biting allusion to Statius' 'Caledonian' campaign of Bolanus. If Bolanus allegedly *entered Thule* he must have reached the *finem Britanniae*. But there are no *castra* to prove it. Agricola's statement rings clear about the camps *he* established at the end of the island and the expedition that *he* sent to Thule—it is now up to the archaeologists to locate the camps in question.

Tacitus' reference to *inertia erga hostes* (*Agr*.16.5, *inactivity with regard to the enemy*) does not tie in with Statius' heroic description.[447] The boast that Bolanus *grabbed a breastplate from a British king* reflects the old republican concept of protagonists representing their armies.[448] But it does not have to mean that the king was killed,[449] any more than Arviragus, who fell from his chariot,[450] or prove that

---

[446] I believe that Tacitus was also familiar with the *Thebaid*. Statius writes (10.8-9) *aegras/secernunt acies* (*they withdraw their exhausted lines*). In the *Codex Aesinas* fol.62 v. (*Agr*.36.3) we find the nonsensical *aegrādiu autstante*. I suggest that *E*'s exemplar read,

                     mi
nimenimequanriseapugnaerat
cumaegrādiuſuſtentanteſaciēſi
mulaequorumcorporibusimpel
lerentur

Enim is a dittographical error and the misplaced *facies* is really *aciē* (contraction for *aciem*). This evolves as *minime aequa nostris ea pugna erat, cum aegram diu sustentantes aciem simul equorum corporibus impellerentur* (*such combat was most disadvantageous to our men, since they had been maintaining an exhausted line for a long time and were being pushed on simultaneously by the bodies of the horses*. Anderson 1922, 137 was correct with *aequa nostris*; the verb *impellerentur* requires a subject. Fighting on uneven ground against charioteers is hardly what the Roman infantry needed. There is no alleged *slope* and no cavalry, cf. note 264 (no general, let alone Agricola, would ever allow his cavalry to fight on a hill). This part of the action (*meanwhile*) is on the *plain*; the horses belong to the chariots.

[447] Cf. Wellesley 1972, 130.

[448] This is another extravagant statement from Statius. A comparison with the winners of the *spolia opima* (*rich spoils*) is suggested here.

[449] There is no reference elsewhere to a king being killed or captured, which would surely have merited mention, cf. Stewart 2001, 386. Shotter 2004b, 23 believes that the king *certainly could have been Venutius or one of his allies*. Tacitus suggests that Venutius got the better of the Romans in the Brigantian War, *regnum Venutio, bellum nobis relictum* (*Hist.* 3.45.1,

Bolanus had a personal hand in it. Republican heroism rarely finds its parallel during the principate. Military commanders had more sense than to search out their counterparts. Tacitus does not tell us that Agricola had such close personal contact with the enemy.[451] The jousting between Agricola and Calgacus is verbal. In fact the prudence of Agricola may be firmly contrasted with the rashness of Alexander who regularly risked his life. All we can be sure of is that the weapons of an enemy king became a trophy: *haec dona deis, haec tela dicavit* (*Silv*.5.2.147 *these gifts, these weapons he dedicated to the gods*).[452] So how can there be *inertia* when Bolanus is actively involved in a war? It is even possible that Bolanus came too close for comfort and nearly lost his life. This may explain why he dedicated his own breastplate, perhaps as a thanksgiving present to the gods for having protected him. The suggestion of *inertia* may be the consequence of policy differences between Agricola and Bolanus,[453] or simply an attempt to boost the image of the *magni duces* whose predecessors fare badly by comparison (*Agr*.20.1). The reality, however, may have more to do with the reduction of the British garrison and the need to plug the gaps.[454]

Tacitus does not link Bolanus specifically to any campaigns beyond Brigantia. Bolanus had possibly two campaigning seasons to deal with Venutius and the Brigantes, sufficient time for forays into southern Scotland and the possible establishment of forts. But it would not suit Agricola's *curriculum vitae* for Tacitus to credit Bolanus with any initiatives. The advantage always lies with Tacitus; he knew from personal contact the details of Agricola's fort-building. What did Statius have to go on? *Fama* and *rumore*? I doubt that Bolanus' achievements were etched in the public memory so long after the event. The Civil War and the crushing of the Jewish revolt may have allowed the focus to switch to the west, even if the propaganda still perpetuated events in the east. But it would take a decade before the province reached headline status and numismatic recognition. The sad fact is that the masses would not be interested in either Bolanus or Agricola, as long as Domitian's *panem et circenses* (*bread and chariot races*) kept them quiet.[455] It is all well and good for Tacitus to claim that *poscebatur ore vulgi dux Agricola* (*Agr*.41.3, *there was popular clamour for Agricola to be appointed commander*). The reality is that no one really cared who would be the next general to *save his guts for Dacian vultures*.[456]

Statius' reference to Bolanus as establishing *late speculas castellaque longe* (*Silv*. 5.2.145 *watchtowers and forts far and wide*[457]) in Caledonia could be a description of the Gask Ridge system,

---

Venutius was left the kingdom, we were left with the war). This is as far as Tacitus takes him, and vague claims by Statius cannot be used as evidence of his later military activities in Caledonia. The fact that his name subsequently drops out of history is not proof of his death by 71 any more than Calgacus' defeat at Mons Graupius is proof of his capture or Cartimandua's rescue by the Romans is proof of altruism. The suggestion by Hanson/Campbell 1986, 83 that Statius' *poetic embroidery* is connected with the rescue of Cartimandua is hard to justify. Venutius, as Tacitus makes clear (*ibid.*), was motivated by his hatred for the Romans as much as by personal problems. He was not interested in what happened to his former wife. The course of events suggest that over the previous fifteen years, whether on his own initiative or more likely prompted by agencies further north, he had been planning to fill the role vacated by Caratacus. The irony lies in the peoples of Scotland envisaging a powerful nationalist leader in control of a buffer state to protect their interests, while the Romans had anticipated the same for themselves.

[450] Juv. *Sat*. 4. 125-6: *de temone Britanno/ excidet Arviragus* (*Arviragus will fall out of his British chariot*).

[451] Tacitus tells us that Agricola *aestuaria ac silvas ipse praetemptare* (*Agr*. 20.2 *reconnoitred estuaries and forests personally*). This does not mean contact with the enemy. Statius likewise attributes the same role to Bolanus, *iter praenosse timendum* (*Silv*. 5.2.41 *knew in advance the dangerous route*). No general of any quality would rely totally on information garnered by his scouts, especially if the terrain was dangerous.

[452] See Appendix 3 for numismatic depiction of trophies.

[453] McCullough 2007, 63 goes a little too far in describing Agricola's position as *deference to a bad leader*. Policies which *did not encourage proactiveness* (62) are not indicative of *bad* leadership. Bolanus is not a *bad* leader simply because Agricola does not get his own way.

[454] Burn 1969, 46; A.R. Birley 2005, 61 f.

[455] Cf. Ogilvie 1967, 293.

[456] Juv. *Sat*. 4.111-2, of Cornelius Fuscus, referring to his death in Dacia in AD 86.

[457] Gibson 2006, 249 replaces the standard reading *late* (MS *vitae*) with Davies' suggestion *victor* (followed by a semi-colon), to be construed with *adfari* (*to address*). I do not see how such a distortion could occur. *Late* is a simple corruption from *vitae*: *uitae*→ *latae* (cf. M's *latae* for *late* in Tac. *Hist*. 3.60.1)→*late. u* and *l* are easily confused (cf. *praelecta/praeuecta*). *Late* goes well with *longe* (*far and wide*, cf. *longe saltus lateque vacantis*, Virg. *Georg*. 3.477, *pastures far and wide untenanted*) and creates a neat symmetry, sandwiching the military installations. To say that *very little is added to the sense* is poor justification for replacing it and then translating it as if it were still there, *far and wide* (?). *Longe* by itself

although no one as yet seems to know what its function was or who really initiated it.[458] Whom were the Romans watching, and why? Statius presents Bolanus addressing his *turmae* (*squadrons, Silv.* 5.2.144), while Tacitus, without mentioning Bolanus, refers to *cohortes alaeque* (*cohorts*[459] *and wings [cavalry regiments], Hist.* 3.45.1). There is no inconsistency here. The Brigantes appear to have been targeted by auxiliary units, which in the event were just as ineffective as they had been in the earlier campaign under Didius Gallus. In any case, the Brigantes posed intermittent problems over the next decade. There is no mention of legions. If they were a handful for Bolanus as well as for Trebellius, one can understand their absence in Statius. It is the legions, not the auxiliaries, whose indiscipline is stressed in the biography. Only in the *Histories* (1.60) do the auxiliaries subsequently join in. Now that Agricola had taken over the Twentieth legion, which had been embroiled in a mutiny, what better chance for him to test his capabilities? A legion had to be based on the Welsh borders, where the natives were clearly a threat, but garrison duty there was a thankless task. No wonder Agricola was upset. The *otium* (*inactivity*) of the troops, *adsuetus expeditionibus* (*Agr.*16.3, *accustomed to campaigning*), had already caused one mutiny. Tacitus disguises the fact that Agricola faced the same prospect. The historian is too glib about Agricola's performance, which reeks of rhetoric rather than reality. One would be inclined to suspect that he faced the same precarious situation which had greeted Drusus and Germanicus in AD 14. The problems which gave rise to the German and Pannonian mutinies were exactly the same as those which alienated *legio* XX: an enemy lurking nearby, barrack-room bullying (*petulantia castrorum*), disputes over pay and conditions. No wonder *miles lasciviret* (*ibid., the soldiers were running riot*), cf. *Ann.*1.16, *lascivire miles*.[460]

Tacitus is patronising towards Bolanus. He is *guiltless* and *well-liked* in comparison with Trebellius, who was not. But Bolanus lacked authority and charisma, which Agricola apparently possessed. How else could he have controlled a recalcitrant legion? Tacitus gives the impression that Bolanus is blocking Agricola's path to glory.[461] The new governor would allow Agricola's merits to have scope for display (*Agr.* 8.2). Agricola's self-restraint under Bolanus is highlighted by Tacitus to provide a contrast with Roscius Coelius' mutinous attitude towards Trebellius.[462]

After balancing the two contrasting versions in whose favour do we weigh the scales? Some may accuse Tacitus of bias, others may accuse Statius of poetic licence. Gibson suggests that it might be *a revisionist attempt to place more emphasis on an earlier figure in the history of Roman campaigns in Britain*.[463] Agricola was too recent a figure. Neither Bolanus nor Agricola deserves total credit, and Cerialis, who bridges the two, must have a powerful say in all this. Perhaps once again archaeology may help us to resolve the problem. I believe that Bolanus *was* operating in the Scottish Lowlands, as Statius claims, and that these activities may have been given less credit than they deserved, due to exaggerated boasts that he had reached Thule. I also believe that his presence in the area was, at least initially, to isolate the Brigantes from any support from the peoples of the Scottish Lowlands. The Brigantes were a permanent menace, a dormant volcano ready to erupt at any time. You cannot put a

---

means *in the distance, far*. The aged Caledonian must have had far better eyesight than Crispinus (*aspicis*, 146, *Do you see them* ?), if he could point out things *in the distance*; or is this poetic licence ?

[458] The only military watchtowers in Caledonia at such an early date belong to the Gask Ridge system. This is a rare instance of Statius approaching the truth. But there is no reason why Statius should have not attributed to Bolanus what was really due to Cerialis. Gibson (249) unfortunately follows Hanson in assigning an Agricolan date to the construction of the Gask Ridge watchtowers—Woolliscroft /Hoffmann 2006, 189 have now made a strong case for them pre-dating Agricola.

[459] The cohorts would be auxiliary units, cf. Saddington 1970, 98.

[460] The parallels are striking enough to cast doubts on the role of Roscius Coelius. There is enough evidence to suggest that he was originally swept along by a torrent he could not control. Mutinies normally originate at grass roots. The *mutatus princeps* (*Ann.* 1.16 *change of emperor*) provides the opportunity.

[461] The point that Tacitus makes about Agricola as *eruditus utilia honestis miscere* (*Agr.* 8.1 *taught to combine interest with propriety*) is seized upon by Bastomsky 1985, 391 as evidence that Tacitus criticises Agricola and he suggests that it *does have a connotation of deception about it and thus becomes a censure of him*. To assume a pejorative nuance is to do Agricola less than justice. Who *taught* Agricola to behave this way? It was not spontaneous. It could well have been Bolanus. There is nothing to suggest self-interest. Why not the interest of the subjects, or of Rome?

[462] Comparisons between Agricola and previous governors lead McGing 1982, 18 to unnecessary generalisations. Of Bolanus he writes, *there is a clear, but implicit, contrast between the lazy governor and the enthusiastic young legionary commander*. This is too simplistic. Bolanus was not generally lazy; he is simply criticised by Tacitus for *inertia* in dealing with the enemy. There may have been good grounds for a policy of inaction.

[463] Gibson 2006, 248.

cap on a volcano nor can you cut off the force that feeds it by building a wall against it, but that is precisely what the Romans had to do in the end.

APPENDIX 5

CALEDONIUS : ALLUSION AND ILLUSION

In his recent dissertation on Valerius Flaccus T.J. Stover makes the following emphatic, but unfortunately ill-conceived, statement: *The use of the adjective 'Caledonius' proves nothing, since it is clearly an exaggeration intended to flatter Vespasian.*[464] He continues: *searching for an event whereby Caledonia may properly have been 'in the news', and using this event to date Valerius' hyperbolic praise of the emperor is misguided.*[465] But *who* is misguided? I see no *exaggeration* nor anything which could be described as *hyperbolic*. We are not dealing with a social climber like Statius. Valerius had nothing to gain either by *flattery* or by *exaggeration*.[466] As D'Espèrey pointed out, he *was not a fawning court poet*.[467] Stover seems to be unaware that Agricola's invasion of Caledonia should be dated to AD 79, not 80, and that Vespasian was *alive* at the start of it and actually initiated it. Hence *Caledonia* was 'in the news' and the sarcastic criticism levelled at Smallwood falls on stony ground.[468] He is equally unfamiliar with the numismatic evidence offered by Mattingly in support of successes in Britain.[469] To rule out Agricola and his immediate predecessors in the context of the prologue is self-defeating. *Caledonius* should be taken at face value. A knowledge of the history of Roman Britain in the second half of the first century might not go amiss.[470] These allegations are the latest in a long line of misconceptions which can be traced back to Momigliano and beyond.

Scholars, working on the Silver Age poets, have spilled too much ink in trying to explain away the significance of the epithet *Caledonius*. This may be attributed in the main to a failure to understand the background and chronology of military and naval operations in Britain during the Flavian period from AD 69 to 83. There is a tendency among some literary critics to work in compartments, specialising in their own fields, clouding the major issues in pretentious language. Often they are unaware, and more often ignorant, of what is happening around them. Archaeological, let alone numismatic or epigraphical, evidence seldom appears in their notes and commentaries. Historians provide cross-references. This should be reciprocated. The need for interdisciplinary co-operation is something I have stressed before.[471] Without an awareness or acknowledgement of the role of other disciplines

---

[464] Stover 2006, 36 f.

[465] I see no reference to *Caledonia* in Diodorus, as Stover claims, 2006, 37 n.63.

[466] Strand 1972, 26: *it should be noted that the introduction to the Argonautica is rather temperate and restrictive in respect of adulation...Also this fact is in accordance with the impression we get of Vespasian's personality and his attitude towards excessive flattery.* Likewise Kleywegt 2005, 14: *his flattery of the emperor is relatively sparing.*

[467] D'Espèrey 1986, 3075, *Valerius n'est pas un poète courtisan, mais Vespasien ne dédaignait visiblement pas cette sorte d'hommage,* cf. Syme 1929, 136 *Valerius was not begging for his bread*

[468] Stover 2006, 236: *apparently it is more 'natural' to flatter a dead man than a living one.*

[469] H. Mattingly 1930, lxxi. The irony here is that Mattingly correctly alluded to successes in Britain, while putting them into an incorrect chronological sequence. This can be a trap for the unwary researcher who does not see the broader historical context. One has only to note the false descriptions in commercial coin catalogues whose compilers often lack the expertise to make a valid judgement or apply a correct reference. See Appendix 3.

[470] For an up-to-date and succinct account of Flavian operations in northern Britain I would recommend Shotter's website article, *Cerialis, Agricola and the Conquest of Northern Britain.*

[471] Cf. Hoffmann 2004, 151 and 162. Her article does not measure up to the demands of its title. An uncritical summary of the textual tradition of the *Agricola*, discussed authoritatively by others elsewhere (cf.note 78), leads nowhere, while the comments on the literary sources for the first century show little evidence of what the sources actually involve. She has made one valid point, *what is lacking in archaeology is serious analysis of the text itself* (156). I assume, indeed I hope, that the author will favour us with her expertise and remedy this deficiency. The absence of a classical background, especially in the field of philology, can lead astray both the historian and the archaeologist. Burn 1953b, 130 in reference to an unnamed German scholar informs us that *scholarship which ignores archaeology can so easily make itself ridiculous.* His argument can work both ways, except that the archaeologist/historian does not *ignore* classical scholarship; he/she in many cases is not conversant with it. James 2002, 27 uses his own case to produce a somewhat jaundiced view. But he is correct on one point. In referring to the study of the Roman military he writes (35), *it is impossible....for any one scholar to master the theory, methodology, exponentially expanding literature and data-sets of all the disciplines.* But it is essential for a scholar, whether classicist, historian or archaeologist to master the basics. A film director may be excused for calling Agricola an emperor, but it is inexcusable for an archaeologist (Bradley 2007, 2) to say that *the emperor Agricola was so anxious to subjugate Orkney* and then to cite Cunliffe to put the circumnavigation in 85. This example reverses Burn's argument; archaeology which ignores scholarship can so easily make itself ridiculous. Scholarship requires a return to original sources, not a reliance on popular coffee-table fiction.

which provide the historical background to literary allusions Classical scholars run the risk of having their theories shredded. Anyone familiar with Livy's *History of Rome* knows that, unless the different parts of the body work together, the outcome is terminal.

We may now turn to the origin of *Caledonius* in Latin epic poetry:

> ...*vaga cum Tethys Rutupinaque litora fervent*
> *unda Caledonios fallit turbata Britannos*

When the tides of the Ocean and the shores of Richborough are seething, the stormy waves are not heard by the Caledonian Britons.

Lucan, *BC* 6. 67-8

Lucan began his sixth book on the *Civil War* shortly before Nero imposed his publishing ban in AD 65.[472] The adjective *Caledonius* (and *Rutupinus*) makes its first appearance here in Latin literature, but it must have been in existence already for Lucan to use it.[473] As Steele pointed out long ago, Lucan added the adjective to Virgil's *Britannos*.[474] He notes that Valerius Flaccus' use *shows the widening of geographical knowledge*. Caledonia, he adds, *can only be said to have widened with further advances into the northern regions under the Flavian governors*. What a pity that no one took him seriously! The use of *Caledonius* in four Silver Age epic poets must surely refer to the same area, i.e. *northern* Britain. Lucan begins the tradition and Silius Italicus ends it. Lucan would have been familiar with events in Britain, especially since the province had been made headline news by the Boudican revolt—which, in Dio's view, Seneca, Lucan's uncle, may have helped to provoke by suddenly calling in his loans to the British elite.[475]

At the time when Lucan inserted this adjective into his poem Petronius Turpilianus had restored the infrastructure of the shattered province and Trebellius Maximus, Seneca's erstwhile consular colleague, was in his third year of office, no doubt fully briefed on the possibilities of trouble in the north, now that the south was secure. The Boudican interlude had been merely a 'blip' in Roman plans for the conquest of the north, where the Brigantes, unreliable and volatile, had steadfastly held their ground for a decade. Further north were the Scottish Lowlands and beyond them Caledonia proper. I believe that the Brigantian problems peaked in the summer of AD 54,[476] and by the time of Claudius' death the 'horse had well and truly bolted'. With Didius Gallus committed to campaigning in South

---

[472] Dio 62.29.4. Rose 1966, 390 notes the rapidity of Lucan's production, the entire epic compressed into less than two years, AD 64-5.

[473] Page 1908, 38 f. refers to this adjective in Lucan's context as *a literary variation for Britain without special reference to the actual place*. The misinterpretation of *Caledonius* by scholars is bad enough without *Rutupinus* being dragged into the same net. Page obviously had not looked at the whole line.

[474] Steele 1930, 337; Virg. *Ecl.* 1.66..

[475] Dio 62.2.1. He refers to Seneca's *hope of receiving a good rate of interest*. The issue is whether the loans were forced upon the Britons against their will, *akousin*, as the MS reads or at their request (*aitousin*), an alternative emendation. The fact that the loans are not mentioned by Tacitus does not mean that Dio, a regular distorter of the truth, is exaggerating in this instance, although it is unlikely that Seneca was the sole offender (cf. Griffin 1984, 226). Seneca's loan probably dates from AD 49 on his return from exile in Corsica. This would coincide with the establishment of the *colonia* and the financial burden faced by the British elite, especially the Trinovantes, in maintaining the Imperial Cult. It is also possible that Seneca's 'investment portfolio' extended to Cartimandua in AD 51. This would have given him a personal interest in Brigantian affairs. The degree of usury and investment in Britain by private speculators in Rome in order to fund 'home-improvement' schemes may have been considerable. The *negotiatores* (businessmen, bankers) who practised in London (Tac. *Ann.* 14.33.1) were only one end of the strings which were pulled by high-ranking personalities. It is only when the situation becomes critical that the 'big boys', like Seneca, are unmasked. Tacitus (*Ann.* 13.42.4) puts into the mouth of Suillius some bitter accusations against Seneca: *Italy and the provinces were sucked dry by his limitless usury*. Enforced loans and high interest rates were not confined to private individuals; they were part of the regular official 'extortion racket' in Britain (*Agr.* 19.4) before Agricola took over the governorship.

[476] Richmond 1954, 50 sets the start of the Brigantian problems in AD 57. This is far too late. It is somewhat surprising that in an article devoted to Cartimandua there is not a single reference to Didius Gallus. Webster 1970, 192 suggests that *when Nero succeeded in AD 54, the position was probably still unstable*. In his footnote he cites Seneca's reference to the Brigantes. They were certainly topical.

Wales we have a scenario similar to that which faced Paulinus on the eve of the Boudican revolt. A pointless partisan struggle for power was not what the Romans wanted. Brigantia required stability, even if only for the short term. Then, after the client status terminated with the death of its queen, the Romans would step in and Venutius would find himself in the same situation as was to face Boudica later on. Before the end of the year the policy for Britain was in the hands of Nero's advisers, Seneca and Burrus, the latter an old soldier, the former a Stoic philosopher whose interpretation of the 'Brotherhood of Man' was that some brothers should be more equal than others.[477] How could he morally reconcile official government policy on Britain with his own vested interests?

Claudius had weaknesses which to this day have unfairly relegated him to the status of a caricature. Seneca, whose career, according to the sources, embraced the roles of chief adviser, philosopher, politician, adulterer, child-minder, usurer and pimp, was also a part-time comedian whose *Satire on the Late Emperor* did more for establishing his reputation among young undergraduates than anything else he ever wrote.[478] This satire contains a reference to the Brigantes,

> *ille Britannos ultra noti*
> *litora ponti*
> *et caeruleos scuta† Brigantas*
> *dare Romuleis colla catenis*

he ordered the Britons beyond the shores of the known sea and the blue-shielded† Brigantes to give their necks to Roman chains

Sat. 12.3, ed. Roncali

Every schoolchild knows that the ancient warriors painted their bodies with blue dye. But the concept of *shields* painted blue beggars belief.[479] Julius Caesar exaggeratedly attributes the application of blue dye to *all* the Britons (*BG* 5.14.3), although his contact was limited to the south-east. There are two points to note about Seneca's lines, firstly the *Britons* are not wearing war-paint, secondly the

---

[477] Suillius (Tac. *Ann.* 13.42.4) sums it up nicely: *by what rules of philosophy had he acquired within four years of royal favour, 400,000,000 sesterces*?

[478] This production probably appeared at the time of the *Saturnalia* in AD 54—I have cited it under the MS title to avoid being drawn into the debate on the meaning of *Apocolocyntosis*.

[479] I do not subscribe to the current texts. *Woad* is used for painting people. Why would they want to paint their shields? Caesar is quite clear that the Britons used blue dye to make themselves look more terrifying. What sort of terror does a *blue shield* instil? This absurdity was noted in the 16th century by Buchanan 1582, 2.45. The oft cited example from Ovid (*Met.*9.307), *flava comas* (*yellow-haired*), is hardly a parallel. A shield is not part of a body. Eden 1984, 134 points out that '*scuta' is exceptional, but not impossible.* I think it is not just implausible but ludicrous. *caeruleos* refers, according to Roncali 1990, 20 in her *apparatus*, '*to the colour of their skin*'. When this adjective is used to describe people, it invariably refers to their skin. So why *shields*? Scholars have never been happy with this. Suggested readings have ranged from the metrically impossible—*cute, Scotobrigantas*—the latter concocted by Scaliger to distinguish the British Brigantes from those in Spain and Gaul (cf. Bernays 1855, 138 f.), the palaeographically impossible (*serva, victa*), the illogical (*curta*: what benefit would the Romans derive from putting *broken necks* in chains?) and the over-salacious (*scorta,* harlots). The Brigantes were a client monarchy, a protectorate of Rome. Cartimandua, as Frere suggests, 1987, 54, had probably thrown in her lot with the Romans as early as AD 43. Their uprising had been crushed by Ostorius, but they 'refused to lie down'. Their relations with Rome fluctuated with the mood of Venutius. But technically they enjoyed a security which others lacked. Seneca's joke is in Claudius treating as prisoners of war natives who had been guaranteed safety under the original terms of the treaty with Cartimandua. Other Britons had been forced to submit to Claudius, the Brigantes were protected. I would suggest changing *scuta* to *tuta* (*protected, safe*). As already mentioned, *c* and *t* are indistinguishable in minuscule, and the *codex optimus* from St.Gall probably derives, like the *Agricola*, from Fulda. Continuous script produces *caeruleostutabrigantas*. Dittography produces a superfluous *s*. The scribe would automatically link *shields* with natives wearing war-paint. The irony lies in natives of a client state being forced to submit *their safeguarded persons* to Roman chains. Although grammatically *tuta colla* would apply to the Britons also, the sense requires that *tuta* be treated as a *zeugma* and be applied to the Brigantes, i.e. he forced the Britons to submit to the might of Rome, and the Brigantes who were protected by it. It is also possible that Seneca added this line later, prior to publication; its omission would not alter the sense of ignorant natives being forced to submit to a nincompoop. The Brigantes had become seriously topical in 54 and their actions may have impinged on Seneca's financial investments. The juxtaposition of *caeruleos* and *tuta* is also ironic. The protection of Rome should guarantee peace, not provoke war. The neck represents that part of the person which bears the yoke and is virtually a synecdoche for *se* (*themselves*). This is merely a suggestion. Scholars may be impressed by blue shields. I am not, and I doubt that the Romans would have been.

Brigantes are *not* Britons.⁴⁸⁰ This implies that at the time Seneca was writing there was peace in the south-east, following the conquest, when Plautius and Ostorius had created the first British province (Tac. *Agr.* 14.1), while those Brigantes now alienated from Rome by Venutius, had donned their war-paint, which rendered them indistinguishable from the tribes further north. Is there any difference between a *caeruleus Brigas* and a *caerulus incola Thyles*? The peoples of Scotland were not called *Picts* for nothing. The Brigantes are being lumped together with the Caledonians, as if they were *Caledonii Britanni*. This would not be surprising if their northern limits actually stretched into Scotland. This is the earliest recorded reference to the Brigantes and, although satirical, is significant. Tacitus may fill in the details in a haphazard and garbled sort of way, but he was writing fifty years later and would have known less about these natives than Didius Gallus or Seneca did at first hand. After all, Agricola, like Lucan, was still a schoolboy when these events occurred, and Tacitus had only just been born.

Whatever policy of containment Didius put into effect would never prevent the Brigantes from receiving support from Scotland, and *rapprochement* for Rome with a divided community was never an option once the nationalists gained the upper hand. Unfortunately for the Romans not all the Brigantes conformed to the stereotypes to be found in Seneca; there were those who knew from the very start that they were being 'taken for a ride'. Some Brigantes were proud and nationalistic, others were greedy and opportunist. The breakdown of a marriage is an excuse for, not the real cause of, internal dissension. The Brigantes had always been pulled in two directions from the moment the Romans first appeared.

So where do the Britons of Caledonia fit into this jigsaw? We need to examine more closely the two crucial lines which many scholars have frequently referred to without, as will be seen, having any idea of their relevance. Duff's translation (1928, 309), *Britons of the North*, clearly passed unheeded. It is obvious what Lucan is saying. The Ocean extends from the English Channel to the Scottish Firths, but the Caledonians are so far away that they are unaware of what is happening in the south. Whether Lucan was specifying a particular ethnic group or simply generalising about northern Britain is immaterial; Duff, for once, was correct.

Two points should be made clear. Firstly, the Romans had established a base at Richborough in AD 43.⁴⁸¹ Lucan would have known that right up to his day *Rutupiae* was the entry point for goods, merchants and dignitaries arriving from the continent.⁴⁸² Secondly, Didius Gallus, would have been aware that the anti-Roman elements among the Brigantes were receiving full sympathy from the as yet 'uncontaminated' nations of the Scottish Lowlands.⁴⁸³ He had actually foreseen that 'if push came to shove', any vacuum would be filled by reinforcements from the north. Brigantian interests coincided with those of its northern neighbours.⁴⁸⁴ Geographical parameters are no barrier to commercial, social

---

⁴⁸⁰ Rouse's translation, 1919, 398, reflects the difference: *the Britons beyond in their unknown seas, blue-shielded(?) Brigantians too*. Likewise Waltz's French version, 1934, 13, *il força les Bretons...ainsi que les Brigantès*. Weinreich's German translation, 1923, 145, solves the problem by omitting *Brigantes* altogether. Braund 1984,5 refers to *Britons and the Brigantes in particular*. This is not what the Latin says. The two are separate. Adding *in particular* is an attempt to square the circle. The issue is trying to explain the division and accounting for why the Brigantes are covered in war-paint and the Britons are not. The role of Venutius here is irrelevant. Where Braund is correct is in his reference to Brigantes in the mid-fifties.

⁴⁸¹The point made by Haverfield 1907, 105, that *there is plainly no reference to a land-locked harbour* is completely pointless. What interest would that be to Lucan? At least Haverfield acknowledged a *contrast between England and Scotland*.

⁴⁸² Cf. note 258. The adjective *Rutupinus* derives from the noun *Rutupiae*. This noun form is found only in Ammianus (cf.note 151), and since Ammianus borrowed heavily from Tacitus, the likelihood is that it occurred in the missing books of Tacitus' *Annals* which covered the Claudian invasion. Lucan must have known the noun form. Lucan's knowledge extends to a description of British osier boats (cf.n.11) operating in the Channel and the North Sea.

⁴⁸³ The armed forces who invaded Cartimandua's kingdom in AD 54 (Tac.*Ann.*12.40.3) came from outside Brigantia, clearly from southern Scotland. This was repeated in AD 69 (Tac.*Hist.* 3.45.2 cf. Frere 1987, 102 n.1). Wellesley 1975, 93 adds his own imagination to the second intervention: Venutius *summoned all the wild men from the north and from the heights*. So for fifteen years the natives of the Scottish Lowlands showed more than a passing interest in what was happening on their southern borders. I do not accept Richmond's argument, 1954, 50, that Venutius and Cartimandua ruled separate cantons and that reinforcements came from within Brigantia. There is no evidence in Tacitus to support this. Salway's suggestion, 1981, 108, that the reinforcements may have been a *war band in exile* is somewhat non-committal.

⁴⁸⁴ *Quod nobis praevisum* (Tac. *Ann.*12.40.3, *we had foreseen this*).

or political links,[485] and where borders may be assumed by the location of mountains and rivers, it would be only natural that peoples should share common values and aspirations.[486] This would become more apparent when faced with the same enemy and freedom was at stake. Because the southern peoples had succumbed to Roman influences, there was no reason why the northern ones should follow suit.[487] The Lowland peoples, in company with those across the Forth-Clyde isthmus, realised that they would be the next victims of Roman aggression; it was only a matter of time—as in fact it turned out. It would be naïve to assume that the natives of Scotland were unaware of Rome's ultimate objectives. *Once southern Britain*, as Braund neatly puts it, *became familiar, Caledonia (and even beyond) became the object of imperialist desire*.[488] The 'domino effect' always starts with an initial push, but the push can come from either direction. Buffer zones are so called because they absorb impact.[489] But if they crumble, the shock may be felt on both sides. Brigantia had been destabilised in a power struggle. The death of Claudius turned a trickle into a torrent. Instability is not what the Romans would have wanted. Tribal factions could be exploited from the north as well as from the south. Brigantia was the rope in a tug-of-war.

Lucan's point is significant. Why would he introduce *Caledonios* unless it had a relevance to events occurring in the principate of Nero? He is not deliberately trying to be clever by incorporating it into Latin poetry for the first time, despite the fact that a polysyllabic adjective looks impressive in a hexameter line and sounds even more impressive and exotic when recited before an appreciative audience.[490] To assume it to be a gratuitous insertion is to give Lucan less than his due. He was doing more than simply filling in a space. I have no doubt that Caledonians featured prominently in the topics for discussion (*suasoriae* and *controversiae*) in the type of school which Lucan attended as a boy in Rome, and which promoted rhetorical themes. What went on in the northern limits of the Roman Empire would have been as fascinating to Roman youth as events in darkest Africa would have been to its British counterpart in Victorian times. Mixing with the elite of Rome in his youth, he would almost certainly have known about Didius Gallus and could well have met Trebellius through his uncle's connexions.[491] By employing the emotive *Caledonios* Lucan was putting *contemporary* history into a poetic setting. Lucan had good grounds for his use of *Caledonios*, and this started the tradition in which the word would have equally *contemporary* relevance in the later epic poets.

The focal point of all the misconceptions on the use of *Caledonius* is Momigliano, whose edicts proved as fatal to Lucan's successors as Nero's were to Lucan. His 'house of cards' terminates with this pronouncement: *it disposes of any theory that takes 'Caledonians' in Flavian sources to allude distinctly and truthfully in every instance to the territory north of the Forth-Clyde line*.[492] The

---

[485] The discovery at Birrens, in Dumfriesshire, of a statuette dedicated to *Dea Brigantia* (*RIB* 2091; Toynbee 1962, 157) is significant, despite the points raised by Breeze/Dobson 1987, 46, who quite rightly are at a loss to explain the function of the outlying forts, *if this territory is not Brigantian*. See also Mann/Breeze 1987, 89: *The possibility that the northern fringes of Brigantia lay north of the Solway cannot be ruled out*.

[486] Tacitus was aware that the Roman policy of 'divide and conquer' blossomed on the self-interest of native communities. In AD 83 the Caledonians united, *docti commune periculum concordia propulsandum* (*Agr*.29.3, *they had learned a lesson— that they had to stick together to avert the danger which threatened them all*

[487] Ogilvie 1967, 178, commenting on Tacitus' distinction between vanquished Britons and *the rest*, includes the Brigantes among *the rest*. The speech which Tacitus puts into the mouth of Calgacus draws attention to the Brigantes, albeit confusing them with the Iceni (*Agr*. 31.4). I hardly think, *pace* Ogilvie 1967, 260, that this was a mistake by Tacitus. Calgacus knew that the Brigantes were the closest tribe to Caledonia and added the sensational distortions to show what could be done. This is not *boastfulness and inaccuracy*. It is good propaganda and good leadership. There would be no point in Tacitus depicting Calgacus as an unworthy and guileless opponent.

[488] Braund 1996, 11.

[489] *Their proper function was precisely to save the employment of the Roman army on peace-keeping duties in remote areas*, Wellesley 1975, 93. Richmond 1954, 52 made a valid point that *if the Brigantes could have been converted into a strong and stable buffer state...Rome would have been saved the great expense and effort of occupying northern Britain*. But would the Romans have been satisfied with anything less than total conquest?

[490] The syllabic values of this adjective restrict *Caledonius* to the position of second word in a hexameter line. It occurs eleven times in Latin poetry and always as *second* word, just as Thule always occurs as *last* word. This may be due as much to tradition as to metrical constraints. Rivet/Smith 1979, 288 note that the correct form is *Calidonius*, as used by Pliny, but that the poetic form took precedence in general usage because it fitted the metre.

[491] *It is not unlikely that the two were friends*, A.R.Birley 2005, 54.

[492] Momigliano 1950, 42.

stipulation that not *in every instance* does the reference apply is a convenient escape clause which allows the author 'to have his cake and eat it'.[493] And why should any Flavian sources distort the truth? In fact, why start with the Flavians? There should be some mention here of the reference in Lucan which began the whole poetic tradition. An argument cannot be supported without a collation of *all* the sources. Why no mention of the Caledonian campaign of Cerialis, alluded to by Pliny, which I referred to earlier? Why no reference to Mattingly's *Coins of the Roman Empire in the British Museum*, where corroborative evidence might have been found? He would obviously be unaware of the archaeological discoveries, made in the last thirty years, which may support Pliny's claims. His misguided arguments have unfortunately influenced later generations of scholars who have taken them as gospel and could not see beyond their own blinkered vision. Scholarship is a continuously evolving process, and yet half a century of evolution still persists in producing its quota of dinosaurs. Momigliano's *DNA* is unmistakable and litters the notes of the gullible. *Simple truth can take a long time to percolate*, but it gets through in the end.[494]

In order to substantiate the usage of *Caledonius* in Valerius Flaccus and Silius Italicus scholars looked back to Lucan as the starting-point for their misguided theories. But they failed to note the contrast that Lucan was emphasising. Lefèvre, blindly following Momigliano, criticises Smallwood for failing to grasp what he himself does not understand, and claims that Lucan's *Caledonia* is a generalisation for *Britain*.[495] Spaltenstein likewise follows suit, claiming that *Caledonius* equates with *Britannus*.[496] Can anything be more illogical than Lucan repeating himself? His mountain of irrelevant examples is built on a lost cause. Could Lucan have made it any clearer? Richborough is *south* and Caledonia is *north*.[497] To claim that *Caledonius* is merely *evocative of England* will certainly not endear him to the Scots.[498] It is a pity that he did not pursue his own suggestion, made in his commentary at *Pun.* 3.598, where he was halfway to the truth. Kleywegt falls into the same trap, claiming that Valerius Flaccus is as vague as Lucan.[499] There is nothing vague about Lucan's sense of direction in his use of *Caledonios*. At least vagueness is better than exaggeration. The addiction to Lucan unfortunately sucks in Río Torres-Murciano who in support of *Caledonius* in Valerius Flaccus observes, *the use of 'Caledonius' for 'Britannicus' may be inspired by Lucan*.[500] So up comes the *British Briton* again! He ignores the reality of the Thule-Caledonia link in Silius Italicus and replaces it with the suggestion that it is *inspired by Argonautic verses*. Such *inspiration* we can well do without. This is a case of one myth replacing another, an illusion based an allusion. The only true parallel which may be adduced is that both Jason and Agricola had reached areas previously regarded as inaccessible.

Such then are the shaky foundations of the edifice which houses Lucan's *Caledonios*. Lucan and his successors would have relished the thought that so much could be conjured up by so many out of so little. More names could be added to this list of mythographers, but I would rather suggest alternative routes for others to follow than impose my own views. I have no more right to tell others what line of reasoning to pursue than others have of claiming to know what Valerius Flaccus was thinking.

---

[493] Shotter 2000b, 193 follows the same line of argument, but whereas Momigliano restricts his observations to the Flavian period, Shotter generalises, in which case he is correct. Later writers do exaggerate. I fully endorse the points he makes about Silius Italicus and Vespasian's principate. But the reference to Thule and Agricola has been missed.
[494] Syme 1979, 1.
[495] Lefèvre 1971, 52. He likewise assumes that Statius' *Caledonian plains* are a general reference to Britain. Can we rely on such criteria? He brings in Martial's *Caledonii Britanni* (*Epig.* 10.44.1) to reinforce his case. I assume that Martial's *British Britons* are to be contrasted with the *British bears* (cf. *Spect.* 9.3). Evans 2003, 256 informs us that *to emphasise its remoteness, Britain was often referred to as Caledonia*'.....*and even more often it is called Thule*. I don't need to repeat my objections to this.
[496] Spaltenstein 2002, 29.
[497] As Susanna Braund put it, 1992, 275, *Britons in Scotland do not notice the disturbances at Rutupiae (Richborough)* in Kent. The current misconceptions were popular among 19th century antiquaries. Poste 1853, 134, referring to the Caledonian Ocean, writes, *it being mentioned in conjunction with Rutupina litora...and the poet mentioning that the waves were a deceitful protection to the Caledonian Britons is a direct allusion that the invading Roman army under Aulus Plautius landed at Southampton*. This a consequence of the total failure to understand the Latin in its context. He was not the only one.
[498] Spaltenstein 2002, 29.
[499] Kleywegt 2005, 14: *Caledonius Oceanus - of course, not in the strict sense*. Why not?
[500] Río Torres-Murciano 2005, 89.

The use of *Caledonius* in the epic poets opened the flood gates for all manner of absurd excuses. If critics had looked more closely at the veiled allusion in Statius to Agricola's conquest of Caledonia, they might have resisted the impulse to regress to the Claudian era. What is relevant in Statius applies equally across the board to other Silver Age poets in their eulogies of the *gens Flavia*. The attempts to demolish the arguments of Peters, who supported a Flavian context for *Caledonius*, are both ludicrous and lamentable. It takes a brave man to raise his head above the parapet; Bernays, Preiswerk, Peters, Moreda and Soubiran were lions, not donkeys. Words such as *flattery, exaggeration, hyperbole, metonymy, synecdoche, magnification*, in whatever language they appear, are flimsy pretexts for justifying poetic licence and reflect a barrenness of ideas. Poets are entitled to some degree of over-elaboration, but there are times when they tell the truth. Not every emperor wants to be faced with exaggeration when he knows that the truth requires no distortion. Would Vespasian really be happy to hear that his recent achievements had been ignored and that ten years of ruling had disappeared down a poetic drain? The same applies to Domitian where references to *Caledonius* appear. Martial refers to *Caledonius ursus* (*Spect.* 9.3 *Caledonian bear*).[501] Are we to assume that this is also a left-over from Noah's Ark? Coleman describes a Scottish bear as *unique in ancient literature. It may be a topical example of Roman propaganda, the first sign of a tendency to suggest that in the year 80 Caledonia was already under Roman control.*[502] The fact that wild animals are only referred to by Tacitus in his last year of operations (*Agr.* 34.2) could indicate that the bear reached Rome in 84, at the same time as Martial's rhinoceros.[503] She was, of course, right in her interpretation, but I would have liked more commitment in her reference to Vespasian's conquest of Caledonia as described in Silius and Valerius. If *Caledonius* is *topical* in Martial, why shouldn't it be topical in his contemporaries? At least Martial's bear in the Agricolan context of Caledonia has much more life in it than a sheepskin dangling from a tree in Colchis. Others would do well to look for allusions to contemporary history in the poets, provided they can make a valid case. All said and done, if I am required to make a judgement, whom am I to believe, Valerius Flaccus and Silius Italicus or those who try to enhance their *CV*s by disparaging them? I find it amusing that scholars can waste so much time in building cases against each other, like pigeons scrambling for crumbs, when a closer examination reveals that there is no case.

What I have discussed in this appendix, together with other points relating to the significance of Caledonia in the latter half of the first century, may be listed as follows:
1. The first reference to Caledonia appears in Lucan, perhaps written only weeks before his death in April AD 65.
2. Lucan was the nephew of Seneca, whose connexions with Britain were both as speculator and as policy maker for Nero.
3. At the end of AD 54 Seneca wrote a satire on the death of Claudius. The Brigantes are first mentioned here.
4. In AD 55 Seneca had held the consulship with Trebellius Maximus, later governor of Britain.
5. Didius Gallus and Trebellius Maximus would be aware of the Brigantian issues during their governorships. Reinforcements from Scotland invaded Brigantia during the governorship of Gallus.[504]

---

[501] Birley 1981, 80, n. 48, 2005, 84 and Grant 2007, 96 refer to this animal as a *Caledonian boar*. This is a misquotation from Martial. The mistake is spread further by Shackleton Bailey's mistranslation in the Loeb edition. Grant goes on to make an erroneous connection with the emblem of *legio* XX and to offer an irrelevant note on the mythological *Calydonian boar*. If Martial's interpretation of *Caledonius* is correct here, then the responsibilities of Quintus Ovidius (cf. note 266) will take him ultimately to *northern* Britain. The reference to Oceanus and Tethys (*Epig.* 10.44.2) is significant in terms of a voyage into a remote area. This would be no problem to one who had negotiated the *aequora Scyllae* (*Straits of Messina, Epig.* 7.44.5). On Q. Ovidius, cf. note 266. Vioque 2002, 278 noted that Ovidius *went with another friend to Britannia*, without suggesting who it might be. Martial likewise is silent on the name. But it was clearly the outgoing governor, Quietus, on whom cf. Birley 2005, 102-4. Nauta 2002, 71 n.113 assumes the friend to be either a governor or legionary legate (the latter unlikely, Birley, *pers.comm.*) rather than an exile following Domitian's reign of terror, as Kleywegt 1998, 272 suggested.

[502] Coleman 2006, 88-90. It is not clear on what evidence Coleman assumes that Roman trade with Caledonia *probably existed long before this date*. Tacitus makes Caledonian isolationism a fundamental point in Calgacus' speech.

[503] It is not known for certain which 'Caesar' is being addressed. That some, if not all, of poems relate to the principate of Domitian is beyond doubt. For the arguments relating to the date of composition, cf. Coleman 2006, xlv-lxiv. For a view of Coleman's arguments, cf. Nobili 2007. For the rhinoceros as evidence for dating between 83-85, cf. Buttrey 2007, 101-112.

[504] Although Tacitus tells us that Trebellius dissociated himself from campaigning, the governor would still be aware of what was happening on the northern frontier. The problems which came to a crisis in AD 69 may well reflect earlier unrest in AD

6. Caledonia and Thule were topical in the last quarter of the first century.

7. Statius, writing c.AD 95 alludes to the conquest of Caledonia by Agricola.

8. Both Silius Italicus and Valerius Flaccus are eulogising the *gens Flavia*. The *Iuli* cover all rulers from Julius Caesar to Nero. The use of *Iuli* in both poets should be identical. If the *Iuli* take second place in the latter, they should take second place in the former.

9. The use of *Caledonius* in both poets, as well as in Statius, follows the tradition set by Lucan who is not guilty of exaggeration.

10. Pliny alludes to the presence of Cerialis in the proximity of the *Caledonian Forest* within three years of Vespasian's assumption of the principate.

11. The coin finds in Scotland, as far north as Strageath (Tayside), comprise comparatively large numbers of early Flavian issues and reflect early occupation from Newstead to the Fife peninsula.[505]

12. Statius' reference to the *Caledonian plains* in the campaigns of Bolanus is possibly connected with the Gask Ridge. Consequently the term *Caledonius* is applicable to any event occurring in Scotland during the decade of Vespasian's rule.

13. The role of the navy is dominant during Agricola's advance north, despite Lang's claims that this was not the case under Vespasian.[506] It must have played an equally dominant role during the campaigns of Cerialis in the same area. The eastern seaboard would have seen naval bases in the Humber, Tyne and Forth, the western in the Dee, Solway and Clyde.[507] The naval push by Cerialis, involving marines and transport ships, must have been authorised by his father-in-law, Vespasian. *Tua carbasa* is appropriate in the poet's address to the emperor and reflects the Flavian activity of the *Classis Britannica* which participated in Agricola's invasion of Caledonia in 79 and achieved its most famous exploit under Domitian in reaching Thule in 83.

14. The numismatic evidence points to AD 79 as a crucial date for Agricola's invasion of Caledonia when Vespasian was still alive. This date ends a decade of Flavian naval involvement in northern Britain under that emperor.

63-4. In that case Lucan would have known about it. The Brigantian problem was always tied up with the freedom movement which was fuelled from further north.

[505] Shotter 2000b, 195-8 provides an excellent statistical analysis, suggesting that *the criteria adopted...offer working yardsticks for the identification of military sites which may be of Cerialian, rather than, Agricolan origin*. Hanson's statement on Statius' *poetic licence*, 1991b, 1750, that *campaigns into Scotland at this juncture probably fall into that category*, needs to be reconsidered.

[506] Lang 2003, 317.

[507] Caruana 1997, 26, listing possible landing sites from the Dee to the Solway, points out that *troops could be landed at suitable points along the coast, and particularly in river estuaries, where they could gain temporary control of river valleys, putting pressure on local groups by separating them from their neighbours*.

Acknowledgement for Maps and Photographs

I would like to express my gratitude to those who allowed me to use their materials and my apologies to any I could not contact:

Ian Keillar, Andreas Pangerl (www.romancoins.info), Classical Numismatic Group (www.cngcoins.com), Harvey Maps (www.harveymaps.co.uk), Robert Berg (www.bergbook.com), Peter Standing, Alan Moar www.alanmoar.flyer.co.uk), Aaron Atsma (www.theoi.com), Wikipedia

BIBLIOGRAPHY

Acheson, G.J. 1938: *Agricola, an English version of a Roman tale*
Adams, J.N. 1987: *The Latin Sexual Vocabulary,* London
Allen, D.F. 1970: 'The Coins of the Iceni', *Britannia* 1, 1-33
Allen, S. 2007: *Lords of Battle - The World of the Celtic Warrior,* Botley
Alonso-Núñez, J.M. 1988: 'Roman knowledge of Scandinavia in the imperial period', *OJA* 7, 47-64
Amm.: Ammianus Marcellinus, *The Histories* Anderson, G. 1922: *Cornelii Taciti De Vita Agricolae,* Oxford
André, J-M and Baslez, M-F. 1993: *Voyages dans l'Antiquité,* Lille
Andresen, G. 1880: *Cornelii Taciti de vita et moribus Iulii Agricolae liber,* Berlin
Angus, C.F. 1934: 'Pytheas of Marseilles', *G & R* 3 no.9. 165-172
Anthon, c. 1850: *A System of Ancient and Mediaeval Geography for the use of Schools*, New York
Armit, I. 1998: *Scotland's Hidden History,* Stroud
Armit, I. 2003: *Towers in the North: The Brochs of Scotland,* Stroud
Augoustakis, A. 2008 : 'Seascapes in Silius and Tacitus' in *Carmen Solutum : interactions of Poetry and History in Flavian Literature,* (abstr), Liverpool
Aujac, G. 1988: 'L'île de Thulé, myth ou réalité', *Athenaeum* 76, 329-343
Aujac, G. 1993: *Claude Ptolémée astronome, astrologue, géographe: connaissance et représentation du monde habité,* Paris
Avienus: *Descript. Orb. Terr.*: *Description of the World*
Ballin Smith, B. and Banks, I. 2002: *In the Shadow of the Brochs - The Iron Age in Scotland,* Stroud
Barlow, C.W. 1938: 'Codex Vaticanus Latinus 4929', *MAAR* 15, 87-124
Barnes, T.D. 1988: *Ammianus Marcellinus in the Representation of Historical Reality,* New York
Barrett, A.A. 1991: 'Claudius' British Victory Arch in Rome', *Britannia* 22, 1-19
Bastomsky, S.J. 1985: 'The Not-so-Perfect Man: some ambiguities in Tacitus' picture of Agricola', *Latomus* 44, 388-393
Bauer, L. 1890: *Silius Italicus Punica,* Leipzig
Benario, H.W. 1979: 'Agricola's proconsulship', *RhM* N.F. 122, 167-172
Benario, H.W. 1991: *Tacitus' Agricola, Germania and Dialogue on Orators, translated with an Introduction and Notes,* University of Oklahoma
Benferhat, Y. 2004: 'Review of P. Dräger, *C. Valerius Flaccus. Argonautica*', *BMCR* 04.01 (on line)
Bentham, R. 1948: *The Fragments of Eratosthenes* [unpublished Doct. Thes. Univ. of London]
Berard, F. 1994: 'Bretagne, Germanie, Danube; mouvements des troupes et priorités stratégiques sous le règne de Domitien, *Pallas* 40, 221-240
Bernays, J. 1855: 'Joseph Justus Scaliger', Breslau
Bernays, J. 1861: *Ueber der Chronik des Sulpicius Severus.* Jahresbericht des judisch seminars, 'Fraenckelscher Stiftung', Breslau
Bernstein, N.W. 2007: 'Fashioning Crispinus through his ancestors: epic modes in Statius *Silvae*', *Arethusa* 40 no.2, 183-196
Berry, P. 1977: *Pomponius Mela, Geography/De Situ Orbis AD 43,* transl., Lewiston
Bianchetti, S. 1998: *Pitea di Massalia, L'Oceano. introduzione, teste e commento a cura di...,* Pisa-Roma
Bird, H.W. 1993: *Eutropius: Breviarium,* Liverpool
Birley, A.R. 1975: *Agricola, the Flavian Dynasty and Tacitus* in *The Ancient Historian and His Materials. Essays in honour of C.E.*
Stevens on his seventieth birthday (ed. Levick, B.), Farnborough
Birley, A.R. 1981: *The Fasti of Roman Britain*, Oxford
Birley, A.R. 1999: *Tacitus, Agricola and Germany, a new translation,* Oxford
Birley, A.R. 2000: 'The life and death of Cornelius Tacitus', *Historia* 49, 230-247
Birley, A.R. 2005: *The Roman Government of Britain,* Oxford
Birley, E. 1946: 'Britain under the Flavians, Agricola and his predecessors', *Durham University Journal* n.s. 7, 79-84
Birley, E. 1953: *Roman Britain and the Roman Army*, Kendal

Birley, E. 1978: 'The adherence of Britain to Vespasian', *Britannia* 9, 243-245

Blockley, R.C. 1973: 'Tacitean influence on Ammianus Marcellinus', *Latomus* 32. 63-78

Blomfield, H.G. 1916: *The Argonautica of Gaius Valerius Flaccus Setinus Balbus. Book 1, translated into English prose with introduction and notes*, Oxford

BMC: *Coins of the Roman Empire in the British Museum, vol.1 Augustus to Vitellius, vol.2 Vespasian to Domitian, vol.3 Nerva to Hadrian* (Mattingly, H. 1923,1930, 1936), London

BMCRR: *Coins of the Roman Republic in the British Museum* (H.A. Grueber, 1970/1910), London

Borzsák, S. 1992: *Tacitus' Agricola*, Budapest

Bosworth, A.B. 2004: 'Mountain and molehill? Cornelius Tacitus and Quintus Curtius', *CQ* 54.2, 551-567

Bowersock, G.W.1994: *Fiction as History: Nero to Julian*, Berkeley-Los Angeles-Oxford

Bradley, R. 2007: *The Prehistory of Britain and Ireland*, Cambridge

Braun, T. 1980: 'Review of C.F.C. Hawkes: the Eighth J.L. Myres Lecture. Pytheas: Europe and the Greek Explorers' *CR* ns.30, 124-127

Braund, D. 1984: 'Observations on Cartimandua', *Britannia,* 15, 1-6

Braund, D. 1996: *Ruling Roman Britain,* London and New York

Braund, S.H. 1992: *Lucan Civil War*, translated with introduction and notes, Oxford

Breeze, A. 2002: 'Philology on Tacitus' Graupian Hill and Trucculan Harbour' *PSAS* 132, 305-311

Breeze, A. 2005: 'Scotland's oldest place-names', Lecture at Scottish Place- Name Society Day Conference, Dollar.

Breeze, D.J. 1978: 'Roman Scotland', *PCA* 75, 24-25

Breeze, D.J. 1982: *The Northern Frontiers of Roman Britain*, London

Breeze, D.J. 1988: 'Why did the Romans fail to conquer Scotland ?', *PSAS* 118, 3-22

Breeze, D.J. 1989: 'The Northern Frontier', in M.Todd (ed.), *Research on Roman Britain, 1960-1989, Britannia Monograph* 11, 36- 60

Breeze, D.J. 1990: 'Agricola in the Highlands', *PSAS* 120, 55-60

Breeze, D.J. 1996: *Roman Scotland - Frontier Country*, London

Breeze, D.J. 2007: *Roman Frontiers in Britain,* Bristol

Breeze, D.J. and Dobson, B. 1987: *Hadrian's Wall*, 3rd ed., London

Brodersen, K. 1994: *Kreuzfahrt durch die Alte Welt*, Darmstadt

Brugnoli, G. 1961: 'La vicenda del Codice Hersfeldense', *RCCM* 3, 69-90

Buchanan, G. 1582: *Rerum Scoticarum Historia,* Edinburgh

Büchner, K. 1955: *Die historischen Versuche, Agricola. Germania. Dialogus*, Stuttgart

Büchner, K. 1960: 'Reicht die Statthalterschaft des Agricola von 77-82 oder von 78-83?', *RhM* 103, 172-178

Bunbury, E.H. 1959: *A History of Ancient Geography*, New York

Burmann, P. 1724: *C. Valerii Flacci Argonauticon libri viii*, Leiden

Burn, A.R. 1949: 'Mare pigrum et grave', *CR* 63, 94

Burn, A.R. 1953a: *Agricola and Roman Britain*, London

Burn, A.R. 1953b: 'In search of a battlefield: Agricola's last battle', *PSAS* 87, 127- 133

Burn, A.R. 1968: 'A new *Agricola*', *CR* ns 18, 314-316

Burn, A.R. 1969: 'Tacitus on Britain', in T.A. Dorey (ed.), *Tacitus*, London

Burton, H.E. 1932: *Discovery in the Ancient World*, Cambridge, Mass.

Buttrey, T.V. 1980: *Documentary Evidence for the Chronology of the Flavian Titulature*, Meisenheim am Glan

Buttrey, T.V. 2007: 'Domitian, the Rhinoceros and the Date of Martial's *De Spectaculis*', *JRS* 99, 101-112

Caes., *BG, BC*: Julius Caesar, *On the Gallic War, On the Civil War* Campbell, D.B. 1986: 'The consulship of Agricola', *Zeitschrift für Papyrologie und Epigraphik* 63, 197-200

Carpenter, R. 1966: *Beyond the Pillars of Hercules. The Classical World seen through the eyes of its discoverers*, New York

Caruana, I. 1997: *Maryport in the Flavian Conquest of Britain* (in *Roman Maryport and its setting, CWAAS* extr.ser.vol.28)

Cary, M. and Warmington, E.H. 1929: *The Ancient Explorers,* London

Cassidy, V.H. de P. 1963: ' The voyage of an Island', *Speculum* 38 no. 4, 595-602

Casson, L. 1991: *The Ancient Mariners*, Princeton N.J.
Casson, L. 1995: *Ships and Seamanship in the Ancient World*, Baltimore and London
Caviglia, F. 1999: *Valerio Flacco, Introduzione, Traduzione e Note*, Milan
Chevallier, R. 1984: 'La vision du Nord dans l'Antiquité gréco-romaine de Pythéas à Tacite', *Latomus* 43, 85-96
Church, A. and Brodribb, W.J. 1869: *The Agricola of Tacitus, with a revised text, English notes and map* (repr.1964), London and New York
Church, A. and Brodribb, W.J. 1877: *The Agricola and Germany of Tacitus*, London
Cic., *Rep., Dom.*: Cicero, *On the Republic*; *On his House*
CIL: *Corpus Inscriptionum Latinarum*
Clarke, K. 2001: 'An island nation: re-reading Tacitus' *Agricola*', *JRS* 91, 94-112
Claudian, *De III, IV consulatu Honorii. On the third, fourth consulship of Honorius*
Cleom., *Cael.*: Cleomedes, *Heavenly Phenomena*
Cody, J.M. 2003: *Conquerors and Conquered on Flavian Coins*, in *Flavian Rome: Culture, Image, Text*. eds. Boyle A.J. and Dominik W.J., Leiden
Col., *RR*: Columella, *On Agriculture*.
Coleman, K.M. 2006: *M.Valerii Martialis liber Spectaculorum*, Oxford.
Columba, G.M. 1935: *Ricerche Storiche. volume primo. Geografia e Geografi del Mondo Antico*, Palermo
Cotterill, J. 1993: 'The late Roman coastal forts', *Britannia* 24, 227-239
Couissin, P. 1932: 'Tacite et César', *RPh* 97-117
Courtney, E. 1996: *A Commentary on the Satires of Juvenal*, London
Cravioto, E.G. 2003: *Viajes y viajeros en el mundo antiguo*, Cuenca
Crawford, O.G.S. 1949: *The Topography of Roman Scotland*, Cambridge
Cunliffe, B. 1991: *Iron Age Communities in Roman Britain*, London and New York
Cunliffe, B. 2001a: *Facing the Ocean*, Oxford
Cunliffe, B. 2001b: *The Extraordinary Voyage of Pytheas the Greek*, London
Curt., *HA*: Quintus Curtius Rufus, *History of Alexander*
Dalby, A. 2000: *Empire of Pleasures: Luxury and Indulgence in the Roman World*, London and New York
Daniels, C. 1989: 'The Flavian and Trajanic northern frontier', in M.Todd (ed.), *Research on Roman Britain, Britannia Monograph* 11, 31-35
Davies Pryce, T. and Birley, E. 1938: 'The fate of Agricola's northern conquests', *JRS* 28, 141-152
Davis, R.B. 1892: *P. Cornelii Taciti Agricola*, London
Dawkins, R. 1976: *The Selfish Gene*, Oxford
De la Bédoyère, G. 2003: *Defying Rome. The Rebels of Roman Britain*, Stroud
Delz, J. 1983: *P. Cornelii Taciti qui supersunt libri, Agricola*, Stuttgart
Delz, J. 1987: *Silius Italicus Punica*, Stuttgart
D'Espèrey, S.F. 1986: 'Vespasien, Titus et la littérature', in W. Haase (ed.) *ANRW* II 32.5 3048-3086, Berlin and New York
D'Hollander, R. 2002: *Science geographique dans l'Antiquité - Connaissance du monde - Conception de l'univers*, Saint-Mande & Marne-la-Vallée Dicks, E.R. 1960: *Geographical Fragments of Hipparchus*, London
Dihle, A. 1994: *Greek and Latin Literature of the Roman Empire*, London and New York.
Dilke, O.A.W. 1964: 'Geographical perceptions of the north in Pomponius Mela and Ptolemy', *Arctic* 37 n.4, 347-351
Dilke, O.A.W. 1985: *Greek and Roman Maps*, London and Reading
Dilke, O.A.W. 1990: 'The Budé Mela', *CR* n.s.40, 285-7
Dillemann, M. 1979: 'Observations on chapter v. 31. *Britannia* in the Ravenna Cosmography', *Archaeologia* 106, 61-73
Di Martino, V. 2003: *Roman Ireland*, Cork
Dio: Cassius Dio, *Roman History*
Diod.: Diodorus, *Library of History*
Dion, R. 1965: 'La renommée de Pythéas dans l'Antiquité', *REL* 43, 443-466
Dion, R. 1966: 'Pythéas explorateur', *RPh* 40, 191-216

Dion, R. 1977: *Aspects Politiques de la Géographie Antique*, Paris

Dion., Perieg. *Orb. Descr*: Dionysius Periegetes, *Description of the World*

Dobson, B. 1981: 'Agricola's Life and Career', *SAF* 12, 1-13

Dobson, D.P. 1936: 'Roman influence in the north', *G & R* 14, 73-89

Dominik, W.J. 1994: *The Mythic Voice of Statius: power and politics in the Thebaid*, Leiden

Dorey, T.A. (ed.) 1969: *Tacitus*, London

Drakenborch, A. (ed.) 1717: *Caii Silii Italici Punicorum Libri Septemdecim*, Utrecht

Driver, G.R. 1965: *The Judaean Scrolls: The Problem and the Solution*, Oxford

Duff, J.D. 1928: *Lucan with an English Translation*, Cambridge, Mass. and London

Duff, J.D. 1934: *Silius Italicus Punica*, vols. 1 and 2. Cambridge, Mass.

Durant, G.M. 1969: *Britain: Rome's Most Northerly Province*, London

Eck, W. 1982: 'Jahres- und Provinzialfasten der senatorischen Statthalter von 69/70 bis 138/139', *Chiron* 12, 281-362

Eden, P.T. (ed.) 1984: *Seneca Apocolocyntosis*, Cambridge

Edwards, K.J. and Ralston, I.B.M. 2003: *Scotland after the Ice Age: Environment, Archaeology and History 8000BC-AD1000*, Edinburgh

Ekwall, E. 1928: *English river-names*, Oxford

Elton, I.E. 1882: *Origins of English History*, London

Enn., *Ann.*: Ennius, *Annals* (ed. Warmington, *Remains of Old Latin*, Harvard and Cambridge)

Ernesti, I.A. 1770: *Taciti Opera*, Berlin

Eutr.: Eutropius, *Abridgement of Roman History*

Evans, R. 2003: 'Containment and corruption: the discourse of Flavian empire' in *Flavian Rome: Culture, Image, Text*, 255-276, eds. Boyle. A.J. and Dominik W.J., Leiden

Fabre, P. 1975: 'Étude sur Pythéas le Massaliote et l'époque de ses travaux', *EC* 43, 25-44

Fitzpatrick, A.P. 1989: 'The submission of the Orkney Islands to Claudius: new evidence?', *SAR* 6, 24-33

Fitzpatrick-Matthews K. 2006: *Britannia in the Ravenna Cosmography*, www.kmatthews.org.uk

Fletcher, J.E. 1999: 'Battle lost', *The Scotsman*, 4th December

Fordun, J.1871: *Chronica Gentis Scotorum* in *The Historians of Scotland 1* (ed. Skene, W.F.) Edinburgh

Forni, G. 1962: *Agricola, ed., commentariolo, instruxit et illustravit*, Rome Fotheringham, W.H. 1859: 'On the Thule of the ancients', *PSAS* 3, 492-503

Fraser, J.E. 2005: *The Roman Conquest of Scotland: The Battle of Mons Graupius AD 84*, Stroud

Freeman, P. 2001: *Ireland and the Classical World*, University of Texas, Austin

Frere, S.S. 1987: *Britannia*, third edition, extensively revised, London

Frere, S.S. 1990: 'Roman Britain in 1989. 1. Sites Explored', *Britannia* 21, 304-364

Frere, S.S. 2001: 'The Ravenna Cosmography and North Britain between the Walls', *Britannia* 32, 286-292

Freudenburg, K. 2001: *Satires of Rome: Threatening Poses from Lucilius to uvenal*, Cambridge

Frick, C. 1880: *Pomponii Melae de Chorographia libri tres*, Stuttgart

Friis-Jensen, K. 1985: 'Propertius 1.8.19, a conjecture', *Class et Med* 36, 173-175

Front., *Strat.*; Frontinus, *Strategems*

Furneaux, H. 1898: *Cornelii Taciti Vita Agricolae*, Oxford

Galimberti, A. 1996: 'La spedizione in Britannia del 43 d.C.E; il problema delle Orcadi', *Aevum* 70, 69-72

Gallivan, P.A. 1981: 'The Fasti for AD 70-96', *CQ* 31, 186-220

Ganiban, R.T. 2006: *The Thebaid and the Reinterpretation of the Aeneid*, Cambridge

Geminus: *Introduction to Celestial Phenomena*

Getty, R.J. 1936: 'The date of the composition of the *Argonautica* of Valerius Flaccus', *CPh* 31, 53-61

Ghael, F. 1838: 'The Gaelic controversy', *The Gentleman's Magazine* 9. 482

Gibson, B. 2006: *Statius Silvae 5*, edited with an introduction, translation and commentary, Oxford

Golb, N. 1995: *Who Wrote the Dead Sea Scrolls? The Search for the Secret of Qumran*, New York

Gordon, R. 1654: *De Thule Insula dissertatio*, in Blaeu's Atlas of Scotland, vol.5, p.6-7, Amsterdam

Gorrichon, M. 1974: 'La Bretagne dans la 'vie d'Agricole' de Tacite. Littérature gréco-romaine et géographie historique', in *Mélanges offerts à Roger Dion*, 191-205, ed. Chevallier R,   Paris

Grant, A. E. 2007: *Roman Military Objectives in Britain under the Flavian Emperors*, Oxford

Gregory, R.A. 2001: 'Excavations along the Moray Firth littoral' *PSAS,* 131, 177-222

Grienberger, T. 1921: 'Codanovia',   *Phil Woch* 41, 1198-1220

Griffin, M.T. 1976: *Seneca. A Philosopher in Politics, Oxford*

Griffin, M.T. 1984: *Nero: The End of a Dynasty,* London

Grimal, P. 1990: *Tacite*, Paris

Grimal, P. 1991: *Sénèque ou la conscience de l'Empire,* repr. Paris

Gronovius, A. 1782: *Pomponii Melae de Situ Orbis libri tres.* ed.3. Leiden

Grueber, H.A. 197x (1910): *Coins of the Roman Republic in the British Museum (BMCRR)*, vols. 1 and 2, London

Gsell, S. 1894: *Essai sur le règne de l'empereur Domitien,* Paris

Gudeman, A. 1898: 'Agricola's invasion of Ireland', *TAPA* 29, 36-39

Gudeman, A. 1928: *Tacitus de Vita Iulii Agricolae*, New York

Hamilton, J. 1968: *Excavations at Clickhimin*, Edinburgh

Handford, S.A. 1986: *Tacitus, The Agricola and Germania*, Harmondsworth

Hansen, U.L. 1987: *Römischer Import im Norden*, Copenhagen

Hanson, W.S. 1977-8: 'Roman campaigns north of the Forth-Clyde isthmus: the evidence of temporary camps', *PSAS* 109, 140-150

Hanson, W.S. 1979: 'The first Roman occupation of Scotland', *Roman Frontier Studies*, 15-43

Hanson, W.S. 1991a: *Agricola and the Conquest of the North, with corrections*, London

Hanson, W.S. 1991b: 'Tacitus' Agricola: an archaeological and historical study', in W. Haase (ed.), *ANRW*, II 33.3, 1741-1784, Berlin and New York

Hanson, W.S. and Campbell, D.B. 1986: 'The Brigantes: from clientage to conquest', *Britannia,* 17, 73-89

Hanson, W.S. and Macinnes, L. 1980: 'Forests, forts and fields', *SAF,* 12, 98-113

Hanson, W.S. and Slater, E.A. 1991: *Scottish Archaeology - New Perspectives,* Aberdeen

Hardouin, J. 1723: *Caii Plinii Secundi Historiae Naturalis libri XXXVII*, Paris

Haverfield, F. 1899: 'Agricola's invasion of Ireland once more', *CR* 13, 302-3

Haverfield, F. 1907: 'Three notes', *CR* 21, 105-6

Hawkes, C.F.C. 1975: *Pytheas: Europe and the Greek explorers*, Oxford

Hawkes, C.F.C. 1977: *Britain and Julius Caesar*, London

Henderson, A.A.R. 1984: 'From 83-1983: on the trail of Mons Graupius', *The Deeside Field Club* 18, 23-29

Henderson, A.R.R. 1985: 'Agricola in Caledonia: the sixth and seventh campaigns', *Classical Views,* 29, n.s. 4, 318-335

Hergt, G. 1893: *Die Nordlandfahrt des Pytheas,* Halle

Herodian, *History*

Heubner, H. 1984: *Kommentar zum Agricola des Tacitus*, Göttingen

Higgins, J.M. 1998: 'The dog in the night-time: Rome's invasion of Ireland', in *Studies in Latin Literature and Roman* History, 401-410, ed. Deroux C. *Collection Latomus,* Bruxelles

Hind, J.G.F. 1974: 'Agricola's fleet and *portus Trucculensis'*, *Britannia* 5, 285-288

Hind, J.G.F. 1985: 'Summers and Winters in Tacitus' account of Agricola's campaigns in Britain' *Northern History*, 21, 1-18

Hind, J.G.F. 2003: 'Caligula and the spoils of Ocean; a rush for the riches in the far North-West', *Britannia,* 34, 272-4

Hind, J.G.F. 2007: 'Aulus Plautius' campaign in Britain. An alternative reading of the narrative in Cassius Dio (60.19.5-20.2), *Britannia* 38, 93-106

Hoffmann, B. 2001: 'Archaeology versus Tacitus' *Agricola*. A 1st century worst-case scenario', Lecture, Dublin

Hoffmann, B. 2004: *Tacitus, Agricola and the role of literature in the archaeology of the first century AD*, in *Archaeology and Ancient History. Breaking down the barriers*, 151-156 ed. Sauer E.W., London and New York

Hogg, J. 1859: 'On the history of Iceland and the Icelandic language and literature', *TRSL* 6, s.2. 324-386

Holder, A. 1896-1913: *Alt-celtischer Sprachschatz*, 3 vols., Leipzig
Holder, P.A. 1982: *The Roman Army in Britain*, London
Hor., *Carm.*: Horace, *Odes*
Hübner, E. 1881: 'Das Römische Heer in Britannien', *Hermes* 16, 513-584
Hübner, E. 1897: 'Boresti', *RE* 3.1, 731
Hunter, F. 2007: *Beyond the edges of empire – Caledonians, Picts and Romans*, Rosemarkie, Ross-shire
Hutton, M. 1914: *Tacitus Agricola*, London
Hyde, W.W. 1947: *Ancient Greek Mariners*, New York
James, S. 2002: 'Writing the Legions: The Development and Future of Roman Military Studies in Britain', *Archaeological Journal* 159, 1-58
Jarrett, M.G. 1976: 'An unnecessary war', *Britannia* 7, 145-151
Johansen, K.F. 1960: 'New evidence about the Hoby silver cups', *Acta Arch* 31, 185-190
Jones, B.W. 1984: *The Emperor Titus*, London and New York
Jones, B.W. 1993: *The Emperor Domitian*, London and New York
Jones, G.D.B. and Keillar, I. 1996: 'Marinus, Ptolemy and the turning of Scotland', *Britannia* 27, 43-49
Jones, B. and Mattingly, D. 1990: *An Atlas of Roman Britain*, Oxford
Jones, C.P. and Smith, R.R.R. 1994: 'Two inscribed monuments of Aphrodisias', *Archäologischer Anzeiger,* Heft 3, 456- 472
Jord, *Get.*: Jordanes, *History of the Getae*
Jørgensen, L, Storgaard, B. and Thomsen, L.G. eds.: *The Spoils of War: The North in the Shadow of the Roman Empire*, Copenhagen
Jos., *BJ.*: Josephus, *The Jewish War*
Journes, H. and Georgelin, Y. 2000: *Pythéas explorateur et astronome,* Ollioules, Provence
Juv., *Sat.*: Juvenal, *Satires*
Kahlos, M. 2002: *Vettius Agorius Praetextatus: Senatorial Life in Between*, *Acta Instituti Romani Finlandiae* XXVI, Rome
Kamm, A. 2004: *The Last Frontier; The Roman Invasion of Scotland*, Stroud
Kavenna, J. 2006: *The Ice Museum: In Search of the Lost Land of Thule,* New York
Keillar, I. 1986: '*In fines Borestorum.* To the land of the Boresti', *Popular Archaeology* 7.3 (April), 2-9
Keillar, I. 2005: *Romans in Moray,* Elgin
Keppie, L.J.F. 1980: 'Mons Graupius: the search for a battlefield', *SAF* 12,79-88
Keppie, L.J.F. 1986: *Scotland's Roman Remains*, Edinburgh
Keppie, L.J.F. 1988: Review of the *Tabula Imperii Romani: Britannia Septentrionalis, CR* n.s.38, 439-440
Keppie, L.J.F. 1989: 'Beyond the northern frontier: Roman and native in Scotland', in M. Todd (ed.), *Research on Roman Britain 1960-1989, Britannia Monograph* 11, 61-73
Kleywegt, A.J. 1986: 'Praecursoria Valeriana 1', *Mnem.* s.4, 39, 313-349
Kleywegt, A.J. 1998: *Extra fortunam est quidquid donatur amicis: Martial on Friendship* in *Toto Notus in Orbe. Pespektiven der Martial-Interpretation* 256-277 (ed. Grewing, F.), Stuttgart
Kleywegt, A.J. (ed.) 2005: *Valerius Flaccus, Argonautica Book 1: a Commentary,* Leiden-Boston
Koestermann, E. 1964: *P. Cornelii Taciti libri qui supersunt, tom ii. Fasc. 2 Germania Agricola*, Leipzig
Köstlin, H. 1889: 'Zur Erklärung und Kritik des Valerius Flaccus', *Philolog* 48, 647-673
Laederich, P. 2001: *Les Limites de l'Empire. Les Stratégies de l'Impérialisme Romain dans l'Oeuvre de Tacite*, Paris
Lang, P. 2003: *C. Valerius Flaccus: Die Sendung der Argonauten,* Frankfurt am Main-Wien
Lefèvre, E. 1971: *Das Prooemium der Argonautica des Valerius Flaccus*, Mainz and Wiesbaden
Legg. R. 1983: *Romans in Britain,* London
Lenchantin de Gubernatis, M. 1949: *De vita Iulii Agricolae liber*, Turin
Levick, B. 1999: *Vespasian*, London and New York
Liberman, G. 1997: *Valerius Flaccus Argonautiques, texte établi et traduit par*, Paris
Lipsius, J. 1574: *C. Cornelii Taciti Historiarum et Annalium libri qui exstant, Iusti Lipsii……eiusdem*

Taciti......Iulii Agricolae vita, Antwerp
Liv., *H*.: Livy, *History of Rome*
Luc., *BC*: Lucan, *The Civil War*
Lund, A.A. 1980: 'De Agricola primo inventore', *Gymn* 87, 275-282
Lund, A.A. 1981: *P. Cornelii Taciti De Vita Agricolae liber*, Odense
MacDonald, G. 1919: 'The Agricolan occupation of North Britain', *JRS* 9, 111-138
MacKie, E. 2001: 'The circumnavigation of Scotland by Agricola's fleet in the early AD 80s: possible evidence from Dun Ardreck, Skye', *PSAS* 131, 432
Madvig, I.N. 1873: *Adversaria Critica* ll, 569-570, Hauniae
Magnaldi, G. 1997: 'Suetonio, Tacito e il codice Hersfeldense', *Prometheus* 23, 119-144, 229-246
Magnani, S. 2002: *Il viaggio di Pitea sull' Oceano*, Bologna
Malloch, S.J.V. 2001: 'Gaius on the Channel Coast', *CQ* ns 51, 551-556
Mann, J.C. 1996: *Britain in the Roman Empire: The Turning of Scotland*, Aldershot
Mann, J.C. and Breeze, D.J. 1987: 'Ptolemy, Tacitus and the tribes of north Britain', *PSAS* 117, 85-91
Mart., *Epig*., *Spect*.: Martial, *Epigrams, Shows*
Martin, C. 1992: *Water Transport and the Roman Occupation of North*
Martin, R.H. 1994: *Tacitus* (repr.with corrections), Melksham *Britain*, in *Scotland and the Sea*, 1-35, ed. Smout T.C. Edinburgh
Martyn, J.R.C. 1974: 'Juvenal and Ne quid nimis', *Hermes* 102, 338-345
Martyn, J.R.C. 1996: *Juvenal: A Farrago*, Amsterdam
Matier, K.O. 1983: 'The poetic sources of Silius Italicus with particular reference to Book 11', *Acta Classica* (South Africa) 26, 73-82
Mattingly, D 2006: *An Imperial Possession: Britain in the Roman Empire*, Mattingly, H. 1930: *Coins of the Roman Empire in the British Museum* (*BMC*), vol.2, London
Mattingly, H. 1948: *Tacitus on Britain and Germany*, Middlesex
Maxwell, G.S. 1984: 'New frontiers: the Roman fort at Doune and its possible significance', *Britannia*, 15, 217-223
Maxwell, G.S. 1989: *The Romans in Scotland*, Edinburgh
Maxwell, G.S. 1990: *A Battle Lost: Romans and Caledonians at Mons Graupius*, Edinburgh
Maxwell, G.S. 2004: *The Roman Penetration of the North in the late 1st century AD* in M.Todd (ed.) *A Companion to Roman Britain*, Oxford
McCullough, A. 2007: *Gender and Public Image in Imperial Rome,* [Doct. Thes. Univ.of St Andrews]
McDermott, W.C. and Orentzel, A.E. 1979: *Roman Portraits,* Columbia and London
McElderry, R.K. 1922: 'Juvenal in Ireland ?', *CQ* 16, 151-162
McGing, B.C. 1982: '*Syncrisis* in Tacitus' *Agricola*', *Hermathena* 132, 16-25
Mela: Pomponius Mela, *Geography*
Mendell, C.W. 1935: 'Discovery of the minor works of Tacitus', *AJPh* 56, 111-130
Mendell, C.W. 1949: 'Manuscripts of Tacitus' minor works', *MAAR* 135-145
Mendell, C.W. 1957: *Tacitus: the man and his work*, Newhaven and London
Michelet, f.L. 2006: *Creation, Migration and Conquest: Imaginary Geography and Sense of Space in Old English Literature*, Oxford
Millar, F. 1982: 'Emperors, Frontiers and Foreign Relations, 31 BC to AD 378', *Britannia* 13, 1-23
Millar, F. 2003: *Rome, the Greek World and the East* vol.2, *Government, Society and Culture in the Roman Empire,* University of North Carolina
Miniconi, P. et Devallet, G. 1979: *Silius Italicus. La guerre punique. Tome 1, Belles Lettres,* Paris
Momigliano, A. 1950: '*Panegyricus Messallae* and '*Panegyricus Vespasiani*', *JRS* 40, 39-42
Mommsen, T. 1895 : *C. Iulii Solini Collectanea Rerum Memorabilium*. 2nd ed. Berlin
Moreda, S.L. 2000: *Valerio Flaco*, Madrid
Mozley, J.H. 1934 (ed.): *Valerius Flaccus with an English translation*, London and Cambridge, Mass.
Müllenhoff, K. 1890: *Deutche Altertumskunde. Band 1*, Berlin
Müller, C. 1883: *Claudii Ptolemaei Geographia*, Paris
Murgia, C.E. 1977: 'The minor works of Tacitus: a study in textual criticism' *CPh* 72, 323-345
Murgia, C.E. 1978: '*Loci conclamati* in the minor works of Tacitus', *CSCA* 11, 159-178

Murgia, C.E. and Rodgers, R.H. 1984: 'A tale of two manuscripts', *CPh* 79, 145-153

Nauta, R.R. 2002: *Poetry for Patrons: Literary Communication in the Age of Domitian*, Leiden-Boston-Koln

Nauta, R.R. 2005: The Recusatio in Flavian Poetry in *Flavian Poetry* 21-40 (eds. Nauta, R.R. Van Dam H-J, Smolenaars, J.J.L.) Leiden-Boston-Koln

Nesselhauf, H. 1952: 'Tacitus und Domitian', *Hermes* 80, 222-245

Nesselrath, H-G. 2005: 'The Greeks and the Western Seas', *G & R* 52, 153-171

Newton, F. 1999: *The Scriptorium and Library at Monte Cassino 1058-1105*, Cambridge

Nicolson, J.R. 1984: *Shetland*, Newton Abbott

Ninck, M.H. 1945: *Die Entdeckung von Europa durch die Griechen*, repr. Basel

Niutta, F. 1996: 'Sul codice Esinate di Tacito, ora Vitt. Em. 1631 della Biblioteca Naz. di Roma', *QS* 43, 173-202

Nobili, M. 2007: 'Review of Kathleen M. Coleman *M. Valerii Martialis: Liber Spectaculorum*', *BMCR* 10.48 (on line)

Norwood, G. and Watt, A.F. undat: *Tacitus: Agricola*, London

Ogilvie, R.M. and Richmond, I.A. 1967: *Cornelii Taciti De Vita Agricolae*, Oxford (cited as Ogilvie 1967)

Ogilvie, R.M. 1991: 'An interim report on Tacitus' *Agricola*', in W. Haase (ed.) *ANRW* II 33.3, 1714-1740

Oliver, R.P. 1951: 'The first Medicean MS of Tacitus and the titulature of ancient books', *TAPA* 82, 232-261

OLD 1984: *Oxford Latin Dictionary*, Oxford

Oniga, R. 1996: 'Tacito, *Agricola* 24.1', *RFIC* 124, 185-191

O'Rahilly, T.F. 1946: *Early Irish History and Mythology*, Dublin

Orelli, J.G. 1848: *C. Cornelii Taciti Opera, vol. 2*, Zurich

Orosius, *HAP*: Orosius, *Against the Pagans*

Ortelius, A. 1570: *TOT*.; *Theatrum Orbis Terrarum*, Antwerp   Ovid *Met*.; Ovid *The Transformations*

Page, W. 1908: *The Victoria County History of the County of Kent*, vol.3, London

Parroni, P. 1984a: *Pomponii Melae De Chorographia libri tres*, Rome

Parroni, P. 1984b: 'Surviving sources of the classical geographers through late antiquity and the medieval period', *Arctic* 37, no.4, 352-358

Parthey, G. 1969: *Pomponius Mela. De Chorographia libri tres*, repr.,Graz

Paus. *GD*.; Pausanias, *Description of Greece*

Pearce, J.W.E. 1899: *The Agricola and Germany of Tacitus*, London

Pedech, P. 1976: *La Géographie des Grecs*, Rennes (?)

Pekkanen, T. 1987: 'Revue of *Pomponii Melae de Chorographia*', ed. Parroni, *Gnomon*, 59, 552

Perret, J. 1950: *Recherches sur le texte de la 'Germanie'*, Paris

Persson, P. 1927: *Kritisch-exegetische Bemerkungen zu den kleinen Tacitus*, Uppsala

Peters, J. 1890: *De C. Valerii Flacci vita et carmine*, Königsberg

Phillips, E.D. 1969: 'Kronion Pelagos: Notions of the Arctic Ocean in Ancient Geography', *Euphr*. ns 3, 193-197

Pitblado, L.O. 1935: *The Roman Invasions. A saga of the Caledonian race*, London

Plin., *Ep*.: Pliny the Younger, *Letters*

Plin., *HN*.: Pliny the Elder, *Natural History*

Plut., *De Def. Orac*.: Plutarch, *On the Decline of Oracles*

Pohlmann, E. 2003: 'Codex Hersfeldensis und Codex Aesinas zu Tacitus' *Agricola*', *WJA* n.f. 27, 153-160

Polyaen. *Strat*.   Polyaenus, *Stratagems*   Polyb., *Hist*.: Polybius, *Histories*

Poste, B. 1853: *Britannic Researches*, London

Preiswerk, R. 1934: 'Zeitgeschichtliches bei Valerius Flaccus', *Philologus* 89, 433-442

Prisc., *Perieg*.: Priscian, *Coastal Navigation*   Prop., *Eleg*.: Propertius, *Elegies*

Ptol., *Geog*.: Ptolemy, *Geography*

QM: The Qumran Scrolls

Quint., *IO*: Quintilian, *The Training of an Orator*

Rackham, H. 1942: *Pliny, Natural History*. vol.2, London and Cambridge, Mass.

Raepsaet-Charlier, M-T. 1991: 'Sources littéraires, Cn. Iulii Agricolae: mise au point prosopographique', in W. Haase (ed.), *ANRW*, II 33.3, 1807-1857, Berlin and New York

Raftery, B. 2005: *Iron Age Ireland* in O' Croinin D. (ed.), *A New History of Ireland*, Oxford.

Ramsey, J.T. 2006: 'A descriptive catalogue of Greco-Roman comets from 500 BC-AD 400', *Selecta Classica*, 17, 106-124

Ranstrand, G. 1971: *Pomponii Melae De Chorographia libri tres*, Göteberg   Rav. Cos. (*RC*): Ravenna Cosmography

RE: *Real-Encyclopädie der classischen Altertumswissenschaft. Neue Bearbeitung*, Stuttgart

Reed, N. 1971: 'The fifth year of Agricola's campaigns', *Britannia* 2, 143-148

Reifenberg, A. 1953: *Israel's History in Coins*, London

Reid, C. 1905: 'The island of *Ictis*', *Archaeologia*, 59, 281-288

Rhenanus, B. 1533:   *P. Cornelii Taciti.....Annalium....libri sedecim....   recogniti..per Beatum Rhenanum....denique vita Julii Agricolae*, Basel

Rhys, J. 1904: *Celtic Britain*, London

RIB 1995: *The Roman Inscriptions of Britain*, Stroud, Gloucestershire

RIC: *The Roman Imperial Coinage, vol.3 Antoninus Pius to Commodus* (Mattingly, H. and Sydenham E.A.1926), London

Richmond, I.A. 1944: 'Gnaeus Julius Agricola', *JRS* 34, 34-45

Richmond, I.A. 1954: 'Queen Cartimandua', *JRS* 44, 43-52

Richmond, I.A. (ed.) 1958: *Roman and Native in North Britain*, Edinburgh

Richmond, I.A. and Crawford, O.G.S. 1949: 'The British section of the Ravenna Cosmography', *Archaeologia* 93, 1-50

Río Torres-Murciano, A. 2005: 'El proemio de Valerio Flaco. Una lectura retórica', *CFCES*, 25 no.1, 79-100

Rivet, A.L.F. 1958: *Town and Country in Roman Britain*, London

Rivet, A.L.F. 1977: 'Ptolemy's Geography and the Flavian invasion of Scotland', *Studien zu der Militärgrenzen Roms* 45-64, Köln

Rivet, A.L.F. and Smith, C. 1979: *The Place Names of Roman Britain*, London

Roach Smith, C. 1850: *The Antiquities of Richborough, Reculver and Lymne in Kent*, London

Robinson, R.P. 1935: *The Germania of Tacitus. A Critical Edition*, Middletown, Connecticut

Robertson, A.S. 1975: 'Agricola's campaigns in Scotland and their aftermath', *SAF* 7, 1-12

Roller, D.W. 2006: *Through the Pillars of Hercules. Graeco-Roman Exploration of the Atlantic*, New York and London

Romer, F.E. 1998: *Pomponius Mela. Description of the World*, Michigan

Romm, J.S. 1992: *The Edges of the Earth in Ancient Thought*, Princeton, NJ

Roncali, R. (ed.) 1990: *L. Annaei Senecae ΑΠΟΚΟΛΟΚΥΝΤΩΣΙΣ*, Leipzig

Rose, K.F.C. 1966: 'Problems of chronology in Lucan's career', *TAPA* 97, 379-396

Roseman, C.H. 1994: *Pytheas of Massalia: On the Ocean. Text, Translation and Commentary*, Chicago

Rouse, W.H.D 1919: *Seneca Apocolocyntosis*. London and New York

Roy, W. 1793: *The Military Antiquities of the Romans in Britain*, London

RPC: *Roman Provincial Coinage, vol.2. part 1, from Vespasian to Domitian* (Burnett, A., Amandry, M. and Carradice, I. 1999), London and Paris

RRC: *Roman Republican Coinage, vols.1,2* (Crawford, M.H. 1974), Cambridge

Rutilius Namatianus, *De Red.*; *On his Return*

Rutledge, S.H. 2000: 'Tacitus in tartan: textual colonisation and expansionist discourse in the *Agricola'*, *Helios* 27.1, 75-95

de Saint-Denis, E. 1956: *Vie d'Agricola, Belles Lettres*, Paris

Saddington, D.B. 1970: The Roman *auxilia* in Tacitus, Josephus and other imperial writers', *Acta Classica* (South Africa) 13, 89-124

Saddington, D.B. 1990: 'The origin and nature of the German and British fleets', *Britannia* 21, 223-232

Saddington, D.B. 1991: 'An Interim Report on Tacitus' Agricola', in W. Haase (ed.) *ANRW* II 33.3, 1731-1741, Berlin and New York

St. Joseph, J.K.S. 1978: 'The camp at Durno, Aberdeenshire, and the site of Mons Graupius',

Britannia 9, 271-287
Sall., *BJ*.: Sallust: *The War against Jugurtha*
Salles, C.E. 2002: *La Rome des Flaviens,* Perrin
Salmasius, J. 1689: *Plinianae Exercitationes in Caii Solini Polyhistora,* Utrecht
Salomies, O. 1992: *Adoptive and Polyonymous Nomenclature in the Roman Empire,* Helsinki
Salway, P. 1981: *Roman Britain,* Oxford
Salway, P. 1993: *The Oxford Illustrated History of Roman Britain,* Oxford
Sauer, E. 2002: 'The Roman invasion of Britain (AD 43): an imperial perspective: a response to Frere and Fulford, *OJA* 21 no.4, 333-363
Scaffai, M. 1995: 'Rassegna di studi su Valerio Flacco', in W. Haase (ed.), *ANRW* II 32.4, 2368-2373, Berlin and New York
Schama, S. 1995: *Landscape and Memory*, London
Schaps, D. 1979: 'The found and lost manuscripts of Tacitus' *Agricola*', *CPh* 74, 28-42
Schoene, A.E. 1889: *Cornelii Taciti De vita et moribus Iulii Agricolae liber*, Berlin
Schulz, B. 1865: 'Zu Tacitus Agricola (cap.x)', *JCPh* 91 Bd. 555-556
Schütte, G. 1917: *Ptolemy's Maps of Northern Europe*, Copenhagen
Sear, D.R. 1986: *Eight Hundred Years of Roman Coinage,* in *Perspectives in Numismatics*, www.chicagocoinclub.org/projects/PiN/
Selkirk, R. 1995: *On the Trail of the Legions*, Ipswich
Seneca, *Ben*.: Seneca, *On Good Services. QN. Natural History, Sat. Satire on the Apotheosis of the late Claudius*
Servius: *Commentary on the Three Works of Virgil*
Shotter, D.C.A. 1994: 'Rome and the Brigantes', *TCWAAS* 94, 21-34
Shotter, D.C.A. 2000a: 'The Roman conquest of the north-west', *TCWAAS* 100, 33-53
Shotter, D.C.A. 2000b. 'Petillius Cerialis in northern Britain', *Northern History* 36. 2, 189-198
Shotter, D.C.A. 2001: 'Petillius Cerialis in Carlisle: a numismatic contribution', *TCWAAS.* NS 1, 21-29
Shotter, D.C.A. 2004a: 'Vespasian, *auctoritas* and Britain', *Britannia* 35, 1-6
Shotter, D.C.A. 2004b: *Romans and Britons in North-West England,* Lancaster
Silberman, A. 1988: *Pomponius Mela Chorographia,* Belles Lettres, Paris
Silberman, A. 1989: 'Le premier ouvrage latin de géographie: la Chorographie de Pomponius Mela et ses sources grecques', *Klio* 71, 571-581
Sil. *Pun*.; Silius Italicus, *The Punic Wars*
Sleeman, J.H. 1914: *Cornelii Taciti De Vita et Moribus Iulii Agricolae*, Cambridge
Smallwood, E.M. 1962: 'Valerius Flaccus *Argonautica* I 5-21', *Mnem* Ser.4. 15, 170-172
Smith, A.H. 1926: 'A military diploma', *JRS* 16, 95-101
Smith, I.G. 1987: *The First Roman Invasion of Scotland,* Edinburgh
Sol., *Coll*.: Solinus, *Collections of Noteworthy Events*
Soubiran, J. 2002: *Valerius Flaccus Argonautiques. Introduction Texte et Traduction rhythmée Notes et Index.* Bibliothèque d'Études Classiques, Louvain-Paris-Dudley MA
Southern, P. 1996: 'Men and mountains, or geographical determinism and the conquest of Scotland', *PSAS* 126, 371-386
Soverini, P. 2004: *Cornelio Tacito. Agricola, introduzione, testo critico, traduzione e commento,* Alessandria
Spaltenstein, F. 1987-1990: *Commentaire des Punica de Silius Italicus,* vol.1,2, Geneva
Spaltenstein, F. 2002: *Commentaire des Argonautica de Valerius Flaccus* (livres 1 et 2), Bruxelles
Spilman, M. 1929: 'Some notes on the *Agricola* of Tacitus', *CPh* 376-393
Starr, C.G. 1960: *The Roman Imperial Navy,* ed.2. Cambridge
Stat., *Silv*.: Statius, *Occasional Verses*
Steele, R.B. 1930: 'Interrelation of Latin poets under Domitian', *CQ* 25, 328-342
Stephenson, H.M. 1894: *Tacitus: Agricola and Germania,* Cambridge
Stern, M. 1974: *Greek and Latin Authors on Jews and Judaism,* Jerusalem
Stevens, C.E. 1951: 'Claudius and the Orkneys', *CR* ns 1, 7-9
Stewart, J.J. 2001: 'Venutius' role in Romano-British affairs', *Latomus,* 60, 380-386
Stichtenoth, D. 1959: *Pytheas von Marseille, Über das Weltmeer*, Weimar

Stover, T.J. 2006: *Fables of the Reconstruction. A Reading of Valerius Flaccus' Argonautica* (unpub. Doct. Thes.), Austin
Str., *Geog.*: Strabo, *Geography*
Strand, J. 1972: *Notes on Valerius Flaccus' Argonautica*, Göteberg
Strang, A. 1997: 'Explaining Ptolemy's Roman Britain', *Britannia* 28, 1-30
Strang, A. 1998: 'Recreating a possible Flavian map of Roman Britain with a detailed map of Scotland', *PSAS* 128
Strobel, K. 1987: 'Nochmals zur Datierung der Schlacht am *Mons Graupius*', *Historia* 36, 198-212
Strut, E. 1912: 'Some Shetland brochs and standing stones', *PSAS* 46, 94-132
Suet.: Suetonius, *Lives of the Caesars*
Summers,W.C. 1894: *A study of the Argonautica of Valerius Flaccus,* Cambridge
Svennung, J. 1963: *Scadinavia und Scandia. Lateinisch-Nordische Namenstudien*, Uppsala and Wiesbaden
Svennung, J. 1974: *Scandinavien bei Plinius und Ptolemaeus*, Uppsala
Syme, R. 1929: 'The Argonautica of Valerius Flaccus' *CQ* 23, 129-137
Syme, R. 1979: 'The *patria* of Juvenal', *CPh* 74, 1-15
TIR 1987: *Tabula Imperii Romani Britannia Septentrionalis* (compiled by S.S. Frere, A.L.F. Rivet and N.H.H. Sitwell), London
Tac., *Germ.*, *Ann.*: Tacitus, *Germany, Annals*
Tanner, R.G. 1991: ' The development of thought and style in Tacitus', in W. Haase (ed.), *ANRW,* II 33.4, 2689-2751, Berlin and New York
Taylor, P.R. 1994: 'Valerius' Flavian *Argonautica*', *CQ* n.s. 44, 213-235
Terwogt, W. 1898: *Quaestiones Valerianae,* Amsterdam
Thomas, F.W.L. 1875: 'Analysis of the Ptolemaic Geography of Scotland', *PSAS* 10, 198-225
Thomson, J.O. 1948: *History of Ancient Geography*, Cambridge
TLL: *Thesaurus Linguae Latinae*
Till, R. 1943: *Handschriftliche Untersuchungen zu Tacitus Agricola und Germania*, Berlin-Dahlem
Till, R. 1944: 'Britannische Streitwagen', *Klio* 36, 238-250
Till, R. 1979: *Tacitus das Leben des Iulius Agricola,* 2nd ed. Darmstadt
Tillisch, S.S. 2005: 'Isles of the North: Greek and Roman knowledge of the North Sea with a focus on the Orcades, Haemodes and Ebudes', *SAF* abstract (Oct.) (web)
Toynbee, J.M. 1962: *Art in Roman Britain,* London
Tozer, H.F. 1964: *History of Ancient Geography,* second ed. with additional notes by M. Cary, New York
Treves, M. 1958: 'The date of the war of the Sons of Light', *Vetus Testamentum* 8 fasc.4, 419-424
Turner, A.J. 1997: 'Approaches to Tacitus' *Agricola*', *Latomus* 56, 582-593
Tzschucke, C.H. 1807: *Pomponii Melae libri tres de Situ Orbis cum notis additis suis,* Frankfurt a. M.
Urban, R. 1971: *Historische Untersuchungen zum Domitianbild des Tacitus,* Munich
Urlichs, C.L. 1875: *Corn. Taciti de vita et moribus Agricolae liber*, Würzburg
Ussani, V. 1955: *Studio su Valerio Flacco,* Rome
Val. Fl., *Arg.*: Valerius Flaccus, *Saga of the Argonauts*
Viansino, G. 2004: 'Cornelio Tacito e Ammiano Marcellino', *Aevum* 78, 109-135
Vioque, G.G. 2002: *Martial Book VII. A Commentary*, Leiden, Boston and Cologne
Virg., *Aen.*, *Georg.*, *Ecl.*: Virgil, *Aeneid, Georgics, Eclogues*
Vossius, I. 1658: *Observationes ad Pomponium Melam de Situ Orbis*, The Hague
Wainwright, F.T. 1962: *The Northern Isles*, Edinburgh
Walters, W.C.F. 1899: *The Agricola of Tacitus,* London and Glasgow
Waltz, R. 1934: *Sénèque L'Apocoloquintose du Divin Claude. Texte établi et traduit*, Paris
Watt, W.S. 1988: 'Siliana' *MH* 45, 170-181
Watson, W.J. 1926: *The History of Celtic Place-names of Scotland*, Edinburgh
Webster, G. 1970: 'the Military Situations in Britain Between AD 43 and 71', *Britannia* 1, 179-197
Weinreich, O. 1923: *Senecas Apocolocyntosis,* Berlin
Welch, G.P. 1965: *Britannia: The Roman Conquest and Occupation of Britain*, London
Wellesley, K. 1972: *Cornelius Tacitus: The Histories Book lll*, Sydney
Wellesley, K. 1975: *The Long Year AD 69*, London

Wex, F.C. 1852: *Taciti De Vita et Moribus Cn. Iulii Agricolae liber*, Brunswick

Whatmore, A.W. 1913: *Insulae Britannicae*, London

Whitaker, I. 1981: 'The problem of Pytheas' Thule', *CJ* 77, 148-161

White, P. 1975: 'The friends of Martial, Statius and Pliny and the dispersal of patronage', *HSCP* 79, 265-300

Whitmarsh, T. 2006: 'This in-between book: language, politics and genre in the *Agricola*', in *The Limits of Ancient Biography*, 305-333, eds. McGing B. and Mossman J., Swansea

Whittington, G. and Edwards, K.J. 1993: '*ubi solitudinem faciunt, pacem appellant:* the Romans in Scotland, a palaeo-environmental contribution', *Britannia* 24, 13-25

Wijsman, H.J.W. 1996: *Valerius Flaccus, Argonautica Book V: A Commentary*, Leiden

Wijsman, H.J.W. 1998: 'Thule applied to Britain', *Latomus*. 57, 318-323

Wilkinson, J.W. 1957: *A Critical Edition of Book 1 of the Argonautica of Valerius Flaccus with introduction and commentary* [unpublished Doct. Thes. Univ. of London]

Winterbottom, M. 1983: 'Tacitus: the minor works', in *Texts and Transmission: A Survey of the Latin Classics* 410-411, ed. Reynolds L.D., Oxford.

Winterbottom, M. and Ogilvie, R.M. 1975: *Cornelii Taciti Opera Minora*, Oxford

Wissowa, G. 1907: *Taciti Dialogus de oratoribus et Germania, Codex Leidensis Perizonianus phototypice editus*, Leiden

Wistrand, E. 1956: *Die Chronologie der Punica des Silius Italicus*, Göteborg

Wölfflin, E. 1867: 'Jahresberichte: Tacitus', *Philol* 26, 92-166

Wolfson, S. 2002: 'Tacitus, Thule and Caledonia, a critical re-interpretation of the textual problems', *myweb.tiscali.co.uk/fartherlands*

Woodhead, A.G. 1947-8: 'Tacitus and Agricola', *Phoenix* 2, 45-55

Woolliscroft, D.J. and Hoffmann B. 2006: *Rome's First Frontier: The Flavian Occupation of Northern Scotland*, Stroud

Yeames, A.H.S. 1906: 'A statuette from Norway', *JHS* 26, 284-285

Zehnacker, H. 2004: 'L'Europe du nord dans l'Histoire de Pline l'ancien' *REL* 82, 167-186

Zissos, A. 2006: 'Review of A.J. Kleywegt, Valerius Flaccus *Argonautica* Book 1: a Commentary', *BMCR* 02.57 (online)

Zúñiga, J.T. 1978: *Vida de Julio Agricola*, Mexico

www.ingramcontent.com/pod-product-compliance
Lightning Source LLC
Chambersburg PA
CBHW041706290426
44108CB00027B/2871